CRAFTING DYNAMIC DIALOGUE

The Complete Guide to Speaking, Conversing, Arguing, and Thinking in Fiction

WRITER'S
DIGEST
BOOKS

**WRITER'S
DIGEST
BOOKS**

An imprint of Penguin Random House LLC
penguinrandomhouse.com

ISBN 978-1-4403-4554-8

Printed in the United States of America
ScoutAutomatedPrintCode

Edited by Cris Freese
Designed by Alexis Estoye

TABLE OF CONTENTS

PART I: AN INTRODUCTION TO DIALOGUE

PART II: CRAFTING GREAT DIALOGUE

PART III: THE BASICS OF DIALOGUE

PART IV: CHARACTERS & DIALOGUE

PART V: DIALOGUE SETS THE STAGE

PART VI: DIALOGUE DRIVES THE PLOT

FOREWORD

BY CHERYL ST. JOHN

> "You're gonna need a bigger boat."
>
> —Sheriff Brody to Quint, *Jaws* (1975)

Most of us can quote numerous lines from our favorite movies and books. Why? Because unforgettable dialogue grabs us.

We all want to write compelling, dynamic, witty and emotional dialogue. We want to seize our readers, make them care about our story and buy in for the duration. We want readers to finish each book so satisfied they immediately look for the next one. Crafting vibrant dialogue is one of the most important skills we can develop.

As soon as I started reading these chapters, I knew *Crafting Dynamic Dialogue* was going to be as valuable as *Creating Characters*—a book filled with insight and morsels of word-crafting genius in which I jot notes, highlight, and pick up time and again.

Effective dialogue sets scenes, brings characters to life, eases information into the readers' consciousness, reveals relationships, sets the tone, creates atmosphere, generates suspense, builds tension, reveals conflict, evokes emotion, and above all moves the story forward. It's also visually appealing in forming white space on the page. Anything that's doing all that should be as seamless as we can make it.

And dialogue must sound natural, yet be lean and evocative. Personally, I love unexpected dialogue. When a character says something I wasn't expecting, it makes me laugh or cry or think. Isn't that what we want from our readers? Stories are about feelings; we want to evoke surprise and emotion. I've spent time analyzing movies, and dialogue that is particularly surprising plays an enormous part in how I react to the characters. Lines of dialogue also make great beginnings because they drop us right into the action. They can ask a question or supply an answer. And, when done well, dialogue can also make a satisfying or thought-provoking ending.

But real-life conversations are messy. So when we're instructed to write realistic dialogue, it doesn't mean it should be true-to-life. In real life we interrupt and speak over each other, we talk about mundane things, run sentences together, say "um" and "er" way too much, jump topics, and chase rabbits. Writing isn't about replicating real-life conversation; it's about giving the *impression* that this is real-life conversation. These chapters will show you how to write realistic dialogue while making it seamless and easy to read.

Writers are born with a storytelling instinct, a desire to share their views and characters with the world, but the technical aspects of the craft require a skillset learned by reading hundreds of books—fiction and nonfiction—by putting thousands of words on paper and often by getting them wrong before ever getting them right. The skills are also achieved by studying those who do it well and are willing to share their experiences.

Books like this become my best friends, because I turn to them so often for sound advice and wise counsel. I believe it's essential to keep learning, to strive for perfection and to season our writing with fresh perspective. None of us reaches a point where the writing process becomes easy or second nature. No matter how many books a writer has under his or her belt, writing will always be hard work, will always take additional effort, will always require more determination than the last time. Take your time reading over these chapters. Go back and read them again. Make notes, highlight, dig in—and then let your characters come alive. Don't be afraid to take risks, to make mistakes, to surprise, to endear.

As a beginner and as a multi-published author, I've attended countless workshops on dialogue, but I have never seen this topic covered with the depth and breadth presented here. Within this book, writers at all stages of experience will discover tips and tactics to strengthen their skills. Many of us cut our teeth on issues of *Writer's Digest* and the pearls of wisdom from many of these great authors. These writers know what they're talking about—they're teachers, bestsellers, and authors from all genres. Having their expertise collected for us is like facetime with the pros.

> "If you want one thing too much it's likely to be a disappointment. The healthy way is to learn to like the everyday things, like soft beds and buttermilk—and feisty gentlemen."
> —Augustus McCrae to Laurie Wood, Larry McMurtry, *Lonesome Dove*

CHERYL ST. JOHN is the author of more than fifty novels, both historical and contemporary, print and indie published. Her stories have earned numerous RITA nominations, Romantic Times awards, and are published in over a dozen languages. She has a chapter in Writer's Digest Books' *Creating Characters*. With a 4.9 star rating on Amazon, Cheryl's best-selling nonfiction book *Writing With Emotion, Tension, & Conflict* (WD Books) is available in print and digital. She keeps in touch with readers and writers on social media and enjoys talking books.

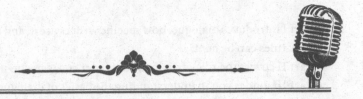

INTRODUCTION

If there's one requirement in fiction, it's to keep the story moving. The easiest way to do that? Dialogue. But you can't just have average, plain conversation between your characters. You need dialogue that sparkles, draws readers in, and keeps them turning pages.

Without excellent dialogue, a story can be jarring. How many times have you started a book and quickly closed it because you were drawn out of the story by a line that didn't feel right? Or because the dialogue felt stilted?

Writing compelling dialogue is difficult. There are a lot of voices and opinions out there that can pull you in different directions. "Dialogue should be believable, but not necessarily true to real life conversation"; "keep your dialogue brief"; "make sure every voice is unique, but don't make someone sound gimmicky."

There are a lot of so-called rules out there. And many are dead-on. But with others, you'll need to pick and choose.

This book is meant to be your comprehensive guide for developing great dialogue. *Crafting Dynamic Dialogue* compiles the very best advice from top writers, editors, and other professionals in the industry on the different aspects of dialogue. You'll find something new and unique to apply to your work in each chapter.

START CRAFTING

Each part of this book will show you the importance of great dialogue, while offering advice and perspective on the best ways to develop it in your writing. Using the tips from experts on the craft, you'll learn what to apply that gives your dialogue a little extra *oomph*.

- Part I introduces dialogue, how specific writers use it, and explains how rules can be bent.
- Part II covers the role of dialogue in reader engagement.
- Part III guides you in understanding the basics of dialogue, including how to make it believable, using dialect or jargon, and quirks of genre-specific dialogue.
- Part IV helps you give voice to your characters, focusing on how to make each one unique.
- Part V delves into advanced techniques, such as setting the pace, revealing background, and creating emotion.
- Part VI shows you how to use dialogue to advance the plot, including creating tension and suspense, constructing conflict, and utilizing internal dialogue.

Each of these sections will arm you with the tools you need to write outstanding dialogue.

Whether you're just starting to write, or are looking to tune your skills for your next submission, there's something in each of these chapters for every level of fiction writer. Start with the first page and work your way through each chapter, line-by-line while taking copious notes, or pick and choose topics that will help you write now—either method will help you gain a total understanding of what good dialogue is.

Let the experts in *Crafting Dynamic Dialogue* guide you every step of the way. When you're finished, you'll find your dialogue doesn't just sparkle, it shines with the best of them.

PART I

AN INTRODUCTION TO DIALOGUE

CHAPTER 1

HE SAID, SHE SAID

BY JACK SMITH

To write great fiction, you must be able to create complex, memorable characters, engaging plots, and vivid settings. You must also be able to create scenes that move, ones that aren't labored or dull. Unless you're writing narrative scenes, this means handling dialogue—and handling it well. When dialogue is rich with energy, characters come alive on the page. The various complexities of the human being are made manifest in what is stated, as well as what is left unsaid—and in the apparent motives behind both speech and silence. It takes some doing to pull all of this off, but that's what it takes to write great dialogue.

THE PROCESS OF WRITING DIALOGUE

Like every other aspect of fiction writing, crafting strong dialogue calls for a process. For T.C. Boyle, award-winning author of fifteen novels and ten short story collections, this process is mostly an unconscious one. He doesn't intentionally set out to energize his dialogue. "It just happens in its own energetic way," he says. "Usually it rides along with me in the way that narration does. It all happens in the unconscious spell that overtakes a writer in the flow of composition." Novelist Amanda Filipacchi reports the same experience in drafting her dialogue. "It's something that comes naturally to me and requires very little conscious effort or calculation."

Of course, plenty of authors prepare to write dialogue by doing some field work. Virgil Suárez, author of several novels and story collections, regularly attunes himself to the various ways people speak. "I like to eavesdrop on conversations, and there are plenty of contemporary places where you can go and do exactly that and no one would notice you sitting there taking it all in." But when it comes to the actual writing, for Suárez this is largely intuitive: "It comes in a variety of ways, sometimes even in sleep. I also hear it as I am writing. The lines that come to me often evolve out of a character's need to speak, to be heard. It also comes from watching characters move from scene to scene. What would they say to themselves?"

All this is nonrational, a matter of feel. And yet Suárez has noticed a set of consistent features that energize his dialogue. Banter is an important one. "I am a big believer in banter between characters ... as it is a way to create dynamic tension through the way the characters speak." Suárez also plays with the margins between silence and sound. "Always present is the idea that silence is often much better for drama than dialogue itself. I like to punctuate my scenes with lots of quiet banter and have plenty of second-level (daily life noise) action going on in the background. My characters never speak in a vacuum; there's always something going on either in their minds or in their setting."

Notice the repartee in Suárez's short story "Blown," from his collection *The Soviet Circus Comes to Havana*.

> "I bet you didn't know I was in Vietnam," you say.
> "A Cuban in Vietnam?"
> You notice how her fingers shake as she takes a cigarette out of the YSL Ritz pack.
> "When the time came, everybody went," you say.
> "Not everybody."
> "You were here?" you ask.
> "Cuba," she says and looks at the man playing the electric piano. He jumps up and down as he starts his solo.
> "Like I said, I went."
> "All right," she says. "How many did you kill?"
> "I got there at the end. Before I knew it I was back."
> "That's anti-climactic."
> "So what?"

Clipped, playful dialogue. Note the man about to gyrate on the electric piano. Banter, silence, sound—these elements tend to pattern Suárez's dialogue, elements ingrained after years of writing, modulated to meet the needs of each new story or novel. It's his stamp of originality.

Originality is also important to Filipacchi, and for her, this means avoiding the predictable. "Dialogue that foils readers' expectations, even in small and subtle ways, can arouse your readers' curiosity and make them pay closer attention. Misunderstandings and misinterpretations between characters can bring entertainment and stress to the reader—two forms of beneficial energy in fiction."

The more you write dialogue, the more you just let it happen, *listening* to your characters speak, you will probably discover your own distinctive approach: energized by the beat or rhythm of your characters' words, their utterances as well as silences, their back-and-forth, their complex, rich voices. Let loose your imagination, your intuitive side. Don't engineer your dialogue. If you force anything, it will come off as fake and inauthentic.

And yet there is always revision. Rethinking, redoing. Like every other element in fiction, you must, at some point, turn a critical eye to your dialogue and demand more of it. Does it reveal character? Does it reveal conflict? Will it keep the reader's interest?

For award-winning short story writer Laura van den Berg, revision strategies come down to several key questions: "Where is the tension? Where is the arc? What is happening underneath the surface?" As she reviews her dialogue, van den Berg pays special attention to this latter issue. "It's crucial to think about what's crackling beneath the surface—where is the subtext? The layers? What is the end game for this conversation for the narrator? What does she want in this moment? These under-layers are a huge part of what brings energy to dialogue."

Notice what's "crackling beneath the surface" in van den Berg's story "I Looked for You, I Called Your Name," from her collection *The Isle of Youth*. Here the narrator, on a honeymoon in Patagonia, is plagued by a series of disasters—for starters a broken nose when their plane makes an emergency landing. You can't help but sense an "under-layer" in the honeymooning couple's conversation with another newly married couple. The narrator replies to a comment about being just recently married.

Crafting Dynamic Dialogue

"Yes," I said. "I suppose we are." I felt as though I was hovering just above the ground. I hooked myself around my husband's elbow. "But doesn't it feel like it's been ages?" I said. "Ages and ages and ages?"

He pulled away from me and leaned toward the Meyer-Stewards. "She broke her nose," he whispered. "During the emergency landing."

Patrick sipped his drink; Susannah sucked on her crab leg.

"You broke it," I said, tapping my cheekbone. "My husband broke my nose."

"What was that?" Patrick asked, rattling the ice around in his glass.

"My husband broke my nose." I felt like signing those words to the entire room. "He broke it with his elbow."

"She doesn't know what she's talking about," my husband said. "It was an accident."

Here, already, on their honeymoon, the narrator feels an unsettling disharmony in her marriage, a potentially broken marriage, symbolized by her broken nose. The spoken, as well as the unspoken, energizes this dialogue. We wonder: What is really going on? What fatal flaw in this marriage has caused the wife to accuse her husband of breaking her nose? The dialogue intrigues the reader to discover the undercurrents, the subtext.

CONSISTENCY OF TONE AND CHARACTER

To zero in on tone, you must capture the core of who your character *is*, his or her sensibility, and so forth. Capturing your character's essential nature takes an imagination that grasps what it's like to be another human being. It requires the writer to get outside herself—to experience empathy. John Keats called it negative capability.

Filipacchi says that, like an actor, you must imagine yourself "in the skin" of your character. You must be aware of both personality and mood. "What kinds of remarks would that personality, in its current mood, utter at that moment? How would that personality and mood react to what has just been said to him or her?" As she writes, Filipacchi automatically asks these questions about all of her characters.

If you haven't pegged the right tone for your character in your initial drafts, do so in the revision stages. For Suárez, getting the tone just right ultimately calls for careful analysis. He tries to match behavior and mannerisms with language—is it a good fit? Additionally, says Suárez, character speech should reflect age, time, place, and thoughts and concerns. "The best trick is always to read the line out loud, play pretend. Block the scene the way a playwright might do it." As she revises, van den Berg also analyzes tone with several criteria in mind. "I think a lot about tics and patterns and habits of speech—is this a polite voice? A voice that curses a lot or is partial to clichés or puns or bad jokes? This can be a way of getting a feel for a voice and distinguishing character."

T.C. Boyle states, "I don't typically work with accents or speech patterns, so it's just a matter of imagining what a developing character might sound like in a given situation." He cites as an example the narrator of *The Inner Circle*, John Milk, an acolyte of Alfred C. Kinsey, the sex researcher. Milk, Boyle notes, "speaks and writes formally, a function of his shyness and uncertainty." The following excerpt, from a scene early in the novel, sets the tone for Boyle's protagonist. A co-ed at IU approaches Milk.

> "Listen," she said, "I just wanted to know if you'd mind getting engaged to me—"
> Her words hung there between us, closing out everything else—the chatter of the group of freshmen materializing suddenly from the men's room, the sound of an automobile horn out on the street—and I can only imagine the look I must have given her in response. This was long before Prok taught me to tuck all the loose strands of my emotions behind a mask of impassivity, and everything I was thinking routinely rushed to my face along with the blood that settled in my cheeks like a barometer of confusion.
> "John, you're not blushing, are you?"
> "No," I said, "not at all. I'm just—"
> She held my eyes, enjoying the moment. "Just what?"
> I shrugged. "We were out in the sun—yesterday it was, yesterday afternoon. Moving furniture. So, I guess, well—"

It's a "pretend" engagement for a college course, as the young woman soon clarifies. We can see in John's stumbling language here, including his "well—," a hesitancy, a sense of unease, which characterizes his speech throughout the novel. Milk's formality is established in his thoughts, his interior language.

Crafting Dynamic Dialogue

BREAKING WITH DIALOGUE CONVENTION

If you break with the traditional method of handling dialogue (double quotation marks), you need a purpose for doing so—don't break convention merely to be fashionable or trendy. As Boyle points out, "The trend lately has been to dispense with quotation marks, but trends by their very nature tend to give way to other trends, which inevitably loop back to standard procedure. Another way to look at it: Each story, each novel, finds its own mode of expression, which may or may not be reflected formally."

"Sometimes," says Boyle, "I dispense with quotation marks as a way (ask old Bill Faulkner) of total immersion, but generally I do use them for the sake of clarity." Most of the time Suárez sticks with quotation marks, too, though he did find reason to break with the standard method in his second novel, *Latin Jazz*. "I had a whole cast of characters to worry about, so I used different punctuation marks for the dialogue to signal which character was speaking."

Van den Berg follows convention, but, she says, "I can think of many stories in which breaking the traditional standards is very effective—when you're trying to dissolve the barrier between thought and speech, for example."

And this is exactly what Filipacchi did in her first novel, *Nude Men*. "I wanted my main character to have imaginary conversations with his cat. I had to decide whether or not to use quotation marks for those conversations. I decided against it, in order to convey that those conversations are taking place in his head." Note the "conversation" between the first-person narrator and his cat, Minou.

> At home, Minou is sitting in a corner of the apartment. That's unusual for her; she usually runs to greet me at the door. I hang up my coat, drink some orange juice, go to the bathroom.
>
> How's the weather outside? asks Minou from her corner.
>
> Fine. Why are you sitting in that corner? I ask.
>
> Because I like it. Did you see any cats more beautiful than I in the pet store window?
>
> No. Only vulgar Himalayans. Are you feeling okay? I've never seen you sit in that corner before.

I'm feeling fine.

Aren't you even going to leave your corner to say hello to me?

I said hello.

First of all, no, you did not say hello, you asked me how the weather was. Second of all, I want one of your usual warm welcomes, I say, walking toward her.

No, she says, cringing farther into the corner.

As we see in this comic exchange, thought and speech are not distinguished by the standard quotation marks because speech is occurring in the narrator's head. We hear the narrator speak; we hear the cat speak. This is dialogue, but it's imaginary dialogue. Dropping the double quotation marks makes sense here: It has a purpose. It's not willy-nilly, and it's not employed merely to latch onto a trend.

TYPICAL DIALOGUE PROBLEMS

Few writers create polished work the first time around. Probably as you revise, you will discover some problems with your dialogue. These issues can fall into one of several categories.

Giving Away Too Much

"Most obvious," says Boyle, "is giving away too much by way of dialogue exposition. We see this in poorly devised sci-fi movies but never, never, never in quality literary fiction. I'm not given to assigning long speeches to characters either, but obviously other writers really run with this (Dostoevsky, anyone?)."

Inauthentic-Sounding Speech

For Suárez, there is a distinct difference between character thought and speech. The former isn't a good fit for dialogue. "I prefer to always split the narrative into what the character is thinking and what the character is actually saying. It's a nice, quick way of getting to know my character right away. It's very true to real life. Ninety-nine percent of the things we think about are never spoken."

Crafting Dynamic Dialogue

Dialogue That Goes Nowhere

"Often I have dialogue in early drafts that is just blather," says van den Berg. "There's language being exchanged, but it's lacking energy and weight and momentum. In revision, I think hard about the role of the exchange in the story—what is being revealed here? Why does this matter?"

Repetition

"A common mistake a writer can make in an early draft," says Filipacchi, "is to make dialogue too long, not only in the back-and-forth between characters but in each individual utterance by each character. Cutting down the nonessential and repetitive portions is the easiest way of energizing dialogue. Ask yourself if the information delivered in that dialogue is crucial. If yes, are there other ways of dispensing that information throughout the novel in a less tedious way?"

SUMMING UP

When dialogue fails, it's because the language of your character seems contrived and doesn't sound real or authentic. It lacks energy. Given your particular character, the tone is off. Powerful dialogue makes us see and hear characters in their own voices, not the author's. It's high octane. It fuels character conflict, and it has an ultimate destination.

TIPS FROM THE PROS

"Follow your instincts. You create and absorb a billion bits of dialogue in your life off-screen. Ask yourself if what you've put in the mouths of your characters sounds real—i.e., as if someone would actually say those words and use those expressions in the very particular situation in which you've put them. I like to set my socks on fire once in a while just to see what sort of expression will emerge from my own vocal apparatus when the flames reach my ankles."

—T.C. Boyle

"Listen. And then listen some more. Crisp, real dialogue comes from watching carefully how people behave, move, and punctuate with gestures. Silence is extremely dramatic and should be reverted to

---

as often as possible. I like to listen to people talk; I like to watch their expressions. Nervous tics and mannerisms are golden. Realistic dialogue is never spoken in complete sentences. Fragmented dialogue sounds real, timely, urgent."

—Virgil Suárez

"Dialogue is more than speech. It's about what's passing between two people. Condense as much as possible. Be as precise as possible. Think about what the characters want and need and fear and love and hate."

—Laura van den Berg

"Add tension and energy. Pique your reader's interest by paying close attention to what a character chooses to divulge to another character. How truthful will the information be? How tactful will a character be? How carefully will she choose her wording? Will the character exercise self-restraint or blurt things he will regret later? Playing with these elements can add tension and energy to dialogue."

—Amanda Filipacchi

JACK SMITH is the author of the award-winning novel *Hog to Hog* (Texas Review Press, 2008), *Icon* (Serving House Books, 2014), as well as numerous short stories and reviews. His fiction has appeared in such literary magazines as *Southern Review, North American Review, Texas Review, X-Connect, In Posse Review,* and *Night Train.* He is a frequent contributor to Writer's Digest's Writer's Market series and was the fiction editor of *The Green Hills Literary Lantern* for twenty-five years.

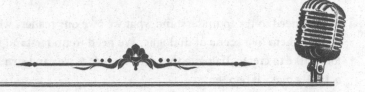

CHAPTER 2
THE PURPOSE OF DIALOGUE

BY GLORIA KEMPTON

You're at the bookstore browsing through the fiction section. You're perusing titles, grabbing books off the shelf and skimming the back cover copy, then finally leafing through the novels one by one. Whether it's conscious or unconscious, guess what you're looking for.

Space. The eye is naturally drawn to space. Plenty of white space on each page. In a nonfiction book, that may mean text broken up with a subhead or a sidebar here and there. In a novel that means dialogue.

Do you remember those novels teachers made us read in high school? *Great Expectations. Madame Bovary. Lord of the Flies.* Page after page of blocks of text. Long passages of boring narrative.

Dialogue not only creates space on the page, which is visually appealing, but it's also what brings characters to life in a story, which is emotionally appealing. We're much more interested in a story's setting when it comes through a scene of dialogue. Dialogue reveals the characters' motives and opposing agendas. Our characters' tense words let readers know where our characters are internally and create suspense for what's ahead in the story. The onset of a dialogue scene immediately propels the story into high gear. Through dialogue, we can give readers a very real sense of a story's setting. If done well, dialogue can even communicate the story's theme. Effective dialogue delivers all of these things to eager readers. This is the kind of dialogue we, as writers, want to create.

How?

We need to try to understand what we owe our readers when we engage them in a scene of dialogue. We need to understand what it looks like to create dialogue that delivers before we can learn how to actually make it happen.

Effective dialogue, the kind of dialogue that connects with readers and makes them care about our characters and their struggles, can accomplish many purposes simultaneously. Let's take a look at them one by one.

CHARACTERIZE/REVEAL MOTIVES

We introduce our characters to our readers through dialogue. Dialogue combined with facial expressions and body language indicates to readers who our characters are. In real life, this is how we get to know one another. We start interacting. Sometimes this goes well, sometimes it doesn't. Through dialogue, we decide if we like someone or not. This is also how our readers decide if they like our characters. As they listen to them and watch them interact with each other, they decide if these are good guys or bad guys or a combination. It's in our power to evoke positive or negative feelings in our readers for our characters through the dialogue we create for them.

When a character speaks in a controlled tone, every word clipped and enunciated clearly, it could be that he's right on the edge, momentarily suppressing a ton of internal rage. On the other hand, if a character's voice is warm and inviting, this could reveal an internal sense of security and well-being. A character who rattles off words faster than the speed of light could be running away from himself, and a character who talks painfully slow may be unsure of himself, experiencing depression, or lacking in social skills.

Every one of your characters is driven by something—they all have agendas, motives, and reasons for what they want in your story. In some sense, motive is the most important element in a story because it drives the character from the inside to go after what he wants. It's the impetus behind and the reason for his goal. Without motive, there's no story. That's how important it is. Let's say you're writing a children's story. The protagonist's goal could be to win the spelling bee. The motive? To earn her father's approval. This could also be an adult story. The goal would be different, but the motive could be the same.

The most effective way to reveal your characters' motives is through their own mouths. Again, in real life, we do this all the time. I remember a friend once telling me that another person had insinuated she had done something rude. "I don't want everyone to think I'm not nice," she told me.

Right away I knew that it wasn't that my friend actually cared if she was nice or not; what she cared about was how others perceived her. What she cared about was her image. I'm not making a value judgment here. I don't have to. She opened her own mouth and revealed her motive herself—wanting others to think well of her. We do it all the time. Whenever your characters open their mouths, they start telling the truth about what's motivating them. This is what you want to do. This is good. You want your dialogue to deliver your characters' motives to your reader. Again, this is how your reader is signaled as to how to feel about your characters. Motives, even more than behavior, reveal whom our characters are deep down inside because behavior is external but motives are internal. Effective dialogue brings up who our characters are at their core. It's powerful stuff.

The following scene of dialogue shows the motives of the antagonist, Sean Dillon, in Jack Higgins' novel *Eye of the Storm*. Dillon is a terrorist, has been one for twenty years, and "he hasn't seen the inside of a cell once," according to KGB agent Josef Makeev. After going undercover and trying unsuccessfully to catch Dillon, Makeev discusses the terrorist, who was also once an actor, with another KGB agent, Michael Aroun.

> "As I said, he's never been arrested, not once, and unlike many of his IRA friends, he never courted media publicity. I doubt if there's a photo of him anywhere except for the odd boyhood snap."
>
> "What about when he was an actor?"
>
> "Perhaps, but that was twenty years ago, Michael."
>
> "And you think he might undertake this business if I offer him enough money?"

"No, money alone has never been enough for this man. It always has to be the job itself where Dillon is concerned. How can I put it? How interesting it is. This is a man to whom acting was everything. What we are offering him is a new part. The Theatre of the Street perhaps, but still acting." He smiled as the Mercedes joined the traffic moving around the Arc de Triomphe. "Let's wait and see. Wait until we hear from Rashid."

A character won't always admit his own motives in conversation with others, usually because he doesn't even know himself why he does what he does. This is often especially true of the antagonist. So having other characters talk about the antagonist's motives is an effective way to show the antagonist's motivation.

EXERCISE

CHARACTERIZE/REVEAL MOTIVES. Consider the background of both your protagonist and antagonist. Write a scene where both of them show up and have to talk to each other, whether they want to or not. In this scene, find a way to insert a bit of motivation into the dialogue so we have sympathy for both characters.

SET THE MOOD IN THE STORY

Every story, no matter what kind, evokes emotion in the reader. Or it should, if you want to hold your reader's attention. The story's emotional pull ultimately creates the story's mood. The mood, the emotion, is what keeps pulling at the reader, compelling her to keep turning the pages. The mood can be setting. It can be the characters and their motives. It can be how quickly or slowly the plot moves.

Dialogue is a tool you can use to create your story's mood. In a mystery or horror story, the dialogue should evoke fear in the reader. In a romance, we're looking for that warm, fuzzy dialogue that budding love brings. In a mainstream or literary story, it may be one of any number of atmospheres we want to create and emotions we want to evoke as we go about creating a scene of dialogue. When characters are interacting, they're exchanging feelings. As the writer, you're in charge of creating the story's mood. Sometimes the mood just kind

Crafting Dynamic Dialogue

of evolves as our characters start talking, but you can also direct the dialogue so you're controlling the mood.

In Anna Quindlen's first-person novel *One True Thing*, the relationship between the protagonist, Ellen Gulden, and her father, the antagonist, George Gulden, is a hostile one. He has convinced Ellen to come and be her mother's caretaker as she wastes away from cancer. Ellen grudgingly agrees, and her attitude toward this task quickly becomes the story's mood. In the following scene of dialogue, we begin to see just what her attitude is.

> "Ellen, there is no reason for the two of us to be at cross-purposes. Your mother needs help. You love her. So do I."
>
> "Show it," I said.
>
> "Pardon me!"
>
> "Show it. Show up. Do you grieve? Do you care? Do you ever cry? And how did you let her get to this point in the first place? When she felt first sick, why didn't you force her to go to the doctor?"
>
> "Your mother is a grown woman," he said.
>
> "Sure she is. But wasn't it really that you didn't want your little world disrupted, that you needed her around to keep everything running smoothly? Just like now you need me around because she can't. You bring me here and drop me down in the middle of this mess and expect me to turn into one kind of person when I'm a completely different kind and to be a nurse and a friend and a confidante and a housewife all rolled up in one."
>
> "Don't forget being a daughter. You could always be a daughter."
>
> "Oh, Papa, don't try to make me feel guilty."

As the story progresses, we watch the plot events transform Ellen, and by the end of the story she's a different person. But this is the mood that permeates the story, and the author often uses dialogue to bring it out.

EXERCISE

SET THE MOOD IN THE STORY. Place two characters in a setting that will enhance the story's mood. A dark, creepy alley in a horror story, a bright island beach in a romance, or you might want to reverse these for something different—a dark alley in a romance or an island beach in a horror story. Write a scene of dialogue focusing on the mood/emotion you want to convey in the overall story.

INTENSIFY THE STORY

We can use dialogue to keep raising the stakes for our protagonist, to keep him in hot water, to keep propelling the story forward. Your character has a goal. He wants something—desperately. In the movie *ET*, we remember one line vividly: "ET phone home." This one line of dialogue—three words—contains the essence of what ET is all about. This little creature just wanted to go back home. Desperately.

Now it's up to you to keep throwing obstacles at your protagonist to keep him from easily getting what she wants. These obstacles come from within and without the character. The other characters come against your protagonist. The protagonist sabotages herself. This is called story conflict, and you can reveal it and keep intensifying it through dialogue. You want to use dialogue to keep reminding the reader just how desperate your character is to achieve her goal.

Every scene of dialogue, in some way, needs to move the story conflict forward. We need to be in a different place at the end of a scene of dialogue than we were at the beginning. The situation should grow continually worse every time our characters open their mouths to talk to one another. Our protagonist is becoming more desperate. Our antagonist seems surer of victory; we know because of the confidence we give to his tone of voice. Our supporting characters keep reminding our protagonist of his goal, of where he's headed on the Hero's Journey. This is dialogue that does not stand still but moves the story forward with each scene.

In Jude Deveraux's romantic suspense novel *High Tide*, the protagonist, Fiona, is being set up for murder. A businesswoman, she is visiting her wealthy client, Roy Hudson, on his boat, when he starts hitting on her. She fights him off, eventually falling into an exhausted sleep on the boat and waking up in the middle of the night with his body on top of hers—his very *dead* body. The hero, Ace Montgomery, and Fiona are talking about the murder in the following scene of dialogue.

> She took a deep breath. "I want to know what's going on," she said as calmly as she could. "I am wanted for murder. The newspaper—"
>
> "No, we are wanted for murder." He'd put the frozen packages back into the freezer and was now looking in the cupboards. "You know how to make pancakes?"

At that Fiona put her arms straight down to her sides, her hands in fists, opened her mouth, and let out a scream.

Ace had his hand over her mouth before she'd let an ounce of air escape her lungs. "What the hell do you think you're doing?" he demanded. "If someone heard you, they might investigate." Slowly, he removed his hand and nodded toward the countertop in the kitchen. "Now sit down while I make breakfast."

She didn't move. "So help me, if you don't tell me what's going on, I'll scream my head off."

"You really do have trouble with anger, don't you? Have you thought of seeing a counselor?"

At that Fiona opened her mouth again, but this time he didn't move. Instead, he just looked at her speculatively.

Closing her mouth, Fiona narrowed her eyes at him. "So why aren't we at the police station, Mr. Do-Gooder? Just hours ago you were telling me that I couldn't be a fugitive from justice, that I had to turn myself over to the police. But now that you're also accused, we're hiding."

"You want blueberries in your pancakes?"

"I want some answers!" she shouted at him.

Since this is a *romantic* suspense, Deveraux has to do double duty in intensifying the conflict in each scene; she has both the plot—the murder—and the relationship between the hero and the heroine to develop. This scene works well on both levels as Fiona is screaming at Ace to give her some answers about the murder—she's scared to death at being a suspect—while furious at him for not being more direct with her. As you probably know, when writing romance, the hero and heroine often start out intensely disliking each other. A scene of dialogue showing this is a lot more fun than the protagonist simply telling us from inside her head.

EXERCISE

INTENSIFY THE STORY CONFLICT. Two characters are arguing about the moral issues concerning abortion, or the death penalty, or assisted suicide, or another hot topic of your choosing. Write a scene of dialogue that intensifies the conflict between these two characters. Show the conflict escalating as they continue to argue.

CREATE TENSION AND SUSPENSE

As a writing coach, I have worked with hundreds of fiction and nonfiction writers over the years, and the weakness I see most often in scenes of dialogue is the lack of tension and suspense. Nothing is at stake. The characters are just chatting about something or other. Making small talk. Having a tea party. Ho-hum.

Dialogue's purpose, and there is no exception to this, is to create tension in the present and build suspense for what's to come. As a fiction writer, you want to remember this. No matter what kind of scene you're writing, no matter the genre, tension and suspense must be included, most often at the core of the scene. Successful authors know this. Robin Cook, the author of a number of successful medical mysteries, is such an author. His stories are full of tense dialogue scene after tense dialogue scene. The following excerpt is one from his novel *Fatal Cure*. It illustrates the kind of tension and suspense in a dialogue scene that grabs the reader by the gut so she couldn't stop reading even if the house was on fire.

The protagonist, Angela, is on a personal mission to find a killer. The reason this is personal for her is because her husband, David, has just discovered a body buried in the basement of the house they recently moved into. Prior to this scene, she confronted the Chief of Police about what she sees as incompetence and indifference in the police's search to find a suspect.

> "Don't you dare paint me as an hysterical female," Angela said as she got into the car.
>
> "Baiting the local chief of police like that certainly isn't rational," David said. "Remember, this is a small town. We shouldn't be making enemies."
>
> "A person was brutally murdered, the body dumped in our basement, and the police don't seem too interested in finding out who did it. You're willing to let it rest at that?"
>
> "As deplorable as Hodges' death was," David said, "it doesn't involve us. It's a problem that should be left up to the authorities."
>
> "What?" Angela cried. "The man was beaten to death in our house, in our kitchen. We're involved whether you want to admit it or not, and I want to find out who did it. I don't like the idea of the murderer walking

Crafting Dynamic Dialogue

around this town, and I'm going to do something about it. The first thing is we should learn more about Dennis Hodges."

Cook creates tension in this scene by pitting Angela and David against each in their different approaches to how this case should be handled. The suspense comes from Angela's determination to *do* something about the murderer walking around her town. She has spoken her commitment out loud and we know she means what she says. She's going to do something and we'll keep reading to find out what she does.

Effective dialogue always, always delivers tension.

JUST FOR FUN

Take a notebook and go to the mall or a park or a café and eavesdrop on a conversation. Chances are, it will be pretty mundane, as is. Now write a scene of dialogue, giving the conversation you just heard a purpose.

EXERCISE

CREATE TENSION AND SUSPENSE. Two characters are in a fender bender. One, the antagonist, has yet to get a learner's permit and was taking the family car out for a joyride without insurance. Write a scene of dialogue that's full of tension and suspense for what's ahead for both characters.

SPEED UP YOUR SCENES

As storytellers, we have a number of writing tools at our disposal—narration, action, description, and dialogue, to name a few. When you're considering how to pace a story, description and narration will move it slowly, steadily, and easily along. Action and dialogue will speed it up—dialogue even more than action. When characters start talking, the story starts moving. Usually. There are always the dull chatting scenes I mentioned above. But we're talking here about effective dialogue—dialogue that delivers.

Dialogue is a way to control the pace of our stories. Getting back to Angela and David—in this scene, David is talking to his daughter about the body he discovered in the basement. The first paragraph is narrative and moves more slowly than the scene of dialogue that follows.

> When it was almost seven Angela asked David if he would take Caroline and Arni home. David was happy to do it, and Nikki came along. After the two children had been dropped off, David was glad for the moments alone with his daughter. First, they talked about school and her new teacher. Then he asked her if she thought much about the body discovered in the basement.
>
> "Some," Nikki said.
>
> "How does it make you feel?" David asked.
>
> "Like I don't want to ever go in the basement again."
>
> "I can understand that," David said. "Last night when I was getting firewood I felt a little scared."
>
> "You did?"
>
> "Yup," David said. "But I have a little plan that might be fun and it might help. Are you interested?"
>
> "Yeah!" Nikki said with enthusiasm. "What?"
>
> "You can't tell anybody," David said.
>
> "Okay," Nikki promised.
>
> David outlined his plan as they continued home. "What do you say?" he asked once he had finished.
>
> "I think it's cool," Nikki said.
>
> "Remember, it's a secret," David said.
>
> "Cross my heart."

In the narrative paragraph that follows this scene, David goes into the house and makes a phone call, and we learn that he's experienced some distress about two of his patients who had previously died. Here things slow down as the author begins feeding us necessary information in narrative. The narrative slows the story back down after the scene of dialogue. What makes dialogue move more quickly than narrative? It's the quick back-and-forth of the character's words to one another, like a tennis ball being batted back and forth across the court.

It's obvious which part of the above excerpt moves more quickly. Of course, there are times when you want a scene to move more slowly, so I'm not saying that it's always best to use dialogue. But when you need to speed up a scene, this is its purpose. This is what it will do for you.

Crafting Dynamic Dialogue

ADD BITS OF SETTING/BACKGROUND

Do you ever find it difficult to get the setting and background into your story in an interesting way? Here dialogue comes to the rescue once again.

As writers, we have a tendency to want to use narrative to set up every scene for the reader before the action starts, which is unnecessary. Once the action in a scene is rolling along, you can use dialogue to throw in what you need us to know at that moment about the setting and story background. In Joyce Carol Oates' novel *We Were the Mulvaneys*, Patrick, the viewpoint character in this scene, and his sister, Marianne, haven't seen each other for a few years. He has just asked her how she did in college and she's told him she had to take a couple of incompletes. Listen to how Marianne describes the town she now lives in, Kilburn, and later how the author slips in a few details of the current setting, Patrick's room.

> "Well—" Marianne squirmed, pulling at her spiky hair. "Things sort of came up. Suddenly."
> "What kind of things?"
> "An emergency at the Co-op, just after Thanksgiving. Aviva who was assistant store manager got sick—"
> "Store? What store?"
> "Oh Patrick, I must have told you—didn't I? In Kilburn, in town, we have a Green Isle outlet. We sell preserves, fresh preserves, fresh produce in the summer, baked goods—my zucchini-walnut bread is one of the favorites. I—"
> "And you work in the store? How many hours a week?"
> Marianne dipped her head, avoiding Patrick's interrogative gaze.
> "We don't think in terms of hours—exactly," she said. She was sitting

on Patrick's sofa (not an item from home, part of the dull spare slightly shabby furnishings of the apartment) while Patrick sat facing her, in a rather overbearing position, on his desk chair, his right ankle balanced on his left knee in a posture both relaxed and aggressive.

Thinking Pinch-style I have a right to ask, who else will ask if I don't? "What terms do you think in, then?"

"The Green Isle Co-op isn't—a formally run organization, like a business. It's more like a—well, a family. People helping each other out. From each what he or she can give; to each, as he or she requires."

Here we get a sense of *who* the town is as a character as well as some physical details. Setting and background can actually be made interesting when incorporated into a dialogue scene. The reader experiences the setting through the viewpoint character's observations, and depending on the character, this could prove very interesting indeed. As long as there's *tension*, of course.

EXERCISE

ADD BITS OF SETTING/BACKGROUND. Find a line of dialogue, either in something you've written or in a novel you've read, that reveals the story's setting. If it's out of another author's novel, study how the writer managed to insert bits of the setting into the dialogue to make it seem like a natural part of the discussion between the characters.

COMMUNICATE THE THEME

In his memoir *On Writing*, Stephen King writes: "When you write a book, you spend day after day scanning and identifying the trees. When you're done, you have to step back and look at the forest ... it seems to me that every book—at least every one worth reading—is about *something*."

This *something* is better known as theme. What's your story *about*? What do you want your story to say to your reader? In its simplest form, theme is your story's conflict and resolution.

Theme is something we need to weave through our stories in bits and pieces, letting it pop up here and there to reveal what the story is

Crafting Dynamic Dialogue

all *about*. Dialogue is definitely a fiction element that pops everything up and out. When characters are talking, whispering, shouting, hissing, grumbling, sneering, or moaning, the reader is listening. If you can sneak your theme into the dialogue, your reader will hear it in a way that it can't be heard in narrative.

In *One True Thing* author Anna Quindlen is an expert at writing about something in the novel and she weaves the theme all through the narrative in the story. Toward the end of the novel, when Ellen is on the stand for her mother's murder, the author uses dialogue to bring it out once more. The prosecutor has just asked her if she loved her mother. This is her answer:

> "The easy answer is yes. But it's too easy just to say that when you're talk-ing about your mother. It's so much more than love—it's, it's everything, isn't it?" as though somehow they would all nod. "When someone asks you where you come from, the answer is your mother." My hands were crossed on my chest now, and the woman in the blue suit turned her rings. "When your mother's gone, you've lost your past. It's so much more than love. Even when there's no love, it's so much more than anything else in your life. I did love my mother, but I didn't know how much until she was gone."

This isn't the entire theme, but certainly one important part of it, and when Ellen speaks these words, the reader knows exactly what she's talking about because the themes in our lives are universal. Dialogue is not only a faster and more effective way to communicate the theme than to use long paragraphs of dry exposition, but it's also more emotional, up-front, and personal with the reader. You have to be careful, of course, that the characters aren't simply preaching and moralizing to each other just to make sure the reader gets *your* message. If you have a philosophy or idea you want to get across in your book—and you should—then it's perfectly natural to have your characters discussing this idea. If the theme is woven in in other ways throughout other scenes, your characters' dialogue about it in any one scene will feel natural. Use dialogue to convey your story's theme to your reader.

GLORIA KEMPTON is an author, writing coach, and former magazine and book editor. She is the author of eleven books, including *Write Great Fiction: Dialogue* and *The Outlaw's Journey: A Mythological Approach to Storytelling*. She's a former contributing editor to *Writer's Digest* magazine and an instructor for WD's online writing courses.

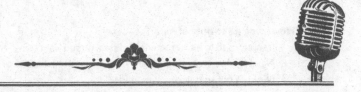

CHAPTER 3
REWRITING THE RULES

BY STEVEN JAMES

Most of us have heard the typical advice about writing dialogue—make sure your characters don't all sound the same, include only what's essential, opt for the word *said* over other dialogue tags, and so on.

While these blanket suggestions can get you headed in the right direction, they don't take into account the subtleties of subtext, characterization, digressions, placement of speaker attributions, and the potentially detrimental effect of "proper" punctuation.

So, let's delve into the well-intentioned advice you'll most commonly hear, and what you need to know instead.

DIALOGUE SHOULD STAY ON TOPIC

In real life we talk in spurts, in jumbles, in bursts and wipeouts and mumbles and murmurs and grunts as we try to formulate our thoughts. We stumble and correct ourselves. We pause and reflect. We backtrack. We wander into tangents, and then get back to the point.

It's often said that on the page, good dialogue doesn't do the same thing. But I disagree.

Tangents reveal character traits and priorities. If dialogue is too focused and direct, it'll become predictable. Readers want to see the motivations, the quirks, the uniqueness of each character. The prudent use of digressions can add texture to a story.

People don't always respond to what was said or to the questions they're asked. They interrupt, change the subject, and attempt to stay on their pre-determined course even after the conversation has taken a turn in a different direction.

"How come it's so hot out here?"

"It's supposed to hit 90 today. Hey, listen, do you want some lemonade?"

"Ninety? Man, I hate this. Remind me why we left Maine in the first place."

"Ninety's not so bad. So, lemonade?"

Even in this brief exchange, multiple conversations are taking place. They overlap, reveal the character's attitudes, and add verisimilitude to what's being said.

At times you'll want your dialogue to pool off into tributaries. This doesn't mean it's unfocused or random, but rather that it's layered with meaning to show the goals of the characters, the social context of the conversation and the subtext that's present in the scene.

In fact, sometimes you'll *want* your characters to discuss trivial things. Subtext brings depth to triviality.

In Hollywood there's a saying: "The scene is not about what the scene is about." In essence, this means that what the readers (or viewers) are witnessing on the surface is not what lies at the heart of that scene.

Scenes that are primarily about romantic tension will often have dialogue in which the characters banter or engage in small talk. But in those instances, it's what's going on beneath the surface that matters most. Identify the core tension of the scene, then plumb subtext and use apparent triviality to your advantage in dialogue. (Caveat: This, like many literary techniques, should be used in moderation. There's no need to show subtext in every scene, nor should you. Chase scenes, for instance, are best approached as *what you see is what you get*. An attempt to layer in subtext will only become a distraction.)

Don't be afraid of digressions. Use them to insert red herrings, foreshadow important events, reveal clues about what motivates your characters, or add new dramatic elements to the story line.

USE DIALOGUE AS YOU WOULD ACTUAL SPEECH

Although in real life people speak primarily to impart information, in fiction a conversation is not simply a way for something to be expressed—it's a way for something to be overcome. As you're writing, rather than asking yourself, "What does this character need to say?" ask, "What does this character need to *accomplish*?"

> A woman wants to confront her husband about his overspending; he wants to watch the game.
>
> The cops are questioning a suspect; she's being evasive.

In both of these instances, the mutually exclusive goals of the characters create tension that affects how the conversation will play out.

When determining your character's response to stimuli, remember that his agenda toward the other person will trump the topic of conversation.

> "There's this crazy thing they invented called the Internet. You can look stuff up on it. You should check it out sometime."
> "Ah. Now, that was sarcasm, right?"
> "Um. No."
> "But that was?"
> "What do you think?"
> "Wait—was that?"
> She looked at me disparagingly.

Words can be barbs. They can be sabers. They can be jewels. Don't let them be marshmallows that are just passed back and forth.

Give each character a goal. The speaker might be trying to impress the other person, or entertain her or seduce her or punish her. Whatever it is, the agenda—whether stated explicitly or not—will shape everything that's said.

> "You're not going to tell him about us, are you?"
> "He'll find out eventually. I should be the one to—"
> "No. Listen, we have something special here. Do you really want to lose it?"
> "It's not just that. I have the kids to think about. What's best for them."

Here, neither question is answered directly. Often you can move the story forward more effectively by having the characters respond in a way that *implies* an answer, showing that they're reading between the lines of what was said or have questions of their own.

OPT FOR SAID

It's true that you'll want to avoid cluttering your story with obtrusive speaker attributions. Having a character consistently *chortle*, *exclaim*, *retort*, *chip in*, *quip*, and *question* rather than simply say anything will become a distraction. Readers will stop being present in the story and will start searching for your next synonym for *said*. They get it. They know you own a thesaurus. Just tell the story.

On the other hand, the use of *said* can become tiresome when it appears repeatedly on the same page. And, when used improperly, it can also be a giveaway that you're an inexperienced writer.

"Bob said" does not equal "said Bob."

To hear how your dialogue reads, try inserting the pronoun instead of the character's name. For example:

> "That's an awesome car," Bob said.

> "That's an awesome car," he said.

Both of those statements make sense. But look at what happens when you write it the other way:

> "That's an awesome car," said Bob.

> "That's an awesome car," said he.

If you wouldn't write "said he" then don't write "said Bob." Stick with placing the speaker's name before the verb unless there's an overwhelming contextual reason not to.

Don't use attributions simply to indicate who's speaking. Use them to create pauses reflected in actual speech, to characterize, and even to orchestrate the pace and movement of the scene.

> "She was strangled."
> "So," he muttered. "Another one."

That snippet of dialogue reads much differently from:

> "She was strangled."
> "So, another one," he muttered.

Additionally, speaker attributions can be used to maintain or diminish status. Compare the two following sentences.

"Come here," he said. "Now."

"Come here now," he said.

See how the placement of the speaker attribution in the first example creates a pause that emphasizes the last word while also raising the dominance of the speaker?

AVOID LONG SPEECHES

Sometimes allowing a character to have her say reveals more about her than forcing her to speak in sound bites ever could.

In this excerpt from my novel *The Pawn*, a teenage girl is speaking with her stepfather after her mother's death in New York City.

"Why didn't you ask me if I wanted to move to Denver?"

"What do you mean?"

"After Mom died. We just picked up and moved. Why didn't you ask me if I wanted to move?"

"Well, I just thought it might be best for both of us to get some space and—"

"For both of us?"

"Yes."

"And how did you come to know what would be best for me?"

"Tessa, I—"

"We're supposed to be a family. Families make choices *together* about what's best for *everyone*, not just for the one in charge."

"Listen, I—"

"You took me away from all my friends. My mom dies, and you make me leave everyone I know and move across the country, and all I ever wanted was a family like Cherise has—a mom and a dad—and when Mom met you, I thought maybe it would happen, just maybe I'd finally have someone to teach me the things dads are supposed to teach their daughters—I don't know, like about life or guys or whatever and maybe come to my volleyball games and make me do my homework when I don't want to and tell me I'm pretty sometimes and give me a hard time about my boyfriends and take a picture of me in my prom dress and then stand by my side one day when I get married ..."

> "I never knew—"
>
> "You never asked!"

The girl's run-on response does more to show her attitude and personality than a back-and-forth exchange would. It also reveals characterization, expresses desire, and provides escalation.

(Incidentally, notice how the dashes are used when a character is cut off, and ellipses when the girl's thoughts trail off. Dashes and ellipses are not interchangeable.)

When deciding whether to let a character launch into a diatribe, consider if she's trying to get her say in before anyone else can interrupt. Also, take into account the buildup of tension that precedes the speech. Like a garden hose, the more pressure, the more dramatic the release.

BE GRAMMATICALLY CORRECT

Always be willing to break conventions when it's in the service of the story and the reader.

> Kyle spoke before Daniel could: "So you told your dad? I mean, about the visions and everything?"

Although some editors might want to replace the colon in this example with a period, the primary issue should be how the punctuation affects the flow rather than how closely it follows a stylebook. Because the urgency of the scene has Kyle speaking quickly before Daniel has a chance to reply, a full stop would undermine that. A colon serves to better convey the scene's uninterrupted pace.

Notice also in the above example that question marks indicate an upward inflection at the end of a sentence, *not necessarily a question*. So your primary concern isn't always "Is this a question?" but "Do I want this to *sound like* a question?"

In dialogue, sentence fragments sound more realistic to readers than complete sentences do. Cut semicolons from dialogue. If you find them, it's usually because you're trying to include complex sentences that wouldn't sound natural if they were spoken aloud. Choose commas and periods instead.

SHOW WHAT THE CHARACTERS ARE DOING WHILE THEY'RE TALKING

Too often this results in on-the-nose writing and an overemphasis on the minutia of body language. If you find your character brushing his nose or repositioning his chair or crossing his legs and so forth for no other reason than to provide a respite from the dialogue, recast the scene.

Just as dialogue should reveal the intention of the characters, so should the actions that they take while they're speaking. When we read that a character folded his arms, we'll naturally wonder why he's doing that. What is it meant to convey about his attitude or emotional response to what's happening? Don't confuse your readers by inserting needless movement. Rather, include action only as long as it adds to the scene or enriches it. If the action doesn't convey anything essential, drop it.

KEEP CHARACTERS' SPEECH CONSISTENT

I used to agree with this until one day I overheard a man in his late 20s talking on his cell phone in a hotel lobby. After a moment or two it became clear that he was a lawyer and was speaking with a client. He was articulate, spoke in complex sentences and sounded well versed in legal terminology.

A few moments later he received a call that was obviously from an old college buddy. Suddenly, his entire demeanor changed. He was joking around and talking more like a frat brother than a law school grad.

If those two conversations appeared in a book they would sound as if they came from two entirely different characters. That man's history with those people affected his tone, word choice, grammar, sentence structure, use of idioms, everything. Even his posture changed.

Dialogue needs to be honest for each character *in that situation*. Don't try to make your characters consistent in the sense of always sounding the same, but rather allow them to remain in character within each unique social context.

So, if a character is highly educated and every time she speaks she's using impressive words, it'll get old. She'll seem one-dimensional. Or if she's from the South and you have her saying "y'all" all the time she'll become clichéd.

Few people are always blunt, always angry, always helpful. We speak differently in different situations. Moods, goals, states of mind fluctuate. This ties in with character believability. Remember: status, context, intention.

Give characters a goal, a history and an attitude toward the other people in the conversation. And always strive for honest, believable responses rather than canned ones.

TELLING DIALOGUE

Say more by saying less. Use dialogue to reveal traits, bring out subtext and escalate conflict.

"We could get in big trouble for this."

"Why? We haven't broken any laws."

In this two-line exchange, not only have we introduced underlying tension, but we've told readers a lot about each character. The first speaker is hesitant, apprehensive, a rule-keeper. The second is more brash, adventurous, more of a risk-taker. Look for ways to evoke and reveal.

HINT: Disagreement can be much more revelatory than agreement.

STEVEN JAMES is a national best-selling novelist whose award-winning, pulse-pounding thrillers continue to gain wide critical acclaim and a growing fan base. *Suspense Magazine*, who named Steven's book *The Bishop* their Book of the Year, says that he "sets the new standard in suspense writing." *Publishers Weekly* calls him a "master storyteller at the peak of his game." And RT Book Reviews promises, "the nail-biting suspense will rivet you." Equipped with a unique Master's Degree in Storytelling, Steven has taught writing and storytelling on four continents over the last two decades, speaking more than two thousand times at events spanning the globe. Steven's groundbreaking book on the art of fiction writing, *Story Trumps Structure*, won a Storytelling World award. Widely-recognized for his story crafting expertise, he has twice served as a Master CraftFest instructor at ThrillerFest, North America's premier training event for suspense writers.

Crafting Dynamic Dialogue

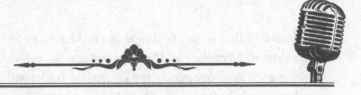

CHAPTER 4

"SAY WHAT?!" QUICK TIPS FOR YOUR CHARACTERS

BY SARAH DOMET

An emotional core, derived from your characters' internal lives, is fundamental to any complex and interesting story.

One problem I've noticed in my students' writings is that they create really interesting, complex, nuanced characters, but they fail to engage them with any of their other characters. In their "real lives" most people tend to be nonconfrontational—especially writer types—and sometimes this rubs off in their writing as well. If you create interesting characters, don't confine them to their own heads; let them walk, talk, and interact with the other characters you've created.

What a person says, too, can go a long way toward revealing her character. Perhaps your character wants to seem smart, so she tries using unusually big words, only to misuse them: "That bombastic cupcake is ostentatiously scrumptious, I decry!" If a character is a scientist or a doctor, perhaps he uses technical terms. Instead of saying "My wife is pregnant," he might explain, "My spousal partner has a fetus in utero." Or if a character is an auto mechanic, perhaps he uses metaphors suited for his profession: "That'd be as embarrassing as an El Dorado with a rusted muffler." Oh, boy. That *is* embarrassing

Consider, too, when what a character *says* differs from what he *thinks*:

> "I love you," said Penelope.
>
> "Uh ... I love you, too," Ricky said, because he didn't know what else to say. He watched her snap her gum, and in this moment she looked even more like a horse. He needed to find a way to let her down easy.

When done artfully, a scene of dialogue can make a reader feel like she is in the room with Penelope and Ricky, cringing at the awkwardness of the exchange. When done poorly, rest assured the reader will be cringing at the author's ill attempt at writing dialogue. Remember, dialogue should sound true to life, and everyone speaks differently. Be sure your dialogue is distinctive and authentic to the character doing the speaking.

Your written dialogue should always be working to reveal the depth, intentions, or actions of your character. A common mistake is using dialogue as "filler" that simply describes the setting or narrates the plot. Consider this scene:

> "What is the weather like outside today?" asked Penelope.
>
> "The sky is blue, and the silhouettes of ducks taking flight to the south are lovely, like planes flying overhead," said Ricky.
>
> "I am going to get in my car and drive to the hair salon," said Penelope. "My strawberry-blonde hair could use a good cut."
>
> "Wait, I hear a knock on the door," said Ricky. "Why, it's the mailman, and he has an important letter from my dying aunt. What's this? She's dead. But she's left me her estate! I'm rich! See you later, horse-face! Don't let the door hit you on the way out!"

A scene such as this one will quickly lead your reader to skip these pages or put down your book altogether. A good general rule to follow when allowing your characters to speak directly is this: Dialogue should always aim to reveal some character trait about the individual who is speaking. If your character speaks a line of dialogue in order to describe the setting, this description should also reveal an element of your character's interiority. What does Ricky's line of dialogue about the lovely ducks flying south reveal about him? Does it indicate that he's sensitive? If so, why does he call his girlfriend "horse-face"? If the spoken line of description doesn't tell us much about your character, that line will be better served in a paragraph of exposition. Dialogue should accomplish two things at once: Describe a setting *and* tell us something about a character; convey plot-forwarding action *and* provide the reader with your character's history; establish tone *and* show how your character's dialogue conflicts with his indirect thoughts. However, each line of dialogue should give your reader insight into your character's mind, personality, or motivations.

Here are some other general rules to follow when writing a dialogue scene:

- Avoid beginning a scene with a line of dialogue. It's a good idea to first orient your reader to the setting and who is present at the scene. Readers process information in the order they receive it, so if you launch into dialogue before setting the scene, they may not know who is speaking and to whom.
- Be sure to describe what your character is doing while he is speaking. When Ricky tells Penelope that he loves her, is he looking at the floor? Is he flipping through channels on the television set?
- Be sure to give some insight into what the characters are thinking versus what they are saying. Such a contrast will provide tension in your scene.
- Be sure to balance dialogue with descriptions of setting and paragraphs of exposition. Dialogue scenes are often a great place to "sneak in" sentences of exposition and character history that might stand out if contained in a separate paragraph. For example:

  > "I love you, too," Ricky said. He doubted there was such a thing as love. His ex-wife told him she loved him all the time, all the while sleeping with his brother, Mickey.

- Less is more when it comes to dialogue. People don't often speak in long paragraphs. At least not without some breaks. Dialogue scenes can quicken the pace of a novel and give your reader a needed rest from long paragraphs of exposition or description.
- Your characters should all speak differently from one another. If you randomly extracted a line of dialogue from your novel, you should be able to tell to whom it belongs simply by analyzing the diction, content, and tone.
- Make sure you include dialogue tags so we know who is speaking and to whom. A simple "he said" or "she said" usually works best and does not draw attention to itself as "He pontificated wildly"

might. Your goal is to aim for invisibility when writing dialogue tags, so this is not the best place to demonstrate your creativity.

- Avoid too many adverbs in your dialogue tags that tell your reader how to "interpret" a line of dialogue. Consider this example: "'I hate you, I hate you, I hate you, Ricky!' Penelope said angrily after Ricky insulted her equine mug." If Penelope is saying something as strong as "I hate you, I hate you, I hate you," we can assume she's saying it angrily. Your dialogue should be able to, pardon the pun, speak for itself. Trust that your reader will "get" it.

- Avoid overusing exclamation points! These can be easily distracting and irritating to your reader! Plus, it makes it seem like your characters are breathlessly exclaiming something, when this isn't always the case! Punctuation should, like dialogue tags, never draw attention to itself! Never ever!

- Always read your dialogue out loud. When you do this, you'll be able to pick up on awkward phrases and dialogue that sounds stilted. It will also help you generate ideas.

ENGAGE YOUR READERS

You need to practice engaging your characters with other characters, and, in addition, to practice writing dialogue to reveal elements of your characters. Keep in mind that what a person says, how she says it, or how it conflicts with her internal musings will do a lot of the muscle work of character development.

First, think of some real individuals you've come into contact with today (waitress, coat-check girl, car-wash attendant, etc.) and place them each in a scene with one of your characters. How will these individuals interact? What might they discuss? You never know when one of these "minor contacts" will have a big impact on a more prominent character. (And if you find one of these minor characters interesting, you may wish to draw up a separate character bio.)

Next, write a short dialogue scene involving your two characters *least likely* to interact in your novel. What might they discuss? You never know when you might learn something about these characters that you didn't know before. (And if you do learn something important, be sure to update your character bio to reflect this.)

Crafting Dynamic Dialogue

Finally, write a dialogue scene involving at least two of your characters who are directly at odds with one another. For now, don't worry if you don't actually envision this as a scene in your novel. Just focus on integrating action, descriptions of setting, and descriptions of your characters' body language. After you've finished, review the general rules for integrating dialogue. Did you adhere to these?

SARAH DOMET is the author of *90 Days to Your Novel* (Writer's Digest Books, 2010). Her fiction and nonfiction also appears in *New Delta Review, The Cincinnati Review, Beloit Fiction Journal, Potomac Review, Harpur Palate,* and *Many Mountains Moving.* She holds a Ph.D. in comparative literature and fiction from the University of Cincinnati and currently teaches in the writing department at Georgia Southern University.

CHAPTER 5

STRENGTHEN YOUR DIALOGUE

BY JERRY CLEAVER

Some writers freeze up when it comes to putting words in their characters' mouths. "How does he talk?" "What would she say?" "It comes out so stiff, wordy, detached." So, what should you do?

The first thing, always, is: Put it down anyway. It's better to write poor dialogue than to write no dialogue. Lower your expectations; take off the pressure to write well. It'll actually help you write more and write better.

Before getting into specific techniques, the how of dialogue, you need to understand the why of dialogue—dialogue's place in story.

The biggest mistake you can make with dialogue is treating it as something separate from the story. If you think you have a dialogue problem, you, in fact, have a story problem. All problems of any consequence are story problems. No matter what the problem appears to be, you must first examine your story to make sure you have the dramatic forces in place to move things forward. If your story or scene is lacking those forces, the dialogue will also be lacking. "The dialogue is stunning, but the story is dead," is something you'll never hear. The fault lies not in the dialogue but in the story.

For example, if you wanted to, you could write a decent line of dialogue with some emotional punch for Romeo, Hamlet, or Scarlett O'Hara. That's because the dramatic forces of their stories made the characters come to life on the page. They were defined by the conflicts in their stories and the specific, personal way each struggled to overcome them: Romeo, by sneaking into the enemy castle for the masquerade ball to see Juliet again; Hamlet, by agonizing over, "To be or not to be," and finally attacking; Scarlett, by trying to seduce Ashley. These characters had no trouble speaking because they had plenty to say in response to plenty of problems.

We experience characters by the way they struggle against the forces opposing them. They're forced by circumstances to speak from the heart and not the head. They have no time to pontificate or philosophize. A character cannot speak in a gripping or arresting way about something he cares nothing about. (Can someone speak passionately about the color of the neighbor's lawn mower?)

The situation creates the dialogue, not the other way around. Here's a quick exercise: Write a few lines of dialogue that work in response to the following situations:

> "Give me your money, or I'll blow you away," he said, shoving a gun in my ribs.

> "I want a divorce," Louise said to John the morning after their wedding.

> "My best estimate," said Dr. Green, "is that you have three weeks to live."

It's not hard to come up with dialogue because the situations demand the right things from you and the character. Dialogue is a natural part of the situation and is drawn out of the characters when the right story forces (pressures/threats) are present—just as it works in life. You don't have trouble finding the right words when you're worked up, desperate or frantic about something.

So when you're having dialogue trouble, forget it, and check the scene. If you don't have a scene with two strong forces (desire plus obstacle) determined to overcome each other, you won't have the dramatic energy to move the characters to speak in a personal and revealing way. You can't write strong dialogue in a weak story.

Another guide that'll keep you out of weak scene/weak dialogue is to remember: There are no discussions, conversations or exchanges of information in fiction—only confrontations. A confrontation doesn't have to be in-your-face yelling or shoving. A confrontation can be polite and careful, but it must be one character attempting to get something from another character—to get someone to do something she doesn't want to do or attempt to make something happen. If that isn't the case in any given scene, your story has stopped dramatically. It's at a standstill, and you risk losing the reader and too often your connection to the story.

Okay, those are the general considerations regarding dialogue. Now, use these tips to make your dialogue stronger.

LOOK INSIDE

Realize that you use dialogue all the time, all day long. Your mind goes at 150 to 300 words a minute every waking hour. It never stops. The words that run through your mind would fill 500 pages a day. The thing to do is to write them the way you would say them. Get out of the way, and put the words on the page any way they want to come out. Then work from there.

How? Don't worry about what the character would say, but first think about what you would say if you were in that situation. Put that down. Then, ask yourself what you'd say if you were the character? That'll get you closer to the words you need. You may not be there yet, but you'll be on your way.

DON'T GET INTELLECTUAL

Dialogue is always direct, emotional, and simple. Even in special cases when someone is being indirect or evasive, it's still emotional and simple.

Emotional language refers to small words that are to the point. If one character said, "I don't love you any more. I want to split up," and the other answered, "I disagree. In addition, it's my firm belief that we have the foundation for a sound and lasting relationship, and I know you're just as cognizant of it as I am. Unless of course there's been some deception on your part as far as honest disclosure of your feelings is concerned—not to mention your activities," you'd wonder what the hell was going on or just decide that it's bad writing. But if the character answered, "No! We're a perfect match. You said so yourself—unless you've been lying to me," chances are you'd find it believable and keep reading.

That example is easy to see, and I made it obvious so it would be, but it's not always so clear. The dialogue can be a lot less intellectual than this and still be stiff and distant—just a touch too intellectual for example. So you need to examine your dialogue carefully. Remember, though, carefully examine as you rewrite and not when you're putting it on the page for the first time.

GET OUT THE SCALPEL

But how do you turn the stiff, intellectual and distant dialogue into immediate, personal and emotional words from the heart? Your best weapon with dialogue and rewriting in general is to cut, cut, cut. Get rid of every word you can do without. Then shorten the words.

Here's a sentence. See what you can do with cutting and shortening:

> This is horrendous. Don't leave me. What's your motive? Ignore that. Motive isn't important. Just tell me. What do you want? I'm willing to consider anything, to do anything.

Here's one solution:

> Don't leave me. What do you want? I'll do anything.

Sometimes the words are short, but it's still too excessive (too wordy) for the situation—especially if it's highly emotional. How would you rewrite this for more emotion?

> "Yes. Maybe you're right. But, I don't think so."

It could be cut to: "You're wrong," or, "Come off it." In this case, you would cut it all and simplify.

LET THEM TALK

The following examples are two versions of dialogue between the same characters about the same problem. Can you read them and identify what technique is lacking or working successfully?

Here's the setup: A young woman sees her husband in a dimly lit parking lot giving a young woman he works with a passionate kiss. That night she confronts him.

> "She just learned her father has terminal cancer. I gave her a peck on the cheek to comfort her. What's going on?"
>
> "That's what I want to know."
>
> "I've never seen you humiliate yourself like this before. She's just a friend. I'm not hiding anything. It was an innocent gesture. So now I suppose you think I'm spending all my free time chasing women."

How does it feel? Was it gripping, strong, direct? Could more be added to it? If so, how? Reread it and think about what you might do to make it better. After you do, read the revised version below. Remember, we're only considering the dialogue and not getting into anything else.

Here's the second version:

> "She just learned her father has terminal cancer. I gave her a peck on the cheek to comfort her."
>
> "That was no peck, and it wasn't on the cheek. I haven't had a peck like that in months. Now I see why."
>
> "What's going on?"
>
> "That's what I want to know."
>
> "I've never seen you humiliate yourself like this before."
>
> "The humiliation is your doing."
>
> "She's just a friend. I'm not hiding anything."
>
> "I could see that."
>
> "It was an innocent gesture."
>
> "I'd hate to see what you'd call guilty."
>
> "So now I suppose you think I'm spending all my free time chasing other women."
>
> "All your time? How about some or any?"

Which version is better? What's the difference? What was done to improve it? There's one simple technique that made the difference. Note that not one of the husband's remarks has been changed. They're identical in both versions. So, can you see what made the difference?

In fiction, everyone gets to speak her mind, but no one should be allowed to go on and on without the other character responding, especially when a response from that character will intensify the situation and reveal the characters all the more. All that was done in the second example was to have the wife respond after each of the husband's remarks. And it wasn't hard to come up with the right words because the situation is so charged with emotion from the wife's desire for a happy marriage (dramatic want) and the husband's betrayal (dramatic obstacle) and her determination to get to the bottom of it (dramatic action).

When you write your dialogue, always consider whether the characters respond to each and every statement the others make. This is also true to reality, because when things are intense and emotional, people can't get away with longwinded speeches while others sit patiently and quietly listening. But, again, this isn't just about dialogue. It's about getting more out of the characters and your story—which happens when the characters are trying to get more out of each other.

FAMOUS BITS

Let these snippets of dialogue excerpted from the pros guide you when perfecting your own writing.

> "You couldn't say something boundless within the boundaries of any language."
>
> —*Dune Messiah*, Frank Herbert

> "Oh, Jake," Brett said, "we could have had such a damned good time together." ...
> "Yes," I said. "Isn't it pretty to think so?"
>
> —*The Sun Also Rises*, Ernest Hemingway

> "Scarlett, I was never one to patiently pick up broken fragments and glue them together and tell myself that the mended whole was as good as new. What is broken is broken—and I'd rather remember it as it was at its best than mend it and see the broken places as long as I lived. Perhaps, if I were younger—" he sighed. "But I'm too old to believe in such sentimentalities as clean slates and starting all over. I'm too old to shoulder the burden of constant lies that go with living in polite disillusionment. I couldn't live with you and lie to you and I certainly couldn't lie to myself. I can't even lie to you now. I wish I could care what you do or where you go, but I can't."

He drew a short breath and said lightly but softly, "My dear, I don't give a damn."

—*Gone With the Wind*, Margaret Mitchell

"Oh, and do you remember"—she added—"a conversation we had once about driving a car?"

"Why—not exactly."

"You said a bad driver was only safe until she met another bad driver? Well, I met another bad driver, didn't I? I mean it was careless of me to make such a wrong guess. I thought you were rather an honest, straightforward person. I thought it was your secret pride."

"I'm thirsty," I said. "I'm five years too old to lie to myself and call it honor."

—*The Great Gatsby*, F. Scott Fitzgerald

"So what about love?" I asked.

"What about it?" ...

"Don't you believe in it?"

"I don't believe in it the way people believe in God or the tooth fairy. It's more like the *National Enquirer*. A big headline and a very dull story."

"So what do you believe in?" I asked her.

"I believe in living as I like. I see a Stickley lamp, a cashmere sweater, and I know I can have it. I own two houses besides this. When the ashtrays are full in my car, I'll sell it."

—*White Oleander*, Janet Fitch

"Good Morning, Miss Ratched ... This is Candy."

"What worries me, Billy, is how your poor mother is going to take this."

—*One Flew Over the Cuckoo's Nest*, Ken Kesey

JERRY CLEAVER was a writer, teacher, writing coach and creator of Chicago's legendary Writer's Loft. Author of *Immediate Fiction, a Complete Writing Course* (St. Martin's Press), he was published in various magazines, ghostwrote several books, and created numerous online courses. His book was published by the Renmin University Press in Beijing and was used by major Chinese Universities to teach the burgeoning field of creative writing in China.

PART II

CRAFTING GREAT DIALOGUE

CHAPTER 6

THE SOURCE OF GREAT DIALOGUE

BY ELIZABETH SIMS

Dialogue—the words people say—is a huge component of good writing. Because fiction or nonfiction, no matter what you write, you're going to write stuff that somebody said. The more convincingly you do it, the more you will awaken your readers' heartbrains (your readers' whole, deepest self) and bind them to yours.

More than anything, I want to help you *understand* dialogue so that you can begin to think about dialogue as professional writers think about it—as a component of writing that's alive and totally your servant.

First off, let's get in the mood.

HOW WE TALK

Gather your writing materials.

Find a comfortable place.

Enter garret mode. (Note: A garret is an attic. Attics are places where you can be alone—hidden, even—and no one will bother you. For our purposes, garrets are real places, but they are also infinitely moveable, changeable, and adaptable to our needs. What a writer needs is psychic isolation, a mental place where you can focus on what you want to do without much chance of interruption.)

Pick one and write about it:

• The first time you found yourself in serious trouble for something you did. Lying, fighting, shoplifting, speeding, perhaps?

- An argument you took part in. Siblings' spat, lovers' quarrel, barroom debate, for instance?
- Have you ever been involved in a proposal of marriage, either the asker or the askee?

What happened? What was said? Write down the words that were spoken as best as you remember. Just write everything as naturally as it came out, without worrying about grammar or sounding stupid or anything.

After this incident, were you like, "Yeah, but I shoulda said ..." Write that too. Just add it on.

Write for as long as you like.

When you're ready to stop writing, stop.

TRY THIS: Read what you just wrote aloud. If you can, read it aloud to somebody else, or better still, have somebody else read it out loud to *you*.

How does it make you feel? Are you engaged with what was happening, does your heart move a little bit?

I thought so.

Does any of it sound fake or weak?

I thought not.

Why is that? Because you wrote something that was totally real to you. You wrote honestly and without strain to make up something. You weren't trying to force anything. You were in flow.

This is a key thing. You now know you can write realistic dialogue. If your book is fiction, when it comes time to make up dialogue for your characters, simply be as relaxed and energetic as you just were a moment ago, and *let it come as if it's already happened and you're remembering it*.

If you're writing nonfiction, just be easy and natural when you're writing what people say. Genuineness is better than precise grammar.

Great dialogue:

- sounds real
- fits each individual character
- develops character
- moves the story forward

We'll get at all of these aspects, but first, I'll tell you something professional authors think about a lot.

THE GREAT PARADOX OF DIALOGUE

Authors must write dialogue that comes across as real. Yet why does actual speech sound so dumb when transcribed onto the page?

Here's an example.

> She: Did you remember to pick up milk? Because Chris had his friends over and they—
> He: Yeah.
> She: —and like I said on the phone I'm going to make pudding, and I need four cups for the recipe.
> He: Yeah.
> She: Yeah you got it?
> He: I put it in the fridge.
> She: What?
> He: In the fridge.
> She: I'm sorry, I didn't hear you.
> He: It's OK. Is anything the matter?
> She: No. Everything's fine.
> He: I have to get ready for bowling.
> She: I think Chris is getting less allergic to sesame seeds. He ate a McDonald's bun in the car with Anders and his mom, and he was fine.
> He: Still, I wouldn't feed them to him because—
> She: I'm not. I totally agree.
> He: I'm gonna eat, then I gotta get out of here about seven.

Fascinated yet? Me neither.

The reason real speech sounds so dumb on the page is that most of what people say is *really boring*!

Why? Because our lives are not like novels or movies. Most speech is self-referential, repetitive, unnecessary, and mundane.

However, there's gold in it. Real people say unique, remarkable things, especially when they're talking about something they feel strongly about, or when they're talking about a memorable event. Those things are like gold nuggets in the fine gravel of a miner's pan. The words and phrases that make your ears perk up, make you laugh out loud, make you cry, or make you seethe with anger are dialogue gold—keep an ear out for anything that makes you *feel*.

The gravel you sift out of your pan is the brainless dreck that people say and forget. It's our job to pan for the gold.

STARTING TO LISTEN

Real people don't speak words alone. They use tone and cadence to get meaning across.

The word *Oh*, for instance, is endlessly flexible.

Like this:

> "Oh," he grunted.
>
> "Oh!" Cassie couldn't believe her luck. "Oh!"
>
> All at once he understood. "*Ohh.*"

You can see the difference on the page, and you can almost hear it. Notice that here we combined the word with punctuation and narrative to add context to the dialogue and achieve different effects. More on punctuation soon.

In plays, you'll see dialogue that might read awkwardly but comes to magical life in the mouths of actors and actresses.

Not long ago when I read a play by the extremely talented Martin McDonagh, *The Beauty Queen of Leenane*, I kept noticing the word *so* at the end of characters' lines, and I was like, I guess that's an Irish-ism. And it sort of is, but sometime later I heard myself say *so* at the end of sentences sometimes, like, "I already ate, so." Which is a trailing off with a precise meaning: "So I won't go along to lunch with you guys."

And I heard myself say that and a bell was ringing in my head, and I remembered those plays where sentences ended in *so*, and I realized, "I *do* that, it's a *modernism*, it isn't totally just an Irish-ism." And I understood another little thing about realistic dialogue there.

Tennessee Williams was a master of dialogue; I recommend reading his plays. Here's an excerpt from *Cat on a Hot Tin Roof*:

> MAGGIE
> One of those no-neck monsters hit me with a hot buttered biscuit so I have t'change!

(Water turns off and Brick calls out to her, but is still unseen ...)

BRICK
Wha'd you say, Maggie? Water was on s'loud I couldn't hearya ...

MAGGIE
Well, I !—just remarked that !—one of the no-neck monsters messed up m' lovely lace dress so I got t' —cha-a-ange ...

BRICK
Why d'ya call Gooper's kiddies no-neck monsters?

MAGGIE
Because they've got no necks! Isn't that a good enough reason?

BRICK
Don't they have any necks?

MAGGIE
None visible. Their fat little heads are set on their fat little bodies without a bit of connection.

BRICK
That's too bad.

MAGGIE
Yes, it's too bad because you can't wring their necks if they've got no necks to wring! Isn't that right, honey?

William Inge was also pretty good with dialogue, and while I'm on the subject of plays and great dialogue, I must tell you to read *Who's Afraid of Virginia Woolf?* by Edward Albee. Raw, wrenching, startling—it's just terrific.

You know that every word you write must serve a purpose, whether to move the action forward or to develop a person.

But dialogue, unlike every other aspect of our craft, is an opportunity to do both at the same time. Reading plays really helps you see that.

Reading screenplays is also a fun way to learn more about good dialogue. They're available in libraries, in bookstores, and online.

HOW TO TUNE IN AND GET GOOD

People talk for different reasons.

They talk in order to:

- communicate neutral information
- give warning
- demand
- complain
- manipulate
- grieve
- process stuff
- keep from thinking or feeling
- keep from listening
- express hurt
- fill silence
- declare love
- boast
- lie

Here's an example of a miner's pan that has at least one gold nugget in it. This is an exact excerpt from an interview I did while putting together an oral history project for a symphony orchestra I was a member of a few years ago.

Wait, what exactly is an oral history?

Simply, the spoken memories of a person or persons, recorded. The recording could stand on its own as an audio version, or it can be transcribed into written form.

This is a female musician talking. A cellist, in fact.

> I remember Leo Sunny, when we were in France, on a symphony tour, and we were sitting in this restaurant, a hotel restaurant. You could always count on Leo to have his violin, and he would always serenade with his little gypsy songs, just wandering around, just this little infectious smile, who could resist that—just serenading everybody, kind of a little bit out of tune and then oh, he would serenade us when we were in the airport when we were sitting waiting, he would serenade us at the airport and also hotel lobbies while we were waiting for the luggage to be packed up.

> Out of sheer nothing else to do, he'd try to cheer our spirits up, keep us preoccupied. Anywhere, you could count on it.

A piece of gold from this excerpt is the phrase, "Out of sheer nothing else to do." You know? It's so real, so informal. I might someday have a character say, "Out of sheer nothing else to do," or not. If that cellist had *written* her memories of Leo Sunny, I guarantee you she wouldn't have written, "Out of sheer nothing else to do," she would have written something more formal. She'd probably have left it out altogether. Which would be a loss, which is why oral histories are so rich.

Another piece of gold in here is "kind of a little bit out of tune." Informal, kinda funky, totally real.

If you ever have the chance to do an oral history project, jump at it. If you go and ask people questions and let them talk into your microphone and you transcribe it, you will learn tons about natural speech. Unfortunately, while speech-to-text programs are freeing writers from the task of transcribing, the same programs are robbing writers of the highly educational duty of transcribing.

If you're doing a nonfiction book, consider recording some interviews for it. You can even interview yourself! You'll get real words you can use.

As you develop your ear and eye for natural speech, you'll sort through the gravel and you'll immediately pick out the gold, and you'll use it.

Now when I say "use it," I don't necessarily mean insert it into your fiction or nonfiction word for word—though you could, depending on your needs. What I mean is to use it to inform yourself as to how people talk.

Read oral histories when you can. I recommend Studs Terkel's *Working*, which I'm not sure is still in print, but that one is really good for developing your ear. There's another one I have on my shelf called *The Life Stories of Undistinguished Americans*, edited by Hamilton Holt, which is filled with compelling examples.

I'd also recommend reading 9-1-1 transcripts, if you can handle it emotionally. You can find these online. Just Google 9-1-1 transcripts, or Google some famous murder case that had a 9-1-1 call, and you'll see how people talk under life-and-death stress. In some of them, the emotion comes through, and in some it doesn't.

As a writer, you should also develop sensitivity to ambient speech, which is the speech that goes on around you, not necessarily involving you. How exactly do you develop sensitivity to ambient speech?

Eavesdrop!

It's simple:

- Watch out for opportunities.
- Listen.
- Make notes!
- Look for context.

First, be very aware of your environment, not merely as it relates to you. When something interesting starts to happen, don't turn away out of politeness; get closer. Be a good witness.

Next, tune in to the speech around you and simply listen, really listen. Coffee shops are the cliché place to eavesdrop, but there's good reason for it. Often two people who haven't seen each other in a long time meet at a coffee shop and talk their heads off, or two people with something important to discuss will go to a coffee shop.

For about a year, I did a lot of writing at a particular Starbucks in my town. Once in a while I would see a certain type of couple: a young man sitting drinking coffee with a much older woman. Their conversations were quiet and exceptionally intense. And I saw this over and over, with a different young guy and older woman every time.

And I started to wonder about it. And I started to quietly, stealthily eavesdrop. I started to look at the bigger picture, and I realized that that coffee shop happened to be a few doors down from an armed forces recruitment center.

And I realized that these young men and ... their *mothers* had just been to the recruitment center. And they came out and saw the Starbucks and decided to come here and talk it over.

And the faces I saw and the conversations I overheard were too intimate to recount here, but they informed me as a writer. I haven't yet used a conversation like that in one of my books, but all of it is inside me somewhere. It adds to my experience as a person and as a writer. Being a good listener, being a sponge, will help you tremendously as a writer, too.

Practicing being sensitive to the human interactions around you is what you need to do.

Third, make notes. This is huge. How many times have you heard something imperishable, but when it came time to recount it, all you could do was weakly paraphrase? Keep paper and pen handy at all times. It's tremendously helpful to scribble down the pieces of dialogue you hear.

Fourth, look at the bigger picture. You want to gain context. Let yourself draw commonsense inferences. Yes, that young man looks like he's trying very hard to be confident. The mother, look at her, she's scared, but she knows the Army might be the best place for this kid. Why? Maybe because he's got lousy posture and a potbelly and this town has a 25 percent unemployment rate. Might be the best thing.

And that could be a story idea right there.

Reality TV is good for learning dialogue, if you can stand it. I got a good line from a reality-type program on bad drivers: "When my husband George is in the car, he becomes very *argumental*." Well, can't you just hear her talking about her kids and the new Diamonique anniversary band that she guilt-tripped George into buying her last month? Can't you imagine her throwing together a tuna casserole while talking to her sister on the phone about the sister's latest bout with Crohn's disease?

Documentaries are good, too, the ones where ordinary people are allowed to talk at length. I'm a fan of Michael Apted's social documentary series ("7 Up," "14 Up," etc.).

As you listen to conversations, you'll realize that dialogue consists of two things:

- content; that is, the words they're using, and
- delivery

Crafting Dynamic Dialogue

Here is a key point for authors: *One is as important as the other.*

As you listen, focus on *how they're saying it.*

Developing your ear for actual speech will let you use the vernacular for your own purposes.

What Does Vernacular Mean?

Simply the everyday speech of a region or group.

My neighbor told me the other day that he had once again, with the greatest determination, picked up *The Adventures of Huckleberry Finn* by Mark Twain, and he was going to read it if it killed him.

Why was he having such a hard time with it? *You* know: the dialect, of course. Twain was totally faithful to the regional vernacular and dialects, both white and black, of the old South, and it requires a bit of work to make your way through it. Once you get it, though, you get it and you enjoy it.

> "Huck, does you reck'n we's gwyne to run acrost any mo' kings on dis trip?"
> "No," I says, "I reckon not."

Today readers don't have much patience for dialect, so my baseline advice is minimize it if you need to use it at all. Furthermore, readers are extremely sensitive to stereotyping. So this is a tricky area for authors.

If you do decide to use dialect, sprinkle little bits of it here and there to suggest it and let the reader use her imagination to fill in the picture.

Ah! Here's our Cockney friend to illustrate:

> "Glad to 'elp, gov'ner, it's the first house on the right."

> **VERSUS**

> "Glad to 'elp, gov'n'r, it's the first 'aouse on the royt."

Cockney is a variation of British English. The second example is actually more accurate than the first, but it gets to be a li'tle much after a woyle.

Here's an example of a common American accent:

> "Elizabeth, your cah has to be moved. You can't pahk on the street overnight."

That example has two words that were changed, to indicate, oh, a Brooklyn or a Boston accent, I guess. You could probably get away with just one and still be successful.

Use your best judgment, and remember, less is better when it comes to accents and dialect.

Your chief goal as a writer of dialogue is to absorb the way people talk and make it your servant.

....

ELIZABETH SIMS is the author of eight successful novels in two series, the Rita Farmer Mysteries and the Lambda and Goldie Award-winning Lillian Byrd Crime Novels. She's been published by a major house (Macmillan) as well as several smaller presses. Elizabeth writes frequently for *Writer's Digest* magazine, where she is a contributing editor. Her book *You've Got a Book in You: A Stress Free Guide to Writing the Book of Your Dreams* (Writer's Digest Books) received special recognition by NaNoWriMo and hundreds of other websites and bloggers.

Crafting Dynamic Dialogue

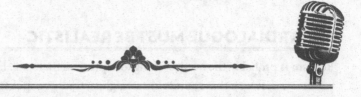

CHAPTER 7
KEYS TO GREAT DIALOGUE

BY JEFF GERKE

What makes great dialogue in fiction? Is it snappy one-liners or trendy phrases? Is it innuendo or inflection or devastating irony? Perhaps it's the unforgettable line: "The problems of three little people don't amount to a hill of beans in this crazy world."

Maybe it's truth that makes dialogue great. Digging down to the essence of the human condition. "I am not an animal! I am a human being! I ... am ... a man!"

Dialogue in movies gives us some of our favorite moments: "Frankly, my dear ..." or "I've got a bad feeling about this" or "The horror ... the horror."

Every novelist wants her lines of dialogue to be as powerful and memorable as these. But how? What's the secret?

And you need to find out because there are acquisitions editors out there (the ones who love fiction, primarily) who will skip over everything in your proposal and flip straight to a section of dialogue in your sample chapters. If you've done your dialogue poorly, they'll put the proposal away right then and won't look at anything else.

I submit to you that I wasn't far off when I suggested it might be truth that creates good dialogue. I believe dialogue is great when it is *authentic*. Dialogue must be realistic, layered, and right for the character and the moment.

GREAT DIALOGUE MUST BE REALISTIC

Realism is probably the hardest thing to capture in dialogue. How can you create dialogue that sounds like it might actually be spoken?

You can't just type up transcripts of actual conversations. Have you ever really paid attention to how we talk? Imagine Brock and Cammie having this conversation:

> "Did you get the ...?"
>
> "Nah. I thought we'd, uh, take the ... thing."
>
> "Okay. Move the shoes, please. So I guess you, you know, are okay with ...?"
>
> "Those aren't my shoes. Oh, I saw Francie at the club. She said we wouldn't ... It's like, she doesn't even ..."
>
> "You're kidding. But she's, you know. And besides, why don't you ... I mean, is it too much to ask to ..."

That's all pretty realistic. But it's not exactly easy to read. It's scattered, multithreaded, and incomplete. This is because real conversations are conveyed through tone and body language as much as actual words.

What you're after in fiction dialogue is something that *simulates* reality but is more intelligible than actual speech.

Let's look at the components of realistic-seeming dialogue.

A Real Boy

First, realistic dialogue is not formal or polite.

> "I believe we will be late if we take that route."
>
> "No, we will not be late. We'll be able to cross over at the Winston Changeover and miss the construction at Seventh."
>
> "Yes, that will be fine."

People don't talk like that. See how nice they are? And see how they take turns and let each other finish complete sentences? Dialogue in real life is much messier (though we need to also keep it intelligible for readers).

> "Don't take Main! You'll make us late. There's—"
>
> "Would you let me drive? We'll take Winston and miss the construction at—"
>
> "Whatever. Just go."

So, lesson one: Don't let dialogue be formal or polite. Don't let your characters take turns and allow one another to express their complete thoughts before speaking.

Second, realistic dialogue is not "on the nose."

Here's an example of on-the-nose dialogue.

> "Bubba, you have bad breath."
>> "No, Cletus, I do not have bad breath. I brushed my teeth this morning."
>> "If you had brushed your teeth this morning, you wouldn't have bad breath. That's what Louanne said, anyway."
>> "Louanne did not say that. She said ..."

By "on the nose" I mean the characters are saying exactly what they mean and responding to exactly what each other actually says. Real-world conversations are not like that.

Words, the deconstructionists tell us, are pitiful vehicles for conveying meaning. And all of us know conversations aren't so much about what is said as what is *meant*.

> "Bubba, you have bad breath."
>> "Dude, look, I'm sorry I dumped your sister. Deal with it."
>> "She deserves better than that. Better than you."
>> "Whatever, Cletus. Besides, I brushed this morning."

In real life, and in simulations of real dialogue, we're never really talking sentence to sentence. It's not the words we use so much as the messages imperfectly carried in those words. We're actually talking meaning to meaning, subtext to subtext.

This is why misunderstandings happen so often in e-mails. When you're left with only the words themselves and don't have the benefit of the tone of voice, body language, and inflection that carry 50 percent of the meaning, we don't communicate accurately.

Lesson two: Let your characters communicate with and respond to the subtext beneath their words, not the words themselves. Don't let dialogue be on the nose.

Great fiction dialogue feels realistic. If your book has dialogue that seems real, your book will be set above many unpublished manuscripts out there. If an editor flips straight to a section of dialogue in your proposal, she will begin to believe you might be ready to be published.

GREAT DIALOGUE IS LAYERED

Authentic dialogue is realistic, layered, and right for the character and the moment. Now let's talk about how to make dialogue layered.

What do I mean when I say that dialogue must be *layered*? This mainly goes back to the idea that conversations don't really take place in a word-to-word manner. It's not the words of the spoken sentences so much as it is the unspoken meaning beneath those words.

For instance, if you're late for work one day, and the boss says, "Nice of you to join us," she's not really meaning what she says. If a non-English speaker heard or read those words, he might think the boss is being polite. But you and I know the boss really meant, "You're late again, and it's disrespectful. Knock it off or suffer the consequences."

Meaning to meaning, not sentence to sentence.

A Seven-Layer Cake

When we talk to people, we're communicating via subtext. The meaning is *layered* beneath the actual words.

And one of those layers often contains old topics or disagreements the characters haven't resolved. Jibes, digs, and stabs. Inside jokes. Covert warnings. Ongoing debates.

For instance: John and Mary are out for dinner with Mark and Martha. All the way to the restaurant, John and Mary have been arguing about whether they should send their rebellious teenage son to boarding school. Now they're in a booth at Chili's talking with their friends.

> "So, Mark," Mary says, "how's your daughter doing? Still an A student?"
> "Well, she does all right. She did get a B on—"
> "I was just wondering because I know she did a year at ... what was the name of that boarding school?"
> John rolls his eyes. Here we go.
> "No, that wasn't actually a boarding school," Martha says. "Bentley is a—"

"And hadn't she been kind of getting in trouble before you sent her there?" Mary asks. "I seem to recall an incident with a boyfriend."

"Mary," John says, "leave it alone."

Martha sits up straighter. "Just what are you implying, Mary?"

"She's not ..." John says. "Mary, let it rest."

"What? I'm just saying that their daughter was rebellious before they sent her to a boarding school, and afterward she became an A student. Sometimes a boarding school is just what a teenager needs to shape up. That's all I'm saying."

"Fine, you win. We'll send him. Are you happy now?"

The four of them sit in silence. Mary reaches for her strawberry lemonade, and the glass shakes as she lifts it to her lips.

Now, not every dialogue will have these undercurrents of subtext. But you should be on the alert for chances to show it, because many conversations in your book will contain these layers.

We're always carrying an agenda. We're always trying to sneak in a few points or secretly strengthen our case. Conversations are just one more arena in the battle between personalities. It's that way for your characters, too.

GREAT DIALOGUE IS RIGHT FOR THE CHARACTER AND THE MOMENT

If you're watching a movie, how do you know when one character stops talking and another character starts talking? You start hearing a new voice, and you probably see the new character on the screen.

But how do you do it in fiction? How do you distinguish between one character and another? How can the reader tell when one person has stopped speaking and another speaker has started?

I'm not talking about the formatting mechanics in a manuscript that signal when speakers change—though you must master this. Nor am I talking about speech attributions, though those are vital.

Great Dialogue is Right for the Character

If you had three characters speaking together, and you removed all beats and speech attributions—which you shouldn't do, by the way, but bear with me—the reader still ought to be able to know which character is speaking at any time.

How? By the way each character talks, of course. By how he speaks, by what he thinks about that comes out in his words, by the vocabulary he chooses, by his syntax and grammar, and by the length of his sentences.

Great dialogue is dialogue that is right for the character.

By their spoken words alone your characters should distinguish themselves to the reader every time they open their mouths. In a sense, the speech they use is all the speech attribution they should need.

In some cases, of course, you need speech attributions, especially when the character is saying something that could be from any character in the scene. "Watch out!" for instance. But for the rest it ought to be clear simply by the way the person speaks.

Here are some classic lines from movies. Can you name who said them?

"We thought you was a toad!"

"Mmm, help you, I can."

"It's not the years, honey; it's the mileage."

"The pity of Bilbo may rule the fate of many."

"For it is the doom of men that they forget."

"Lawsy, we got to have a doctor. I don't know nothin' 'bout birthin' babies!"

"Of all the gin joints in all the world, she walks into mine."[1]

Ah, good memories, eh? Each one of these can take you not only right into the world of the movie it's from but right into the head of the character who said it.

A major component of developing a character is finding his voice, the unique way of speaking that distinguishes him from everyone else in the novel.

---

1 Answers: (1) Delmar in *O Brother, Where Art Thou?*; (2) Yoda; (3) Indiana Jones; (4) Gandalf; (5) Merlin in *Excalibur*; (6) Prissy in *Gone with the Wind*; (7) Rick in *Casablanca*.

I often see unpublished manuscripts (and some published ones) in which all the characters sound the same. And in fiction, if they all sound the same, they all *seem* the same to the reader. Which means you've got a novel of nothing but the same character talking to himself throughout the book. It feels more like the author doing a puppet show and playing all the parts himself than an eyewitness account of what actually happened when real individuals got together for the story.

It also usually results in uneducated people talking exactly like university professors and non-English speakers from Guam sounding exactly like Professor Higgins in London.

Please, for the sake of your story, do the work to be sure each character's dialogue is right for that character.

Good Dialogue is Right for the Moment

No matter what your particular character sounds like, he or she won't sound the same in every situation. If he has to scream above the noise of a battle, he's not going to speak in full sentences. If she's out of breath from running, she's going to use shorthand.

And yet I see the opposite in some of the manuscripts I work with. No matter what's going on, the characters talk as if it's a calm moment in the drawing room. Don't do that. Make sure the dialogue that comes out of a character's mouth is not only right for him to say, but is right for the context in which he is currently saying it.

Characters also change their vocabulary and other elements of their speech when in different company. His vocabulary may go up when he's speaking with a college professor, or down when he's speaking with a child or non-English speaker. Her volume may go up when speaking with someone hard of hearing, and down when she's in a theater. Be mindful of the context a character is in so her dialogue is correctly suited for that situation.

Characters also change their dialogue based on how they want to be perceived by the person they're speaking with. If she wants to get in good with the boys, a character may suddenly talk about football and refrain from using long words, peppering her remarks with "stuff" and "thing" instead. If he wants to get in good with a girl, a character may drop all the foul language and instead quote scripture or Shakespeare.

If it's the last minute before the bomb goes off, he's not going to be speaking in complete sentences. If she's in an interview, she's not going to use slang. And if she's a young teen texting with her best friend, she's going to text like a teen.

Read over your dialogue and be sure to make it appropriate not only for the moment but for the character saying it.

JEFF GERKE trains novelists how to better do what it is they're trying to do. He trains through his books for Writer's Digest: *The Irresistible Novel*, *Plot Versus Character*, *The First 50 Pages*, *Write Your Novel in a Month*, and *The Art & Craft of Writing Christian Fiction*. He trains through the many writers' conferences he teaches all over the country every year. He trained his authors when he ran Marcher Lord Press, the premier publisher of Christian speculative fiction, which he sold after an award-winning five-year run. And he trains through the freelance editing he does for his clients. Jeff is known for his canny book doctoring skills and his encouraging manner, which leaves writers feeling empowered and like they really can do this thing after all. He lives in Colorado Springs with his wife and three children.

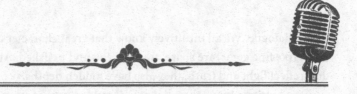

CHAPTER 8
HOW TO CRAFT FLAWLESS DIALOGUE

BY ELIZABETH SIMS

Among the many folktales I absorbed in my spongelike childhood, a particularly disturbing one stands out. A morality fable called "Toads and Diamonds," it concerned a nasty widow who lived in a backwoods hut with her two daughters—one good, one awful just like her mother. The mother favored the one like her, and forced the sweet one to haul water every day from a faraway spring.

One day while the girl was drawing water, a bent old crone appeared and asked for a drink. The girl kindly gave it, whereupon the crone revealed herself to be a magical pixie who bestowed a charm: Whenever the good sister spoke, flowers and precious gems would fall from her lips. The girl ran home to share the news, spewing beauty with every word. The greedy mother wanted the same gift for her other daughter, and nagged her to hike to the spring to offer a drink to the old hag.

When the awful daughter got there, a beautiful lady dressed in finery happened by. She asked for water and the girl answered rudely, observing that the lady could easily help herself. Whereupon the shapeshifting pixie leveled a curse that caused snakes and toads to fall from the nasty one's mouth when she spoke.

I've never heard any story that more literally captures the essential nature of dialogue.

Everybody uses terms such as "a gem of an expression" and "pearls of wisdom." Book reviewers frequently praise "sparkling" or "crystal clear" dialogue. We all intuitively know that great character conversations, like fine gems, are spare, transparent, and polished. And while they reflect light and truth, they also have hidden depths.

Good writers know that dialogue should always serve more than one purpose. It can help establish and develop virtually every other essential element of fine fiction, including plot, theme, style, mood, your voice as an author, your characters' voices, backstory, setting (both place/region and time period), pace, tension, conflict, and subtext.

Great writers dig even deeper, mining for opportunities to use dialogue to advance the story specifics of their genre. Instead of info-dumping via a narrator, use speech to:

- drop clues, plant red herrings, raise questions (mystery/thriller)
- explain the realities of the world you're building (sci-fi/fantasy/paranormal)
- gain trust, betray it, create poetry (romance)
- explore philosophical questions (literary)
- give warnings and ignore them (horror)
- establish the limits of law and lawlessness (Western).

Let's see how to create and serve up your own box of jewels (while keeping the toads at bay).

MINE FOR GEMS

One way to get good at writing dialogue is to make a point of noticing *real* dialogue. (Keep a notebook or smartphone app handy to capture memorable snippets.) Think back to an argument or intense discussion you had in the recent past. Write it out as best you remember. I'm thinking about the guy I confronted at the carwash for deliberately cutting ahead of me in line. As we watched our cars go through, we had this exchange:

> Me (with a smile): You know you cut in front of me, don't you?
> He (after pause of incredulity): I don't know what you're talking about!
> Me (nicely, quietly): Well, I was over there, waiting for Jerry to signal—
> He (louder): I don't know what you're talking about!

Me: Well, see—
He: I didn't come here to be ACCOSTED! I didn't come here to be
ACCOSTED!

There's no way I would have come up with that line; it sounds real because it was real—and well worth capturing. By the way, all caps (used sparingly) can signify volume; italics (ditto) can signify emphasis.

Another way to get some terrific dialogue literally under your fingers is to copy a passage from a great novel or play. Just head to your bookshelf, grab a book you love, find a scene of dialogue, and write or type it word for word, punctuation mark by punctuation mark. I guarantee you'll learn at least one key thing to apply to your own work.

YOUR CHARACTERS MUST WEAR IT WELL

The basic protocol for dazzling dialogue development starts with getting your cast together. Determine the *minimum* number of characters you need for the scene at hand. Then:

- See it. Taking time to first visualize the scene in your mind's eye will make the writing go more smoothly.
- *Hear* them talk.
- Give them all the words they need.
- Edit later.

A simple, effective way to characterize through dialogue is to individuate your players with vocal markers. Such distinctive markers are shamefully easy to cook up and drop into dialogue. Dashiell Hammett made the character of Casper Gutman in *The Maltese Falcon* memorable by endowing the cold, calculating fellow with elaborately mannered speech: "Oh come, come, my boy ...".

You can invent endless possibilities for this kind of thing:

- An insecure character might end sentences with "... I *think*," or begin them with, "Well, lemme see ..."
- A character who has served in the military might call men "sir" and women "ma'am."

Current or period slang can also individuate well:

> "That kills me."

> "Check those gams."

> "Yeah, he gave his full drunkalogue at the first meeting."

Dialogue is not only a vehicle for adding life to your characters, but also for revealing who they really are.

Let your characters' words betray their opinions.

> "You expect to get all the way to Cheyenne in two days, hitching?"

> "Don't underestimate me. I killed seven men in Venezuela, all in the same night."

Show your characters clawing for their deepest desires by making them talk around the point.

> Norah, noticing Ted's stained jacket and pants, steered him into the kitchen. She offered tea.
> "Well, I'm homeless again!" he declared joyfully.
> "You don't say." She poured a large mugful for him.
> "Looks like I might have to—you know, sleep rough for a while."
> "What happened? You just got settled into that nice—"
> "If you're going to grill me like a criminal, I won't stand for it. But, hey, is that back bedroom still open?"
> He never said *your* back bedroom.
> "No. I'm using it as my music studio. I give lessons there."

This is an example of subtext. If you read between the lines, it's obvious that Ted wants Norah to offer to take him in, and it's equally obvious that Norah doesn't want to, but their sparring makes the interchange more interesting—and real—than if either of them were up front about it.

JEWELS NEED A SETTING

Bring the talk (and your setting) to life by putting in a detail of your characters' surroundings, or a bit of physical business. This can be a part of the dialogue, or an aside that breaks up an exchange:

> "Is this snow *ever* going to stop? It's obliterating our tracks!"
> Jordan fiddled with his tie clip as he listened.

CUT AWAY THE EXTRANEOUS

We've all bumped into someone who was wearing too much bling. Jewelry is supposed to complement a person's inherent beauty or handsomeness, not overpower it. The watchword here is *economy*.

In real life, people often exchange pleasantries before getting down to brass tacks. A recruiter for a new government agency might ask the nervous interviewee how the crosstown traffic was, before inquiring about his experience as a CIA operative in Syria. It's of no consequence, just something to disarm the person. But in fiction, unless there's significance to the job-seeker's experience on the crosstown bus, it goes away. You might write:

After a minute of terse small talk, Bonner got to the point:

> "I want somebody who can tell me who ran the village of Al-Masrab from 1986 to '91."

Half of Elmore Leonard's reputation was built on dialogue, which itself made up half of his books. He had a superb ear for lingo, and he was economical as heck. From *Road Dogs*:

> "I didn't cut the man up, I shot him in the head."
> "After you robbed him?"
> "The man dissed me."

Herman Wouk kept the pace moving in *The Caine Mutiny* by having his characters interrupt one another rapid-fire, changing course as they went:

> "Well, I like Mozart," Willie said dubiously, "but—"

"She's cheap," said Mr. Dennis.

"Cheap?"

Even the briefest dialogue, if done well, can quickly establish character and motivation. It's especially appropriate when one of the speakers is a child. Consider the quickness of mind and limited vocabulary of the young. This from Stephen King's *The Shining* (note that the opening lines of dialogue are two sentences, and the rest are each only one):

"He's nice, but he's also a grown-up. And he's very careful not to say things like that in front of people who wouldn't understand."

"You mean like Uncle Al?"

"Yes, that's right."

"Can I say it when I'm a grown-up?"

"I suppose you will whether I like it or not."

"How old?"

You can do the same. Compare the following examples. Which is stronger?

"Did you set the parking brake?"

"No! Isn't that obvious?"

"You forgot?"

"I was only gone a minute!"

"Screw it, let's get out of here."

VERSUS

"You forgot to set the parking brake?"

"I was only gone a—"

"Screw it, let's get out of here."

APPLY PRESSURE

Tension escalates when one character is reluctant to tell something and another wheedles it out. A good way to do this is to have a character posit something false, thus goading another to spill the truth. (In real life, you can learn this technique from passive-aggressive personality types.)

"So I guess Zoltan gets off scot-free, right?"

"It's none of your business."

> "Everybody says you didn't hold him accountable."
> "Well, that's just not so!"

It's okay for a character to simply blurt something, indicating that the internal pressure has become just too great. This is fun to do with children or childlike characters:

> "I know you're not allowed to say, so don't worry about it."
> "Dammit! Dammit! Josephine and Estelle are having an affair! There! Are you happy now?"

It works, it's funny and it unquestionably moves the story forward.

An abrupt shift also can work wonders:

> "The Thames is pretty down here by Greenwich, isn't it?"
> "To be sure."
> "You and Esther enjoyed many a happy hour together on that very bank, didn't you?"
> "Yes, we did, picnicking. I miss her terribly."
> "Well, when you murder someone, it's easy to start missing her, isn't it?"

On a more subtle note:

> "I hope you fellows have found the car by now."
> "We did. Looks like someone stripped and dumped it on the east side."
> "The *east* side?"

APPRECIATE RAW BEAUTY

Often aspiring dialogue writers fall prey to Term-Paper Grammar Syndrome, in which everybody speaks in complete sentences, with correct punctuation. Steer clear by dropping words once in a while and letting characters relax into their speech:

> "How'd you know the pteranodon was even there?"
> "Saw it out of the corner of my eye."

It's also okay to (sparingly) use more crudely phonetic passages to characterize a voice:

"Don't be so ump-patient!"

Avoid giving narrative explanations of dialogue:

> "Get out of my face!" he yelled. Sometimes he just got sick of her, and this
> was one of those times.

The second sentence is unnecessary.

Consider most adverbs and unusual dialogue tags your Kryptonite, and above all avoid the dreaded combo:

> "I win," he uttered sneeringly.
>> "Not again," she groaned loudly.
>> "It's true," he proclaimed in a whisper.

DON'T OVER- (OR UNDER-) DO IT

Economy is great, but how do you really know when you have too much dialogue, or not enough? When you get to the polishing stage:

- Break up megaparagraphs, whether narrative or dialogue. That is, let neither your narrator nor your characters get long-winded.
- Opt for dialogue over narration when possible. If it needs to be said, can dialogue do it?
- Be as sparing with dialogue as with description.
- If you feel your characters are flat, ask yourself if they're talking enough.
- Trust your beta readers. If your reliable writing group, agent, or editor says there's too much dialogue or not enough, consider tinkering.

If you follow even a few of these guidelines, you'll be surprised at how much livelier your fiction will feel. You'll enjoy your writing and revising time, your readers will be delighted, and perhaps one day you'll be stumbling over piles of pearls, rubies, and rave reviews.

PART III

THE BASICS OF DIALOGUE

CHAPTER 9

MANNER OF SPEECH

BY JEFF GERKE

Most plot-first novelists rely on a funny way of talking for the beginning and end of their character-building work.

Ah, he's the Scotsman. And she's the one with the perfect diction and impressive vocabulary. He's the one who always says, "Whatever." She's the chick with the lisp.

How are characters differentiated in movies? Easy: They walk onscreen. Instantly the audience perceives that she is not the other girl who was here earlier. She looks different. She's taller. She dresses differently. She's a blonde. But you can't do that in a novel. You can write "Julie entered the room," but that doesn't do anything, by itself, to distinguish Julie from Hannah. You can keep saying, "She toyed with her blond hair" and "The sun glinted off her blond curls" to remind us of what she looks like, but it's never the same as the luxury you have in movies. (Plus, it's annoying to the reader, so don't.)

To differentiate characters in fiction, you have to show them doing and saying things.

So to a novelist, giving a character a funny way of speaking would seem like the perfect solution. I'll make him a Frenchman and let him be the only Frenchman in the book and then everyone will recognize him at the first "Oui, oui!" Or I'll make her talk only about the Dallas Cowboys so she'll start every sentence with "How 'bout them Cowboys?" Perfect! I'm set!

That's a shallow approach. A character must be defined by more than one single topic of conversation or by his accent. The Dallas

Cowboys girl may love the Cowboys, but she will have other interests or personality quirks as well. Not everyone in France will look, act, and speak exactly like your Frenchman.

THE DEUCE YOU SAY!

The way a character speaks can be magical. If you've done your work up to this point, you should be able to craft a character whose identity doesn't even have to be spelled out every time because the reader knows who is speaking.

> "Bond. James Bond."
>
> "Fasten your seat belts, it's going to be a bumpy night."
>
> "We thought you was a toad!"
>
> "I've always relied on the kindness of strangers."
>
> "Go ahead, make my day."
>
> "If you only knew how much I loved you. How much I still love you."
>
> "For it is the doom of men that they forget."[1]

Can you hear those in your head? Do you get an instant gestalt for the characters speaking? Sure, they're movie quotes not novel quotes, so maybe it's not a fair test, but the point is that the way a character speaks gives you perfect insight into who he or she is.

> "Fortune is arranging matters for us better than we could have shaped our desires ourselves, for look there, friend Sancho Panza, where thirty or more monstrous giants present themselves, all of whom I mean to engage in battle and slay, and with whose spoils we shall begin to make our fortunes; for this is righteous warfare, and it is God's good service to sweep so evil a breed from off the face of the earth."
>
> "What giants?" said Sancho Panza.
>
> "Those thou seest there," answered his master, "with the long arms, and some have them nearly two leagues long."

---

1 Quotes are from the following films respectively: Any James Bond movie, *All About Eve*, *O Brother Where Art Thou?*, *A Streetcar Named Desire*, *Dirty Harry*, *Casablanca*, and *Excalibur*.

"Look, your worship," said Sancho; "what we see there are not giants but windmills, and what seem to be their arms are the sails that turned by the wind make the millstone go."

"It is easy to see," replied Don Quixote, "that thou art not used to this business of adventures; those are giants; and if thou art afraid, away with thee out of this and betake thyself to prayer while I engage them in fierce and unequal combat."

So saying, he gave the spur to his steed Rocinante, heedless of the cries his squire Sancho sent after him. ... "Fly not, cowards and vile beings, for a single knight attacks you."

—Miguel de Cervantes, *Don Quixote*

You could take out every instance of speech attributions from Sancho and his master and not have a bit of trouble knowing who is speaking. That's the gold standard.

The trick is to grow a character's manner of speech from the inside out. Instead of saying, "He's the Cajun," say, "He's a janitor from a single-parent home with a passion for wounded animals who happens to be from New Orleans." Your character may sound like Forrest Gump, but he will *be* who he really is. The speaking is how his essential character leaks out for the world to see; it is not the sum total *of* his character.

The manner of a character's speech is to fiction what an actor's appearance and costume are to cinema. What we "see her say" in quotation marks must do in a novel what a shot of her doing in a movie will do in film: tone of voice, volume, rate of speaking, vocabulary, inflection, emphasis, pitch. All of these are expressions of who she is on the inside.

And, yes, this includes topics of conversation. She might really talk about the Dallas Cowboys if she loves them. She might even find ways to lead all conversations back to the Cowboys. But that's her as a person having fun and expressing her character. It is not the sum total of her character.

It includes her idioms and colloquialisms. If he's an ophthalmologist he might really say, "We take a dim view of such things" and "I'll keep an eye on it" and "Here's the way I see it," and might not even realize what he's doing. But that's because he has been impacted by his chosen career.

It includes her use—or lack of use—of word pictures or exaggeration or jocularity. These and so many more aspects of what she talks about and how she says it are to be found in her temperament and upbringing.

A person's manner of speech is her marker, her name tag, and her résumé rolled into one.

In 2009 there was a news story about a couple who somehow got past the Secret Service and crashed a State Dinner at the White House though they were not on the guest list. There are now-famous photos of these people shaking hands with President Obama, Vice President Biden, and many more dignitaries. The Secret Service had a terrible time explaining how complete strangers got within striking distance of the leader of the free world—not two hundred feet from the Oval Office itself.

These two people were pretenders. They wanted to run with the big dogs. They wanted to be somebodies. But they weren't on the list. They didn't want to do the hard work of actually becoming people who would be invited to a State Dinner with the president. They wanted to cut ahead to the finish line. It's like those people who try to join marathons in the last mile to receive the accolades without doing the work.

Likewise, characters who are nothing more than an accent are pretenders. And the novelists who write them have not yet done the hard work of creating real people. They've tried to cut ahead to the finish line, to sneak into a party they don't belong in, in order to appear as if they've created real characters.

But you're not like that, I know. You're here doing yeoman's work to produce authentic, inside-out characters who speak as they do because that's what comes out when you pair this temperament with this background and realistic parameters. She speaks this way because when you squeeze her, that's what comes out.

ARTICULATE MUCH?

Most novelists are highly intelligent, highly articulate people. They are adept at saying, with precision, exactly what they mean.

That's not to say they always come up with the perfect thing to say in the moment. One of the reasons I'm a writer is that I usually don't come up with the awesome comeback until the moment is over. So I write fiction, during which I think long and hard about the right lines, and then create characters who *do* always say the perfect thing at the perfect time. Revenge!

Perhaps because of this or perhaps even without realizing it, novelists tend to write characters who are as articulate as they are.

That doesn't sound so bad at first. Real life is too full of miscommunication and unclear meanings, so of course we take the opportunity in fiction to bring clarity to our corner of the universe. Fiction isn't about hyper-realism as much as it is about verisimilitude, after all. We don't want reality; we want truth.

Realistic dialogue goes something like this:

> "Hey."
>> "Hi."
>> "How was your ... thing? With your review-whatever."
>> "Oh, good, I think. She was late."
>> "I'm—"
>> "And then she was there but ... Here's your deodorant."
>> "Thanks. I tried to—"
>> "So she was running late and forgot about— I think she forgot we were ..."
>> "You're kidding."
>> "Yeah. So everything was like, 'Hi, you're reviewed, no more leaving early, now get out, I have a lunch.'"
>> "Oh, that's—"
>> "I know. But ..." [shrugs]

That may be an accurate transcript, but it's not great dialogue for fiction. Still, you don't want to completely clean it up and clarify it or you'll end up with dialogue that feels "on the nose" and overly polite—and completely unrealistic.

The goal is to hit something in the middle. And you probably won't achieve that with perfectly comprehensible characters saying perfectly logical things all the time.

So how do you write unclear dialogue? It goes against your nature to write something that is intentionally ambiguous, I know. Not all your characters have to be confusing and not every conversation has to go like the one that follows, but many of your characters will demonstrate some unclear communication at some point in the book.

The roommates we're overhearing below are brushing teeth and getting ready for bed. They've been talking about switching to electric toothbrushes and the like.

JENNY
How long do you have your two?

LAURA
My tube? [thinking tube of toothpaste]

JENNY
No, your two.

LAURA
My two what?

JENNY
Your two students. [sounding exasperated]

LAURA
Oh, I thought you said tube. I thought we were still on toothbrushes.

JENNY
No.

LAURA
You mean my tutoring students?

JENNY
Yes.

LAURA
Oh, they're one hour each.

JENNY
No, how long do you have them?

LAURA
[pause] Um, well, one is in the math program, which is twelve weeks, and the other two are in the reading program, which is—

JENNY
No, I mean for two hours.

LAURA
[pause] I'm sorry?

JENNY
When one is gone?

LAURA
Oh! You mean how long will I have only two students because my third is on vacation?

JENNY
Yes.

LAURA
Oh, just Monday and Wednesday. My third student comes back on Friday.

Poor Jenny, bless her. She probably realizes on some level that her communication was unclear, and it may frustrate her more because she doesn't know how to disambiguate it. But to her it all makes perfect sense. In her mind, it was very clear.

Here are some principles of confusing dialogue, should you choose to write some for your characters.

How To Be Confusing

Begin with a non sequitur. Change topics without signaling. They had been talking about toothbrushes, so when Jenny changed to another topic, Laura was still sitting on topic one.

For best results, use statements that could have meaning with topic one but actually pertain to topic two. Like:

> "Yes, that ball game was the best I've seen in a long time."
> "When did you see the last one?"
> "I actually caught last week's game."
> "No, when did you see the last Dalmatian in the park?"
> "What?"

To be confusing, mumble so that key words are unclear. "Did you say, 'Do I have a tube?' A tooth? A 'tude?"

As you seek to clarify, use no helper words to give meaning. Simply keep stressing the same word or phrase over and over. "No, a two, a two, a *two*!"

Phrase your sentences so as to have multiple meanings based on context (while concealing context). "How long will you have them?" "Have what?"

Use malapropisms at key points:

> "Will you have to stay in lieu of teaching?"
>> "No, I'll both stay and teach. Is that what you meant?"
> "But after your teaching, do you also have to stay?"
>> "Oh, you mean in addition to, not in lieu of. In lieu of means instead of."
> "Are you making fun of me?"
>> "No, I ... what was the question?"

Add a dose of frustration as the other person proves too dense to get what you're saying.

The person being unclear isn't trying to be that way. Indeed, it may cause her great mental angst to realize that she's being unclear and even more angst that she can't find her way out of the maze.

You may try this and find that it becomes too obtrusive for your book. It may turn into a character who is nothing but a comic wrong speaker, like the nurse in *Romeo and Juliet*. Don't let it become a stereotype, of course.

It may be that you try this but decide it doesn't fit for this character or even the whole book. That's fine. Just be conscious about not letting all your characters speak with perfect articulation, like you do. Vary it realistically, based on the other homework you've done for each character's personality.

CHAPTER 10
BELIEVABLE DIALOGUE

BY DEBORAH HALVERSON

Dialogue is more than characters gabbing at one another. It's a powerful tool for exposing characters in ways they aren't aware of, for stimulating them into action they wouldn't otherwise take, and for revealing vital plot information in a way that intrigues readers rather than info-dumps them into a dead-eyed stupor. Above all, it creates a sense of immediacy and intimacy essential for readers yearning to connect with your character.

Your job is to make all that rich story-building stuff happen while sounding convincingly like a real person. The techniques and strategies below tap into multiple storytelling elements to influence and support the words you put in your characters' mouths, even as you wield technical between-the-quotation-marks mechanics. The result will be flavorful, convincing conversations that'll enrich the entire reading experience.

STRONG DIALOGUE IS AN AMALGAM OF STRONG CRAFTWORK

Dialogue is a team event. Plot, characterization, setting, sensibility … they all play roles in what a character says, when she says it, and how she says it. Sometimes, those elements even do the talking in place of spoken words, as in the case of actions that reveal what that character is thinking without her uttering a sound. Those actions and anything else you can stuff into the *narrative beats*—the narrative material between lines of dialogue during a conversation—contribute to the effectiveness of the words you position within the quotations marks. For example, the unremarkable words, "Honey, I'm home," can be drenched with a tidal wave of sinister irony when you couple those peppy spoken words with action in the narrative beat:

> "Honey," he crashed his boot through the center of the door, then put his sneering face to the hole, "I'm home."

If you leave it to the words within the quotation marks to do all the talking, you miss out on depth like this. You end up instead with flat dialogue that, when you really need some emotional pow, swings into overwrought melodrama. Let's look at that same scenario of the booted dude trying to gain entry again, only this time I won't support or contribute to the dialogue with other elements. The spoken words between the quotations marks must shoulder the whole load:

> "Let me in! Now!"
> "This is *not* the day to be locking me out. ... I don't have the patience for this. ... Open the door!"
> "I'll bust down this door if you don't let me into my own home!"

Those examples show how fussy punctuation can get when the dialogue is overburdened, with exclamation points and ellipses trying to convey the emotion. Dialogue tags like "he shouted" or "she hissed" often accompany this heavy-handed treatment of dialogue as the writer does her utmost to wring emotion out of the spoken words alone. Dialogue like this earns the critique, "The dialogue feels forced instead of natural." Authors aware of the need to give a conversation rhythm may toss in some generic action so that it's not just a page of dialogue, but although their hearts are in the right place (they are trying to write an emotional scene), they aren't making full use of their writer's toolbox.

> "Let me in! Now!" he shouted, pounding on the door.

In that example, the pounding shows us an *excited* guy in action, and the verb *shouted* lets us know his voice is raised in case we didn't figure that out from the twin exclamation points. Of course, my offering this snippet out of context leaves room for you to argue that other things in the scene would clarify whether he's *happy* excited or *angry* excited or *desperate* excited, but isolating this line shows us that the elements in this sentence certainly aren't conveying specific emotion themselves. They could easily do so, and should, and that's what this section is about.

I'm going to arm you with five ways to unburden your dialogue by teaming it up with other core elements of storytelling, including your setting, your sensibility, and your characterization tools like body language and prop interaction. Use the strategies in this section to relax your dialogue so that it feels more natural and it works with the other elements to contribute to the scene rather than depending on the rest of the scene for full meaning. Successful conversations require all the elements to work in concert for balance, for effectiveness, and for a lovely emotional wallop.

1. Sync Their Dialogue with Their Sensibility

You need to consider the age and background of your character when writing dialogue. It may be tempting to put advanced vocabulary in the mouths of teens or new adults as a way to make them sound older, but we need to keep in mind that handing a kid his high school diploma doesn't kick his vocab growth into hyperdrive. Rather, what does change are the thoughts these newly independent kids express as they finally get to venture into the wild on their own and start gaining experience and worldliness. With that experience comes a greater tendency to take other people into account, an increased sophistication in the way they frame their thoughts, and a new focus on issues that all young people encounter as they duck and dodge and press forward through new adulthood. What young people talk about and the way they talk about it should reflect the way they now think.

· Teens and new adults still have some of the self-focus of adolescents, but their perspective is turning outward year by year, experience by experience. You can evidence each new adult character's degree of self-focus when they talk. And you can consciously adjust that at certain

Crafting Dynamic Dialogue

times in the story, such as in times of distress, when you can have them backslide into talking about how the situation affects them first and foremost. So on a calm day, when all things are good, your young guy might say, "The commander has a lot going on. He'll want this done fast." But with that stressed-out commander on his case threatening severe reprisal if the job isn't completed *right here and now, buddy,* the dialogue can be worded with more self-focus: "I gotta get this thing done or I'm screwed." Younger new adults may do this more often. Teens, of course, do it a whole darn lot. It's part of our maturation process to expand our focus outward as we get older, like ripples in a pond, moving from our immediate social circles outward, from grade school through middle school and high school and then into the big, round world.

Your new adults can also talk in ways that reveal their growing self-awareness, or ability to be cognizant of why they're doing what they're doing. They're still well short of being psychoanalysts, of course, so let them mess up when they try to self-analyze or analyze other characters. Let them talk to others as though they understand the other's motives, perhaps even sounding condescending or judgmental in how they word that analysis, and in the end saying the absolute wrong thing and worsening their problems. After all, when you try to tell other people why they're doing what they're doing without having a fully developed tact filter, the things that tumble out of your mouth can land you in deep doo-doo. With life experience will come increased tactfulness.

All this is not to say that you can't work in more advanced vocabulary than a teen might use; just be measured about it. Your character can sound too old or just plain unnatural if she's spouting fifty-cent words all the time. Even adults don't normally speak with extreme erudition in real life, not during informal conversations, at least. Consider the circumstances of each scene while you're writing it. Your leading lady's vocabulary is likely to improve when her boss is in the room. Her vocabulary will also reveal her energy and mood. I'll talk more about word choice later in this chapter when I get into nitty-gritty sentence crafting techniques.

2. Combine Characterization and Conversation

Who your characters are influences what they say and when they say it. Highly educated, underprivileged, sarcastic, conservative, devil-may-care … their personalities and their lives before page one of your novel inform the thoughts they think and the words they use to utter them in your book. That's why basic character prewriting work is useful even when you're not an outliner. You should have at least a vague sense of who your character is before you start writing her dialogue. Eventually, it will seem like she's talking on her own, but it's you who sets her mouth in motion.

Hearing directly from characters creates a sense of intimacy, of connection, for readers. In speaking for themselves, the characters reveal things about themselves—often beyond the information they articulate. For instance, they can reveal "facts" about their background, their values, their priorities, their IQ. I'm not talking about delivering facts as info-dumping statements, such as "I went to Miles McKearney High School, which was the poorest school in the whole state." Rather, I'm talking about having your character make comments about things he envies or admires or perhaps finds ridiculous:

> "That guy over there in the preppy vest, we would have eaten him alive at my high school. I'm so done here. C'mon, I need a Bud."

When a character talks about his impressions and reactions, we *feel* his past influencing him as a person rather than hearing it as a biographical fact. This is more of the *showing* instead of *telling* approach that's so crucial to fleshing out a character. Thus, dialogue contributes to characterization even as your characterization influences what your character says.

Your character's personality will play into her way of speaking, too, as will her mood in each scene. A confident character can make statements such as, "Put it in the cauldron," whereas a character lacking self-confidence may frame things as questions: "Put it in the cauldron?" If your character is at the beginning of her book's journey and totally clueless or unwilling to venture a guess at the next action, she might just blurt, "What do I do with this?" You don't have to say a word about her feeling clueless in the narrative now—in fact, doing so and then following with this dialogue will feel like beating your reader over the head with characterization.

Relationships are revealed in dialogue, too. What your characters choose to discuss with each other shows the depth and nature of their relationship. Dialogue that has characters not answering direct questions—practicing "artful dodging"—may indicate a relationship lacking in trust or perhaps clue us in that one person isn't that into the other. If you want to show long-time close friends, you can have them completing each other's sentences or uttering incomplete thoughts that the other character totally understands. Remember to think about every secondary character's relationship to your protagonist when you introduce that character to the story.

Dialogue helps readers get to know the character, but it also helps you get to know them, too. Many authors will "interview" their characters before or during a book as they look for insights. The authors listen to the answers and to the way the character talks back to them, picking up clues just as readers do. Character interviews can also be helpful if you need to work yourself through a rough spot in the story.

3. Link Their Dialogue to Their Setting

Your characters' physical location influences what they say and when they say it, so manipulate your settings with an ear for adding zip and depth to dialogue. When you're choosing a setting for a scene, consider ways you can use that setting to stimulate the gab. For example, you can tell a lot about a person by the words that pass his lips—and nothing gets those words flowing better than a setting that challenges him. Imagine the words of someone you send trudging through brackish swamps in sandals or stumbling through a screen door he didn't see.

The props in your location can provide vital touch points for conversations between characters. Imagine two characters sitting at a café discussing a plan. Since sitting and talking is ho-hum action, you're likely to try to make the spoken words more emphatic or emotional, which burdens the dialogue. That's not fair. Move those characters out of that setting or do something to that environment to give your characters something to do besides look at each other, frown, nod, and laugh while they're there. In the example below, I've moved that discussion out of the café and assigned a prop to the narrative character to give the guy something to focus on besides the emotion I'm trying to convey and the facts he must discuss:

> "So then he told me they come out at sundown and to not be outside after the sun sets," she said. "Jim?"
>
> He jiggled the key. Stupid lock was stuck again.
>
> "Jim."
>
> Goddamn stupid lock, how many times did he have to call the super to get the thing fixed? How had Vinny not been fired yet? He twisted the key, jerking and shoving, then pulling and yanking as the key stuck fast. It popped out abruptly, causing him to fumble it to the floor. What a lazy waste of flesh—
>
> "Jim!"
>
> "Wha—ow." He rubbed his head where he'd banged it on the doorknob picking up the key. "What?"
>
> She held up a new key, its pristine silver glinting next to her pink nail polish.
>
> "Where'd you get that?" he asked.
>
> "I just told you, Vinny was at the meeting. He gave it to me and said don't leave after sunset unless you like being wolf bait. That's not how I plan to go, thank you very much. I plan on getting old and grey and hobbling around with a walker and fifteen grandkids running around my ankles."
>
> The new key turned smoothly in the lock. "I'm not cowering inside all night. The flintlume powder will do its job."
>
> "It didn't for Wexler."
>
> "Wexler didn't add felium. I did. I told you, we're safe."

We get the facts, but more than that, we get a juicy glimpse into this couple's dynamic. I chose to give the male character clipped, impatient dialogue as he tunes out the long-winded girl and gets worked up by that key prop.

Social context is part of a story's setting, and it can be as vocally inspiring as location, with your character reacting to changes in the dynamics of her social group or simply talking in jargon that reveals the community or era she grew up in:

> "I suspect the Emperor has other plans for your highness. Severe plans, I dare say."

> "JD's gonna shove that crown you think yer wearing right up yer ass, *princess*, and I'ma help him."

> "Your inciting of the public is not acceptable. There will be an investigation, but I assure you it's merely a formality. You would be wise to prepare for a lengthy imprisonment."

> "Ooh, uh, maybe not the best idea, you know? You might want to, like, take it down a notch?"

If you're receiving critique feedback that your dialogue feels forced or unbelievable, don't automatically start hacking at and repunctuating the words within your quotation marks. Instead, take a gander at the setting and see if tweaking things there can lighten the burden on your dialogue and strengthen the whole conversation in the process.

4. Strike a Balance Between the Dialogue and the Plot

Dialogue is an important tool for revealing plot as well as for pushing it forward, but you can't be too literal about those tasks. When you have characters talk about story facts, readers can feel like they're being fed information. As I touched on in number three, full conversation about plot facts can become a dry, task-oriented lump of an info dump. So what do you do when characters need to talk about the events in their lives and their plans for dealing with them, particularly when you've got a complicated plot? Teach yourself to think of authentic dialogue as reactive rather than as a delivery tool. Have your characters' conversations focus on their reactions to the situation, on their hopes for what they'll be feeling about it after they take action. This way, the characters aren't delivering plot info but rather reacting to that information. To do this, turn the facts into a back-and-forth. For example:

VERSION 1: INFO-LADEN

"We need to put a wagon under that window. I'll fill it with straw so you can jump out of the window into it, and then I'll drive off. Trust me, we'll be gone before they realize you're even out of the room."

VERSION 2: REACTIVE

"See that window?"

"Oh no. Uh-uh. I know what you're thinking."

"It's just a few feet."

"Feet is what I'm thinking of—as in I don't want mine broken."

"I'll fill it with straw. It'll be soft as a pillow."

"That won't—"

"Yes, it will. Trust me, will you? You'll land like a marshmallow on a pillow, and then we'll be gone before they even know you're out of the room. Come on, you know you've always wanted to fly. And I've been looking for a chance to drive me a wagon. Bonnie and Clyde, right here. Me and you. Boom-chaka, baby."

As we see in the example above, dialogue is a powerful way for one character to manipulate another, and for you to manipulate your readers and force them to make judgments, too. Imagine what that wagon example could be after you've added setting and character-revealing action to the narrative beats. What's their body language like? What props are they manipulating? What could those things reveal about the situation and the relationship of these two people?

As the back-and-forth about the wagon demonstrates, being patient with revelations allows those revelations to suffuse the story rather than to smack readers upside the head. Don't succumb to the temptation of having two characters sit down for a backstory discussion. It's just not fun to read scenes like that. Be patient, and reveal in pieces across the scene, the chapter, and the story. Focus on the characters' dynamics, their reactions, their hopes and fears. Those are what drive the plot forward, not simple facts.

Another deliciously patient tactic of revelation is to have a character intentionally withhold information. Your characters may lie, they may dodge questions, they may say one thing while meaning another or thinking another or while they're really talking about something else entirely. There are plenty of reasons a character will refuse direct answers: lack of confidence, having something to hide, playing their cards close to their chest, distrust, uncertainty, avoiding trouble, avoiding commitment, and stalling for time, to name a few. The point is, conversations don't always have to be so direct, with straight answers and head-to-head confrontation. Add interactivity to the scene by making readers figure out what is *not* being said or when what is being said is deliberately misleading. When you set up a dynamic where characters are less than forthright with each other, readers have to fill in holes and parse out motives, which is excellent interactive reading.

A fabulous technique for making conversations feel layered and land-mined is subtext. *Subtext* plays a character's words against what he's really thinking, using his behavior to alert readers when his talk contradicts his thoughts or feelings. Subtext is the reality behind the words. We're probably most familiar with it in the context of a villain who talks charmingly as he presses the button that blows up the planet. The villain wants to appear as civil as any refined Good Guy, but his innards are the height of incivility and what he wants can only be accomplished via inhumane behavior. But this clash between saying things to make others believe the opposite of what's in a character's heart, mind, and spirit isn't just for villains. Good guys deliberately say one thing when they think the opposite. From little white lies to active manipulation of other characters for their own ends to protecting themselves from judgment or reprisal, every character can mislead. This makes for fun scenes where characters (and readers) have to parse and guess and eyeball each detail to work out what's what. It's a useful tool for thrillers and mysteries, obviously, but any story can use subtext to stoke tensions between characters and to patiently reveal things to readers about what the character really, super deep down inside, wants and thinks.

5. Bring it All Together for Emotional Resonance

Step-by-step, I've encouraged you to think more about dialogue beyond the obvious words within quotations marks. Tapping into a character's mind-set and sensibility will affect what she chooses to talk about, working in sophistication that reflects her age and stage in life will affect her spoken words, and manipulating the setting and the plot will enrich her dialogue. All of that contributes to one final whiz-bang aspect of dialogue: emotional resonance.

Your characters' emotions influence what they say and when they say it, and those emotions then affect readers' emotions. Emotional resonance is vital to a positive reading experience. Readers want to connect with their characters, and dialogue is a powerful bridge for that connection. Emotions should be crackling in your story.

I've spoken several times about overburdened dialogue that emotes the hell out of itself. We call that melodramatic dialogue. *Melodrama* is exaggerated emotion, to the point of hokiness, and it makes readers think, *Oh, gimme a break. No one would say that in real life.* Check out this bit of melodrama:

> "I hate you! You're a lying, cheating jerk, and I want nothing to do with you *ever*. You deserve to rot in hell!"

Ouch, right? No, not the sentiment—although being wished an eternity in Hades does pack some sting. I mean ouch about the visual assault of italics and exclamation points and the feeling of overwrought writing. That sample line gets the emotion across, sure, but powerful storytelling is more than bludgeoning readers with your message. I'm encouraging you to be a merciless manipulator, not a reader beater.

Instead of resorting to melodramatic dialogue, score emotional resonance by turning all the storytelling elements into a happy team. You're a conductor, really, directing a symphony of storytelling elements for one beautiful composition. The following example incorporates all the things I've talked about, all to score a single, powerful emotional connection with readers:

> "Aren't you thoughtful?" She took the rose he'd handed her and walked to the sink where she kept her vase. Two other roses rested in it, one from the week before, wilting slightly. Both were peach, matching the tight bud in her hand. He loved to give her flowers but dismissed red roses as cliché.

Crafting Dynamic Dialogue

"I stopped by Sue's apartment today," she said, turning on the water, her back to him. "She had a rose on her kitchen table." She reached forward, past the running water, past the vase, to the switch on the wall. Resting her finger on it, she turned and smiled sweetly at him. He'd stopped in the doorway, one glove off, the other dangling from his fingers. He wasn't tugging on it anymore. "A peach rose in a tall vase," she said, "right there next to her violin." She poked the bud's stem into the garbage disposal then flicked the button. The grinder roared as it sucked the flower down, flecks of peach petal flicking free, but he heard her clearly: "You told me you hate musicians."

This woman's pain has penetrated into her soul, settled deep down where it could seethe, finally coming out of her mouth not in a screaming tirade of accusation and condemnation but in quiet statements, the final one making you cringe from the intensity of its delivery. Everything leading up to that final delicate statement, all the action and the facts about the rose color, helps build up the tension for that final statement, which says nothing about the rose but is all about that rose. In fact, this passage focuses on the roses but is about something entirely different: his fidelity. This patient, richer emoting can be sustained for an entire book, whereas a book full of screaming, dish-throwing outbursts gets overwhelming.

TECHNIQUES FOR CRAFTING AUTHENTIC DIALOGUE

Even as you intertwine spoken words and core storytelling elements, you've got glorious mechanical techniques you can apply to the words between the quotations marks to make the dialogue feel realistic, youthful, and emotional. For example, freaked-out, worried, tense characters can use sentence fragments and incomplete thoughts. Impatient characters can interrupt others. Nervous characters may let their dialogue trail off using ellipses, or they may ramble, or they may express their thoughts as questions, as in, "I have to go there? Myself?" High emotions often involve exaggeration, as in, "This always happens" (even if it doesn't really *always* happen). We get to focus on those nitty-gritty techniques now, aiming for dialogue that hits readers' ears as rhythmic and wholly natural. We want readers forgetting that they're *reading* dialogue and instead simply hearing the characters talk. We want them praising your dialogue as "real."

Real. A misleading word when it comes to dialogue, but a popular way for readers to describe dialogue that works. Here's a very important thing to keep in mind as you make your decisions with dialogue: Strong dialogue is not real, it's realistic. Real everyday speech is meandering and sometimes boring and often flat-out incoherent when typed onto a page. Real speech is full of *ums* and *uhs* and *you knows*, and *likes*. It contains run-on sentences that change topic midway, sometimes even multiple times. *Realistic* dialogue strips out the babble and civilities of everyday exchanges. None of the "Hey, what's up?" "Oh, not much. What are you doing?" business, and none of the babbling we do as we think and talk on the fly. Here's real talk, unfiltered:

> "He was like—I don't know, I never saw him that way before, you know? All strung out, and, well, just strung out and looking like he couldn't take another thing, you know? It's all just, so, jeez, I don't know, stupid is what it is. Stupid. We gotta get out of this, okay? I mean, like, right this very second, you know? Before he just collapses and then it's all on us because no way do we want this thing on our heads. Let's just take off. Right now. Seriously, just run and be done with it."

Here's the realistic version, streamlined for pacing, clarity, and personality:

> "He was totally strung out. There's no way he can handle another thing. We were stupid to get involved in this. Idiots. Let's get out, now, before he collapses and it's all on us. Let's just go."

I've left in repetition for emphasis and to convey desperation and a casual speaking style, but the passage isn't bogged down with verbal ticks that readers would have to filter through. In real-life conversation, your ears may not pick up those things coming from a live person sitting across the table, but on a page, verbal ticks and filler words are distracting. Worse, they bury the heart of what's being said.

Here's the other doozy advice you need to keep in mind as you strategize and craft your realistic dialogue: *Strong dialogue is inseparable from the narrative that surrounds it.* That's been the theme of this chapter, and if I could, I'd string it with flashing neon lights right here on the page. I'll have to settle for italicizing the sentence, leaving the neon to your imagination. I'll lead this technical section with a big spotlight on the narrative surrounding your character's spoken words and the tags (the *he said, she said* stuff) that tell us who says what. I'll follow that up with a host of specific techniques to build emotion and tension and create the natural cadence of authentic conversation.

Making the Most of Narrative Beats

I touched on narrative beats earlier in this chapter. They're like the mayo in a ham sandwich—you've got a sandwich without it, but it's a dry one. Narrative beats are essential in a conversation, adding pauses that let the readers breathe and soak in what was just said, even as you set them up for the next line of dialogue. Authors seem to instinctively get this rhythmic use of narrative beats, perhaps because authors tend to be avid readers themselves and so have internalized rhythm over their reading lifetime. But too often they fail to realize that these beats are more than rhythmic pauses—they are opportunities to deepen the emotion in the conversation, to reveal things about the character, and to deliver information in interesting ways. Those authors will fill the beat with some generic action like pushing bangs out of eyes or smiling or looking. Readers' eyes slide right over that—opportunity wasted.

Make the action count by inserting revealing action that supports or contributes to the dialogue's meaning or emotion, or that illuminates characters' mood or psyche. There's value in using revealing physical actions to embody our characters. Narrative beats are fabulous places to reveal physical details. Don't waste them on blah items like:

> "Reporting for duty, sir," Maven said, pushing his blonde bangs out of his eyes.

Sure, readers love help in picturing the character, but this generic bang-pushing isn't boosting our understanding of Maven's attitude here. That beat could reveal something about Maven's eagerness for duty, making the entire exchange an insight into the dynamic between a hardened warrior leader and his eager (or not) plebe:

> "Reporting for duty, sir," Maven said, blowing his blonde bangs out of his eyes. He should have gotten a haircut before reporting to the commander.

Or:

> "Reporting for duty." Maven's blonde bangs hung in his eyes, and his uniform lay crumpled on the cot. The commander didn't blink. *I'll get Tex back for this.* Maven sighed, straightened his back, slid his feet together, then raised his hand to forehead. "Reporting for duty. Sir."

We know a lot more about that Maven guy now, don't we?

I went further with my second, longer revision of Maven's narrative beat in order to show you how you can use multiple elements within a beat. I included internal dialogue, setting props, and exposition that lays out what's happening with the commander. Don't do this with every beat, because it can get to be too much, and because you can easily interrupt the flow of a conversation. Instead, vary the length and depth of your beats throughout a conversation to keep it from sounding staccato or choppy. Again, it's about establishing balance through variety.

Sometimes a narrative beat will be simply the dialogue tag that identifies the speaker or just provides the basic rhythmic breather, like "… he said." Note that you don't need dialogue tags as often as you might think. Overuse can make a conversation sound choppy. Sometimes you don't need tags at all. Use them for clarity and rhythm, not automatically.

I want to caution you against filling your narrative beats with adverbs (usually -*ly* words) and clauses that describe how the line of dialogue was delivered, as in:

> "… he said eagerly."

> "… he said, saluting crisply."

> "… he said as he saluted."

Crafting Dynamic Dialogue

If you do the rest of the dialogue work I've outlined in this chapter, you won't need to tell readers that the action was done eagerly because they'll know that from all the other clues. Adverbs can be a sign that you're telling instead of showing, and they can make a piece of writing sound like it's trying too hard to makes its point.

I recommend sticking with the most basic tags to avoid calling attention to them: *said*, *asked*, and *replied*. Readers register those and thus know who is talking, then move on to the important stuff. Also, don't use tags that are physically impossible. *Hissing* can let us know there's a heavy whisper going on, but if there's no *s* in the words being hissed, you can't hiss them. *Laugh* isn't a speaking verb, and neither is *smiled*. If you want your character to laugh, you can do so once in a while (using that verb often sucks the power out of it, reducing it to unrevealing filler action), but stick it in the narrative beat as an action instead:

She laughed. "Stop it."

Choosing Your Words and Constructing Your Sentences

In most circumstances, there's a casual quality to a character's speech, even if that character is living in a more formal time or culture. The following techniques inject casualness, many utilizing the underlying strategy of relaxing the grammar.

1. Embrace Run-ons

Constructing complete and proper sentences is hardly at the top of our list when we're chatting with people, so using run-on sentences in your dialogue helps the realistic quality. However, real-life run-ons can be more like run-aways, with people addressing one point at the beginning of the sentence but wandering off to something new mid-sentence, and ending up who knows where by the end. In your dialogue, harness that run-on quality to emphasize your character's point, to rush the pace, and to tweak the rhythm of the conversation, but always keep clarity in mind. Play these run-offs against shorter sentences to give them added oomph:

"I ran, but he just kept chasing me and so I hid and he still kept coming and, oh my God, Tory, I totally thought I was going to die."

"It was my first concert, what did I know? I thought, you go to a concert and you listen to music and dance around and hang with friends and maybe get a little high and what's the big deal? Now, here I am, fired. Lovely."

2. Be Repetitive

Run-ons are well served by repetition, where a piece of dialogue circles back on itself to create emphasis. A character who repeats himself signals his priorities to the other characters and to readers:

"All I wanted was a little help. But no, nobody would give me the time of day even though all they had to do was stop for five seconds. Five seconds was all I needed, and I would have reached her in time. My sister's dead because nobody on this goddamn planet can spare five flipping seconds for a stranger."

The character's obsession with the five seconds shows his frustration by focusing on the timing, even as we get the dramatic punch of a single mention of death—the very thing you'd think a person would focus on. This character focuses on the five-second delay. For him, life and death is in that five seconds, and readers are aware of that because of the repetition tactic.

3. Trail Off, Blurt, and Interrupt

Blurting can give your dialogue a different quality. It can push the story forward as the characters worsen their problems with ill-considered words. Also, they may start to speak, only to have their tact filters kick in halfway through the utterance, in which case they cut themselves short (punctuated by em-dashes: —) or trail off (indicated by ellipses: …). Ellipses also indicate hesitation, and em-dashes can indicate interruption by someone else. All of these add great variety to dialogue and help reveal what a character is thinking or feeling at that moment. Interruptions and cut-offs are also super ways to speed up your pacing. I just caution you not to get too generous with ellipses and em-dashes, as a page filled with dots and horizontal lines is visually distracting. This is yet another "make it count by being judicious" item.

4. Strip Out the Mumble-Jumble

This is about clearing out the minutiae of real conversations. We talked about this previously when comparing real and realistic. As tempting as it is to fill the dialogue with "like" and "you know," that's distracting to readers. Never sacrifice the content of the dialogue in your quest for authenticity. The same with fillers like *um* and *uh*. Yes, those are useful for showing hesitation, so writers tend to fall back on them. But "falling back" is not powerful storytelling. This takes us back to the writer's toolbox, where you have other ways to convey hesitation that are more flavorful than:

> "You're coming with me, right?"
> "Um ... yeah, I guess."

Instead, you can create a narrative pause with a simple beat—a *he said* or *she said* tag, or maybe just a quick action. Or it could be a longer beat that uses the moment to reveal the relationship or the character attitudes, as in this example:

> "You're coming with me, right?"
>> She glanced at the book in her lap. Her evening could be Romeo and Juliet, or smarmy frat boys looking for a buzz and a babe. Why did Sara always do this to her? She closed the book and heaved herself up.
> "Let me change, at least."

5. Chill on the Slang

It's tempting to use slang to make characters sound youthful. There are indeed times when a generation's slang may be useful for the overall effect of a story, like one set in the 1970s where the culture of the era is a conspicuous story element, making terms like *groovy* natural vocabulary. Most of the time, however, slang can date your story, and it's likely to sound forced. People may say, "Hey, dude, what's up, man?" or "That's rad" in real life, but in fiction it can come across as trying too hard to sound real. Instead, use phrasing that conveys the sense of super informality that you're reaching for with the slang. For example, "He was totally in my face about it," sounds hip without being heavy-handed.

6. Make Your Swearing Purposeful

If you're writing books where explicit sex is fair game, profanity is certainly allowed. Having that freedom, however, is no reason to fill your fiction with four-letter words. Only swear if swearing is organic to your story and you believe the readers of that particular story would appreciate it. A guy hanging with his frat brothers at a tailgate party would very believably and organically say, while ogling a passing girl, "Nice tits." That said, there's no need to risk alienating readers when you can just as easily skip the cuss words. Yes, people in real life do respond to extreme situations by swearing: "Holy shit!" And yes, people in real life do use swearing as natural emphasis: "I was fucking pissed." But often, this is like using italics for emphasis—that is, you're taking the easy way out and selling your story short in the process. Instead of the "Holy shit!" response to something extreme, how about using setting and body language?

> He blinked once, twice, three times. Then, his face a mask of silent fury, he spun and punched his fist through the stained glass window.

Much like carefully timed exclamation points, a carefully timed cuss word can have more dramatic impact than a page full of them. Make sure you're swearing because it's the right thing for that character, at that moment, in that particular story, not because that's the first thing that popped into your head or simply because "real people cuss in real life." Strong dialogue isn't about being real; it's about being realistic and contributing to all the other elements of the story.

MAKING SENSE OF THE VOICES IN YOUR HEAD
Readers want insight into their protagonist's hearts and minds, and internal dialogue can provide that. Internal dialogue, also called interior monologue and direct thoughts, is really dialogue that stops on the tip of the character's tongue. It's often italicized but doesn't have to be. Most fiction

---

Crafting Dynamic Dialogue

eschews the italics treatment, often requiring the tag "he thought" to make it clear that this is a thought and not a regular part of the narration.

> He pushed back the curtains and peered into the darkness. Ten guards flanked the wooden gate. *It's over.* There was no way he'd get past ten guards, not without any weapons.

> He pushed back the curtains and peered into the darkness. Ten guards flanked the wooden gate. *It's over,* he thought. There was no way he'd get past ten guards, not without any weapons.

> I pulled back the curtains. It was dark, but I could make out ten guards, five on either side of the gate. *It's over.* There was no way I'd get past ten guards.

If you choose to italicize internal thought, you don't need a dialogue tag. You do need to write internal dialogue in present tense, just like regular dialogue.

Make sure your internal dialogue truly sounds like a snippet of dialogue that's bitten back just before utterance. Sometimes writers will set a first-person narrator's mental mulling in italics as a direct thought when actually those are *indirect thoughts* and should be treated just like any other piece of narrative. For example:

> I pulled back the curtains. It was dark, but I could make out ten guards, five on either side of the gate. *It's over. There's no way I can get past ten guards, not without any weapons.*

Incorporate mullings or narrative observations into the regular narrative. Save the italics for true internal dialogue so you don't bog down your pages with passages of italicized text:

> I pulled back the curtains. It was dark, but I could make out ten guards, five on either side of the gate. There was no way I could get past ten guards. It was over.

Some writers rely too much on internal thoughts to convey plot information or to pose hypothetical questions meant to force readers to ask those questions, as in, *I wonder what he's thinking? Could he be after my money? Or am I just another notch on his bedpost?* A string of italicized hypothetical questions can make an otherwise strong narration feel forced. It seems to scream, "Pay attention to me. I'm going to ask the questions I want you to be asking yourself, reader." The subtlety of making a reader wonder things gives way to you feeding the questions to readers.

If you're writing in third-person point of view, you can easily work this into the regular narrative. Or just trust that the reader is already wondering those things because you've used all the techniques and strategies in your writer's toolbox to push the story to the brink of those questions.

If you've chosen first person for your story, you probably won't have a lot of internal dialogue because the whole narrative is being presented as the narrator's thoughts. Your narrative is already one big insight into the protagonist's heart and mind.

DEBORAH HALVERSON is the award-winning author of *Writing New Adult Fiction* and *Writing Young Adult Fiction for Dummies*, as well as the teen novels *Big Mouth* and *Honk If You Hate Me* and other books for young readers. Formerly an editor at Harcourt Children's Books and now a freelancer specializing in New Adult Fiction, Young Adult/Middle Grade fiction, and picture books, Deborah has been working with authors—bestsellers, veterans, debut, and aspiring—for twenty years. She is also the founder of the popular writers' advice site DearEditor.com and serves on the advisory board for the UC San Diego Extension "Children's Book Writing and Illustrating" certificate program.

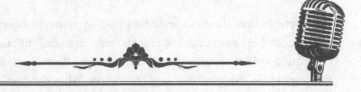

CHAPTER 11

HANDLING DIALECT & JARGON

BY JACK SMITH

Great fiction almost always includes great dialogue. As with drama, we get to know characters by what they say and by what others say about them. If the dialogue is flat, the characters will be flat. If the dialogue seems off, or not believable or real, we won't trust the characters as authentic beings. Grant Tracey, author of three story collections and editor of the *North American Review*, emphasizes the importance of dialogue in solid character development: "Dialogue is about giving characters space to breathe, to step out from the author's controlling voice to speak from a real authentic place of their own. Through dialogue characters are at their most autonomous and free." It's this distinct speaking voice, in the larger context of the story's narrative voice, that fiction writers need to master

Writing dialogue of course presents many challenges, especially to authors whose characters tend to come from diverse backgrounds. Speech patterns vary from region to region of the country—and the world. Characters from different ethnic groups and social classes speak differently. Different trades have their own jargon. To create authentic characters and authentic-sounding dialogue, writers can sometimes depend on their own background or experience, at other times on research of various kinds, and sometimes on imaginative powers.

REGION AND CULTURE

Robert Garner McBrearty, a winner of the Sherwood Anderson Foundation Fiction Award, likes "doing 'Texans.'" He grew up with that language on his "ear and mind" and has a feel for handling the regional speech patterns.

Still, he emphasizes, there's some skill involved—you have to make sure you don't overdo it. As an example, he cites his story "Episode," the title story of his winning collection, which has a "distinct Texas flavor in the dialogue." The language is "fairly subtle," says McBrearty. "They don't sound like a bunch of hicks."

When it comes to handling regional dialect, Catherine Brady, cowinner of the 2002 Flannery O'Connor Award for Short Fiction and author of *Story Logic* and the *Craft of Fiction*, emphasizes that the writer has "to develop an ear—to be alert for the idiosyncratic qualities of speech and to respect them." She warns against such variant spellings as "I lak to be goin'" for "I like to be going"—word corruptions that are "implicitly condescending" as well as "sloppy." What's needed instead, says Brady, is a close attention to "the syntax and expressions that characterize a particular dialect or slang."

Steven Wingate, winner of the Bakeless Prize for his collection *Wifeshopping*, spots one thing writers tend to ignore about dialect—overall characterization: For one thing, says Wingate, writers need to attend to "body language, which can reveal a great deal about how a character communicates." And they should keep this principle in mind: "If a character is rendered well overall, dialect or jargony speech patterns will be easier to do—and more effective in small doses—because characterization doesn't depend so much on them."

Handling dialect well is one thing; making it fully accessible to your readers is another. Josh Weil, like McBrearty, has a close familiarity with his subject—the Appalachian South—along with the speech patterns or dialect of its inhabitants. Yet the challenge for Weil has been how to make the Appalachian dialect harmonize well with the rest of the narrative. In the first two novellas of *The New Valley*, which won the Sue Kaufman Prize for First Fiction, Weil connects dialect and speech inflections tonally with narrative voice. "So the rhythms and patterns and musicality of the way people speak in the mountains crept organically into the voice in the narration." At first glance, this may not seem all that important, says Weil, yet it is: "It creates a subtle connection between the music of the narrator and the musicality of the characters' speech." This tonal harmony between character speech and narrative voice "eases the reader into a more easy acceptance of the dialect in dialogue."

The writer's challenge may be how to handle dialect in another country, in a completely different culture. Midge Raymond, author of the prize-winning *Forgetting English*, drew on her experience living in Taiwan to write her title story, which required a strong sense for Chinese speech patterns. Had she not lived and traveled throughout Asia, she wouldn't have known, for instance, which English words native Chinese speakers have problems with pronouncing and which articles (*a*, *the*, etc.), they regularly leave out of English sentences. Since she was learning Chinese at the time, Raymond says, this enhanced her understanding of Chinese speech patterns.

Yet authors sometimes have neither direct experience—at least not the sustained kind that Midge Raymond had—nor geographical or cultural roots to draw on. Yet a particular character they're introducing requires that they write outside their own language background. Doing this will take "comprehensive research," Catherine Brady states, "but it comes in the form of talking and listening rather than reading." Ellen Sussman, author of both nonfiction and fiction, most recently the novel *French Lessons*, says: "When I'm trying to learn a new voice, I try every possible way to first hear those voices. I'll rent movies where the characters speak that dialect. I'll find YouTube videos with characters from that world." David Hubbard, a short story writer from Carlsbad, California, even makes trips to different areas of the country to listen to the way people talk to each other. But as we've seen, getting a sense of the regional dialect, while absolutely necessary, is only the beginning. The rest is putting it into play—and not overdoing it.

ETHNICITY

Carolina De Robertis, author of the prize-winning *The Invisible Mountain*, speaks of the "added challenges" writers face in writing outside their own cultural or ethnic background. "There is the potential danger of falling into stereotypes—especially when the cultural group we're writing about is historically marginalized. There is plenty of bad writing, and even decent writing, that falls into this trap." Ethnic stereotypes need to be avoided, says De Robertis. "Stereotypes are not only sociopolitically problematic; they also bleed the vitality from fiction." This second result alone, De Robertis believes, should prompt writers to be sure their characters reflect as much "complex humanity as possible"—and dialogue plays a critical part in characterization.

It's this complex humanity that Irina Reyn, the Russia-born author of *What Happened to Anna K*, respects as she writes ethnic characters, and in her case it means opting for "very little dialect." She wants to develop her characters fully as individuals. "I usually allow speech patterns, tone and voice to guide presentation of a character," says Reyn. "I am very sensitive to the dangers of representing otherness."

So is Joe Benevento, the author of *The Odd Squad*, a finalist for the John Gardner Fiction Book Award. Benevento believes that accurately representing slang, dialect, and words peculiar to a given ethnicity is quite important. He feels comfortable, he says, doing a Cuban storeowner as well as an Italian-American grandmother but not a Cajun character since he lacks the sufficient firsthand experience to do so. But from what Benevento has seen, his own emphasis on verisimilitude is surprisingly not shared by a lot of agents, editors, and readers. For Italian-American language, for example, most people, says Benevento, seem to be ignorant of certain linguistic nuances, as when Mickey Rourke's supposedly Italian-American character in *The Pope of Greenwich Village* responds to the question "*Capisc?*" ("You understand?") with the ridiculous response "*Capisc*" ("You understand") instead of "*Capisco*" ("I understand"). As for fiction, "I've rarely seen working class dialogue done right—Italian Americans are always stereotyped, even though not all of us are Mafia wannabes, and the other dialects I also know about, Latino, black, Jewish, etc., are also usually botched. But it doesn't seem to matter." Why is this? Benevento explains that a "veneer of verisimilitude" is apparently enough if readers are sufficiently hooked by the characters and plot. Yet this is problematic for Benevento, who holds that writers who ignore verisimilitude create ethnic stereotypes and "botched" representations of ethnicity of several kinds.

Midge Raymond also believes dialogue should be accurately represented. She avoids writing dialogue for a given ethnic group unless she's sure she "can get it right." While extensive research might conceivably work, Raymond does believe the best way to capture the dialect of ethnic groups outside one's own is immersion: "hearing voices firsthand." But what if you can't gain such firsthand experience? There is one resource to consider, as a second option, says Raymond: the Library of Congress's Center for Applied Linguistics Collection has recorded 118 hours of audio documenting North American English dialects, and this is available online.[1]

One controversial issue that sometimes arises is whether or not a writer not of a given ethnicity even has a right to create a character from an ethnic background not the writer's own. Writers are sometimes criticized for doing this, just as male writers are sometimes criticized for creating female protagonists. Cliff Garstang, author of the award-winning *In an Uncharted Country* and editor of *Prime Number* magazine, calls such criticism "ridiculous." For him, "A fiction writer is free to assume any identity he or she needs to for the purpose of telling a story; the only obligation is to do it well, and that's a whole other challenge."

SOCIAL CLASS

DeWitt Henry, founder of *Ploughshares*, came from an upper-middle-class background, certainly not the working class that he wrote about in his novel *The Marriage of Anna Maye Potts*, winner of the inaugural Peter Taylor Prize for the Novel. Yet, growing up, Henry did have a good deal of exposure to different social classes and ethnic groups, including working-class idiom and speech patterns. For his novel he was able to draw on this fund of language experience. The question for Henry was how to do it well.

"A primary focus for me," says Henry, "in writing *The Marriage of Anna Maye Potts*, was to translate articulate perceptions into the vocabularies and idioms of my characters." Since each character was quite different, Henry found this to be "painstaking, slow work." He found himself initially writing speech/thought in his "own literary vocabulary," then struggling for a "translation, which was sometimes silence and gesture and sometimes vernacular and cliché." The right technique comes, Henry believes, from developing "an ear" or "an eye"—and this takes a regular regimen, which he likens to the rigors of an athlete's training.

While Robert Garner McBrearty has sometimes depended on his Texas roots, he's also done informal "field research" such as watching movies, television, and the news to create working-class characters. Working different jobs and eavesdropping on the way working-class people talk has been

1 http://memory.loc.gov/ammem/collections/linguistics

one avenue that has really paid off. Then the challenge is to get these characters down in writing. McBrearty tends to start from just a little and take it from there, relying on his imaginative powers. "The idea is sort of like if one gets a little piece of the character, then the writer goes to work filling the character out." Once McBrearty gets that first line down, he's usually able to "tap into the way the person speaks"—that is, if he writes from "inside the character" versus "planting dialogue in someone's mouth." On the whole, he does feel more comfortable creating characters he's familiar with, and yet he's seen successes with material gained from eavesdropping too.

HISTORICAL FICTION

The issue of realistic speech, along with dialect, naturally arises in historical fiction. But here the reach of years, when the writer goes deeply into the past, can present an additional problem. How does a writer obtain all the linguistic information he needs? And then, how does he handle it?

Edmund White is the author of many commercial press works of fiction, including *Fanny: A Fiction*, set in the pre–Civil War period, and based on the life of Fanny Trollope, mother of the famous novelist Anthony Trollope. In this work White includes a runaway black slave named Jupiter Higgins. To handle Higgins with authenticity, he did extensive research, reading "slave narratives and fiction written before 1900 in which there were black characters." He didn't read "any technical linguistic studies on black speech of that period," but White says he would have if he'd come across them at the British Library, where he conducted his research. He did skim hundreds of books there. As far as Jupiter Higgins's speech patterns and dialect, White notes that he "had him quote from the Bible, from hymns and from the oratory of preachers." White did have one distinct advantage. He could draw on his growing up in the South, where he picked up the speech patterns of Southern blacks, including "their ways of emphasizing a word and many of their vocabulary choices."

As with contemporary regional dialect, handling dialect in historical fiction can be quite demanding. In *The Circus in Winter*, some of which takes place before the Civil War, Cathy Day sought to capture her characters' voices "accurately, but not literally"—a difficult balance to achieve.

Crafting Dynamic Dialogue

With her novel-in-progress, set in the Gilded Age, Day faces new challenges. "How did people of that cultural milieu speak?" For answers, she's been doing considerable research: reading *Edith Wharton*, the first edition of Emily Post's *Etiquette*, and the society pages of the *New York Times*. The tone, as well as the vocabulary of this Edwardian era, is quite different from our own, Day points out, and she hopes to get a firm handle on "the lilt and cadences and rhythms of those voices." Day doesn't believe she needs to cover every base, though, just a few "dated phrases, old-timey words"—just enough to make her characters' speech sound real.

Josh Weil has wrestled with black slave dialect in his novella *Solarium*. He feels comfortable with white Southern dialect, picking this up from neighbors in Virginia. Handling slave dialect, however, has called for a lot of research. He finds this dialect "fascinating and wonderful and full of music." As a result, he says, "for a long time, I stuck to my guns, writing the first person slave sections in full-bore slave dialect." Yet this dialect led to problems: first, the difficulty of reading it; second, the fact that it was so "overpowering" that it caused readers to focus "on the way the words sounded instead of what they were saying." So Weil reduced the amount of dialect and left just enough that the dialect now adds to, versus detracts from, the story. In the current version of his novella, it isn't used in first-person narration, but only "when a narrator is relaying the speech of others." This technique makes the slave dialect easier for the reader to accept, Weil believes.

WORKPLACE JARGON

Ellen Sussman has eavesdropped for a few days at a time at a garage in order to pick up "mechanic talk." To pick up jargon she believes you have to be in the language as much as possible: "The research is best when it's real immersion—then we can find our way to characters who really speak the language."

Once you've gathered the material, again the question is: How do you handle it? With jargon this means finding a way not to explain it.

For Grant Tracey it has to be "real, natural sounding." To make sure this happens, Tracey says: "Whatever job a character has let the dialogue reflect the milieu of their environment without worrying about explaining what they're talking about to readers outside that environment. Trust readers to get it through context." John Yunker, author of *The Tourist Trail*, solved the issue of exposition in his environmental novel by introducing outsiders to the world of penguin naturalists and animal activists so that the characters pick up the jargon themselves. This technique helped him avoid "overtly painful exposition."

TAKING THE CHALLENGE

As we've seen, sometimes you can depend on your background or experience when writing regional or ethnic speech patterns, or dialect, or group jargon, but you may need to do research if you lack the needed background. But wouldn't you be wise simply to avoid dealing with characters outside your own ethnic, cultural, or language background? Wouldn't that be playing it safe? Why risk being "off"?

Catherine Brady urges writers to take the challenge: "It's actually hard for me to imagine an American writer whose social world is so insular that s/he never encounters other dialects or speech patterns, and I also think that dialect and slang and regional (or even generational) speech patterns enrich dialogue—they're its 'poetic rhythm.' So I would encourage any writer to try to render differences in speech pattern while always remembering that s/he's not trying to create a sociologically accurate composite but a believable individual."

Mark Wisniewski, author of *Confessions of a Polish Used Car Salesman*, also sees a problem with writerly insularity, especially when it leads to autobiographical fiction: "I recommend using dialect that's not your own. It forces you out of your own manner of speaking and encourages you to write about characters unlike yourself. Semi-autobiographical (and certainly autobiographical) work, as most fiction editors will tell you, is often mundane, probably because the ego clouds the writer's perception of what engages the average reader. Anyway the use of dialect can keep you from falling into the I'm-so-interesting trap."

Skip Horack, author of the historical novel *The Eden Hunter*, reminds us of an important truth: If writers had always avoided certain kinds of characters, there would be "a whole lot of great fiction that never would have been written."

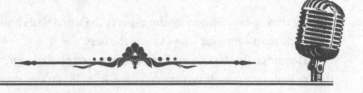

CHAPTER 12

THE QUIRKS OF USING DIALOGUE IN SCIENCE FICTION & FANTASY

BY STEVEN HARPER

A character from Louisiana doesn't speak the same way as a character from London, and a character from three dimensions over won't sound like a native to this world. And imagine the slang that might spring up if elves publicly showed up and made themselves at home in Detroit. Introducing supernatural elements to a book naturally changes the way the characters speak and will likely have a significant impact on the narration.

THE IMPORTANCE OF DIALOGUE

Human conversation grabs the mental ear—it's a chance to eavesdrop on something fascinating—and it's the reason dialogue remains the main thing readers want in a book. In fact, dialogue is one of the stronger opening hooks you can use.

Dialogue performs a number of functions. It moves action forward by telling the reader what's going on. It sneaks in exposition. And most importantly, it tells the reader what your character is like.

Establishing Character

Everyone has his own speech patterns. This means no two people talk alike, not even ones from the same part of the country. Part of it is upbringing, but part of it is also outlook. People's ideas and attitudes shape the way they speak. Someone who expects the worst will choose different words than someone who expects the best.

All your characters should be differentiated by dialogue, whether they're ordinary people or supernatural ones. If you can reassign the dialogue in a given scene to another character without changing any of the words, it means you haven't done your job well.

Dialogue differences can be very overt. Tony DiTerlizzi and Holly Black use wildly different forms of dialogue among their fairy characters in The Spiderwick Chronicles books. Thimbletack the brownie speaks in rhyming couplets. In *The Seeing Stone*, Jared meets a caged hobgoblin named Hogsqueal, and the difference between the ways the two characters speak shows clearly:

> "You're not very chicken-beaked for a nib-head," the hobgoblin grumbled. "I'm in [this cage] for letting out one of the cats. See, I like cats, and not just 'cause they're tasty, which they are, no mistake. But they got these eyes that are an awful lot like mine, and this one was real little, not much meat there. And she had this sweet little mewl." The goblin looked lost in his memory, then abruptly looked back at Jared. "So enough about that. Let me out."
>
> "And what about your teeth? Do you eat babies or what?" Jared had not found the goblin's story very reassuring.
>
> "What is this, an interrogation?" Hogsqueal groused.
>
> "I'm letting you out already." Jared came closer and started to cut the complicated knots on the cage. "But I want to know about your teeth."

The differences between Jared's and Hogsqueal's dialogue stand out sharply. Hogsqueal's word choices have a New Jersey flavor to them with some invented fairy slang (*chicken-beaked* and *nib-head*) mixed in. DiTerlizzi and Black are going for humor here, since no one would expect a fairy to talk like a New York cab driver, and the resulting dialogue very quickly paints a picture of a crude but crafty creature. We also learn that Hogsqueal likes to eat cats. Jared is meant to be a nine-year-old boy who could be from anywhere in the country (since the books don't get specific in their setting), so his dialogue is free of regional dialect.

Christopher Moore's characters in *A Dirty Job* speak differently from one another as well, though the difference is subtler. Here, Charlie is talking to Mr. Fresh about what it means to be Death—or a death.

Mr. Fresh shrugged. " ... Surely you've noticed that no one sees you when you're out to get a soul vessel."

"I've never gone out to get a soul vessel."

"Yes, you have, and you will, at least you should be. You need to get with the program, Mr. Asher."

"Yeah, so you said. So you're—uh—we're invisible when we're out getting these soul vessels?"

"Not invisible, so to speak, it's just that no one sees us. You can go right into people's homes, and they'll never notice you standing right beside them, but if you speak to someone on the street, they'll see you ..."

"So that's how you got to be a—what do they call us?"

"Death Merchants."

"Get out. Really?"

Here, Moore doesn't even need to tell us who's talking. Partly it's that he gives us a cue up front when he writes that Mr. Fresh shrugged and then slips in a cue when Fresh addresses Charlie as "Mr. Asher," but mostly it's the dialogue itself. Fresh has a more formal, polished mode of speaking. Later we learn he can drop it and speak much more informally—the polished dialogue is part of an image he tries to project. His attitude affects his dialogue. Meanwhile, Charlie's dialogue is peppered with fits and starts. He also uses *yeah* whereas Fresh uses *yes*. The differences are subtle but clear. You certainly couldn't put Charlie's words into another character's mouth without serious changes.

EXERCISE

Read the following dialogue.

Evan strode into the dark room and flung back the curtains. "How much did you pay for this place?"

"Enough." Abby set her suitcase on the threadbare carpet and glanced around the tiny cottage's living room. "Come on, it was a steal and you know it. It has a fireplace."

"We only get a week together. I just wanted it to be someplace nice. Romantic. Not a ... well, not here."

"There's romantic and there's romantic," Abby said. "The place isn't important. We are."

"I know. I do. I'm just worried." Evan checked his smart phone. "Six days, fifteen hours, and forty-two minutes before full moon. You know what happens then."

Now rewrite it in two different ways, changing only the words of the dialogue, not the interstitial material. You may not change the overall intent of the dialogue, only the wording.

CHANGE #1

Evan is furious—but not with Abby. (Perhaps he's overt and straightforward, or maybe he shows his anger through sarcasm, or maybe has another method.) Abby is on a hair-trigger herself but is trying to hold it together.

Also, Abby and Evan should speak differently from one another. Differentiate their dialogue choices in some way. Perhaps they're from different regions, or even different countries.

CHANGE #2

Evan is frightened of Abby. Abby is in control of this relationship and knows it. Continue to differentiate their word choices.

Now pick the version you like best and add several more dialogue exchanges.

WRITING GOOD DIALOGUE

Every year when we begin the Shakespeare unit, my ninth graders take one look at the dialogue and inevitably ask, "Did people really talk that way back then?" And my inevitable answer is "No way."

Characters in books, plays, movies, and TV shows don't talk at all like people in real life. Dialogue for real people is full of stammers, stutters, and verbal clutter such as *like*, as in "He was, like, no way, and I'm like, yeah we are." Real people ramble when they speak and natter over details no one cares about: "The bus was rushing straight toward me, and I didn't know what to do. I remember that it was Tuesday because my oldest has his lessons on Tuesdays, and I was taking his clarinet to him because he'd forgotten it *again*. The boy would forget his head if it wasn't attached. So anyway, the bus ... " Yeah. Real people rarely say anything worth putting into a book—not without heavy editing, anyway.

But here's the thing—a lot of people *think* they speak well. They don't notice the annoying verbal clutter, the rambling, the number of times they say *um*, or the fact that they start every other sentence with *You know*. So when they read or hear dialogue that doesn't have any of that stuff in it, it sounds good and natural to them.

Good dialogue *sounds* natural without being the slightest bit natural. It's all part of that illusion of reality you're creating. There are a number of ways to create realistic-sounding dialogue, even for unrealistic characters, and a number of traps to avoid.

Speech Tics

All of us have little verbal tics we use when we speak. As previously noted, we end our sentences in *yeah?* or say *Goodness me!* a lot or misuse the word *literally,* as in *My boss will literally kill me if I'm late again.* Our problem is we use these tics too often, and they would become annoying on the printed page.

You can and should assign speech tics to your characters. The key is to use them *sparingly,* as in no more than once or twice per scene. You want to give the flavor of a speech tic without annoying the readers with it.

Supernatural characters can have their own otherworldly speech tics. We already saw Hogsqueal's odd slang in The Spiderwick Chronicles. Gina, the fashionista vampire in Lucienne Diver's *Vamped,* has a number of teenage girl speech tics, including the words *like* and *totally.* In chapter four, Gina says, "What I mean is, we're, like, beyond the law. Renegades, right? No reflection, so probably no image left behind on pesky security cameras." The word *like* doesn't appear again in dialogue for the rest of the chapter—or in the next. Gina's dialogue retains the flavor of teenage dialect without actually *being* teenage dialect, and it gets the idea across in print very nicely.

In a more extreme example, Dobby, the house elf from J.K. Rowling's books, avoids pronouns for himself and other people, referring to himself as *Dobby* instead of *I.* He also addresses Harry in third person indirectly and by his full name Harry Potter. In *Harry Potter and the Chamber of Secrets*, for example, Dobby says, "Dobby has come to protect Harry Potter, to warn him, even if he *does* have to shut his ears in the oven door later … *Harry Potter must not go back to Hogwarts.*" This speech tic makes Dobby's dialogue quite distinctive and, as I said, a little extreme, but Rowling gets away with it because Dobby is an extreme character. She wisely avoids this with her main characters.

Supernatural Swearing

Okay, this one can be a delicate topic, but it needs addressing. Some novels have explicit swearing in them, and some don't. Which it is depends on what the author has decided is appropriate for the audience. If your book doesn't use swear words, you can safely skip this section.

In English, swearing revolves around two things: bodily functions and religion. Other languages have other standards for swearing. In China, it's a dreadful insult to call someone a turtle, for example. Swearing is based on the forbidden—in English-speaking cultures we're not allowed to say our swear words because the concepts they're based on are considered impolite, disgusting, or profane.

This gets tricky when you have a character from another culture, say from the other side of a mystic gate. What if that culture treats sex as a public act but drinking is considered private, and even a little shameful? The tricky part isn't creating the swearwords, actually—the tricky part is getting away with having a character who stubs his toe and yelps, "Drink!" It can be done. You just have to use it consistently and have other characters react appropriately, forcing your reader to accept it.

One way to create new swearwords is to leave the powerful ones alone but create mild ones for your culture. *Oh my God* or just *God* are common mild swearwords in our culture (though they used to be much more powerful), and a number of paranormal books have characters swear in the plural, saying *Oh my Gods* or *Gods*, or mentioning deities by name instead.

Finally, in a supernatural setting, swearing might have consequences that go beyond social censure. Not that long ago, people were reluctant to mention the devil's name in case calling it out got his attention. ("Speak of the devil, and he is like to appear.") The ancient Greeks were equally reluctant to call on the god of death Hades for the same reason. J.K. Rowling's characters dislike saying the name of the dread wizard *Voldemort* aloud, and everyone reacts as if it were a dreadful swearword. And in a world where magic or the gods are real, swearing might create real consequences. In *The Sword in the Stone* by T.H. White (which is high fantasy but still worth mentioning here), Merlin experiences a moment of frustration toward young Arthur and shouts, "Castor and

Pollux blow me to Bermuda!" He instantly vanishes and reappears a moment later, hair and robe wildly disheveled. When Arthur asks what happened, Merlin only replies, "Let that be a lesson to you not to swear."

Sounding Realistic

Conversation has a natural rhythm, a give-and-take that's not always easy to capture perfectly on paper. Your dialogue should always sound natural. One of the best ways to see if it does is to read it aloud to yourself. Does it sound natural? Could an actor say it on a TV show and sound normal? If not, go back and revise. Try saying the words aloud first and writing them down second. Become a one-writer show. You'll need some privacy—or a lack of concern for what others think of you— but you might like the results. However, this rule applies more to human characters who live in our world.

Otherworldly and Inhuman Dialogue

Readers are willing to accept that characters who aren't human, or who didn't grow up speaking human languages, won't speak the way the humans do. (This is why Hogsqueal's speech patterns are funny— they're the opposite of what readers expect.) Dobby the house elf's speech patterns are outlandish and don't really pass the read-aloud test, but Rowling pulls it off because Dobby isn't human. The same goes for Thimbletack's rhyming couplets. These characters, however, can't occupy center stage for long because their strange dialogue tends to overwhelm everything else that's happening in the scene. There are ways to show odd dialogue without overwhelming the character.

One convention to show otherworldliness is simply to avoid contractions and add a touch of formality to the dialogue. This makes it sound like the speaker's first language is something other than English and the speaker is therefore speaking carefully. Look at the difference between these two sets of dialogue:

> Dennis stared up at the centaur in awe. "But how did you get into a public park?"

"I'm not certain," the centaur replied. "One moment I'm grazing, the next I'm here. Didn't you see anything?"

"Er, no." Dennis glanced around uneasily. "Look, I'm supposed to meet my girlfriend in five minutes. Is there someone I should call? I have my cell."

The centaur stamped a hoof. "What's a cell? You're trying to capture me? But I've done nothing to you!"

Here, the otherworldly centaur speaks like a modern American, despite his professed ignorance of American culture. But we can shift it a bit:

Dennis stared up at the centaur in awe. "But how did you get into a public park?"

"I am not certain," the centaur replied. "One moment I was grazing, the next I was here. Did you not see anything?"

"Er, no." Dennis glanced around uneasily. "Look, I'm supposed to meet my girlfriend in five minutes. Is there someone I should call? I have my cell."

The centaur stamped a hoof. "What is a cell? You are trying to capture me? But I have done nothing to you!"

This is serviceable enough—the lack of contractions makes his dialogue sound more formal, more careful, as if English weren't his first language. However, it still comes across as a bit stilted, so we can modify the centaur's dialogue a bit more:

Dennis stared up at the centaur in awe. "But how did you get into a public park?"

"I am uncertain," the centaur replied. "One moment I was grazing, the next I was here. You saw nothing?"

"Er, no." Dennis glanced around uneasily. "Look, I'm supposed to meet my girlfriend in five minutes. Is there someone I should call? I have my cell."

The centaur stamped a hoof. "A cell? You wish to capture me? But I have done nothing to you!"

The touch of formality in the third version adds yet more otherworldliness to the centaur's speech patterns. All we need is a touch, though. We don't want to go too far:

Dennis stared up at the centaur in awe. "But how did you get into a public park?"

"I am in doubt," the centaur replied. "At one moment I was grazing the tender shoots, the next I stood here on this fair plain. Did you not see the event?"

"Er, no." Dennis glanced around uneasily. "Look, I'm supposed to meet my girlfriend in five minutes. Is there someone I should call? I have my cell."

The centaur stamped a hoof. "A cell? You are attempting to seize my person? And yet I have done nothing to you!"

Too far. The near-Shakespearean language overwhelms the dialogue like too much garlic in a soup. A taste is plenty.

Naomi Novik uses this technique with her dragons. Most of her dragons speak with a formal lilt, but Temeraire, a Chinese dragon, speaks even more formally, which accents the fact that he's an alien among dragons as we see here in *Victory of Eagles*:

"Well, old fellow, I am afraid we will have to swap."

"Swap?" Temeraire said, puzzled, until he divined that Requiescat meant caves. "I do not want your cave," adding hastily, "not that it is not very nice, I am sure; but I have just got this one arranged to suit me."

"This one is much bigger now," Requiescat explained, or by his tone thought he was explaining, "and it is much nicer in the wet; mine," he added regretfully, "has been full of puddles, all this week; wet clear through to the back."

"Then I can hardly see why I would change," Temeraire said, still more baffled, and then he sat up, outraged ... "Why, you are a damned scrub," he said. "How dare you come here, and behave like a visitor, and all the time it is a challenge? I never saw anything so sly in my life ... you may get out at once."

Novik is one of the few authors around who uses semicolons in dialogue, incidentally, and this small touch serves to accent the fact that we're in a different time and place. In this passage, Requiescat's dialogue has a bit of formality to it, but it's not completely so—the phrase *old fellow* is slangy, or it was for the time. Temeraire, however, uses much more elevated dialogue, complete with extra-complicated sentence structure, as we can see when he says, "you may get out at once" (instead of a simple "get out") and "How dare you . . . behave like a visitor, and all the time it is a challenge?" (instead of "How dare you pretend to be a visitor when all the time you wanted to challenge me?"). Temeraire's careful speech doesn't fall into the ridiculous—Novik is too careful for that—but it does show us that he is neither human nor native to England.

You can also add elements from another language that you're familiar with. Play with grammar and word order to give sentences an exotic feel. Perhaps your dwarves have a Germanic bent and their sentences reflect Germanic influence. "Come you in. It will soon give rain" is German translated straight into English, for example, and could sound very much like a dwarf with a Germanic background.

EXERCISE

Pick a nonhuman character such as a dragon, unicorn, winged horse, elf from the fairy realm, or whatever you like, and pair it with a modern-day human. Write a dialogue in which the nonhuman speaks with the same speech patterns as the human. Then rewrite the dialogue so the nonhuman speaks markedly differently from the human in a way that also shows the character isn't human.

They Said Beautifully

There are a number of ways to indicate who said what, and since fiction writers spend a lot of time with dialogue, few mechanical aspects of writing generate more heated discussions. Let's take a little look at what's going on.

The little bits like "he howled" and "she murmured" that writers sneak into dialogue are called *speech tags*. The most common one of these is "said," as in *"Close the door before the werewolf gets through," Norman said.* There are a bunch of others: *growled, murmured, yelled, whispered, roared,* and so on.

For some reason, the speech tag *said* is much maligned. I once attended a writing seminar in which the instructor told the attendees that good writers never, ever use *said*. "It's boring, it's pedestrian, and it shows lack of imagination," he said.

Oops. Did I just use *said*?

And did you notice? Probably not. There's really nothing wrong with using *said* as a speech tag. It's quiet, it's innocuous, and it doesn't call attention to itself. There are really only two rules about using *said* in dialogue.

Crafting Dynamic Dialogue

First, you don't want to *over*use it. If you use *said* for every single speech tag, you'll call attention to it by accident. Use it twice, maybe three times if you're stuck, and then avoid it for a bit before going back to it.

Second, you want to avoid *modifying* it, especially with an *-ly* adverb. Tags like *he said softly* are weak, and you're better off replacing it with something more specific such as *he murmured* or *he whispered*. Besides, *ly* speech tags are prone to *Tom Swifties*. Tom Swift was a science fiction hero of the pulp era, and the books were written quickly, with little editing. It became a joke among readers to spot such lines as *"Cut the rope!" Tom said sharply*, which were unintentionally funny and became known as Tom Swifties. So avoid *said -ly* speech tags, but feel free to use *said* by itself in moderation (he said authoritatively).

Another way to indicate who's speaking is to use blocking within the same paragraph. Rules of grammar require a new paragraph every time you get a new speaker, so the identity of the speaker is easy to discern: *Tanya slammed the door and leaned against it. "I think we're fine."* We know Tanya is the speaker, since the dialogue comes in the same paragraph as her action. However, you have to be careful that only one person acts in the paragraph. Otherwise you can get confusion. *Norman pressed an ear to the wood. Tanya joined him. "What do you hear?"* In this case, either Norman or Tanya could be speaking, and you want to avoid such problems.

A third way is to let the dialogue run its course without any speech tags once you've established the back-and-forth pattern of the speakers. If the reader will know who the speaker is, there's no need for the author to interrupt for a reminder:

> "I can't hear a thing," Norman whispered.
>> Tanya bit her lip. "Is that a good sign?"
>> "Probably. We burned the stupid book and scattered its ashes over—"
>> "Shh! What was that?"
>> "I don't know," Norman said. "The stupid door's too thick."
>> "What are we listening to?" whispered the werewolf.

Just make sure there are enough cues that we don't lose track of who's speaking. Drop in a speech tag every now and then to remind us, as the above example does.

Using Current Slang: Okay or Gag Me with a Spoon?

Paranormal novels that use a modern setting with modern characters naturally lean toward modern language. YA authors especially want to use up-to-the-moment words and phrases so they can identify characters with their audiences. The big question is: How far should you go?

When it comes to recent slang, you *have* to know what you're doing. If you aren't a member of the group who uses the slang, you need to *sound* like you are. Teenage readers especially will spot fake slang users faster than Holden Caulfield can finger a phony, and you'll instantly lose all credibility with your audience if you make a mistake. So if you don't have an absolutely sure hand with current slang, avoid it.

Another problem with current slang is that it dates your novel. You might be good with the idea that your book is firmly set in a particular year or decade, especially if you're writing an historical novel, or your story surrounds a famous event, such as a particular presidential election or the start of the Gulf War.

However, if your book is set in a timeless present (as most modern-day books try to be), you want to avoid anything that could date your book, including current slang.

Some slang has become eternal, and you can definitely use it without worry. Words like *yeah*, *okay*, and *cool* have been part of the American scene for so long, many people have forgotten they're slang.

Really Foreign Languages

Ranadar the elf drops into our world from his own. He's never visited this world before, and his culture has never crossed our own. How does he communicate?

This is kind of tricky. Realistically, Ranadar shouldn't be able to speak or understand English. Even gestures are culturally based. In America, we ask if someone wants to eat by miming a plate with one hand and scooping a handful of invisible food toward our mouths with the other. But in China, people mime a bowl with one hand and over it they waggle two fingers from the other hand—chopsticks. Would Ranadar, who grew up on another world entirely, understand either one? There's also the mirror image of this—the character from our world who goes to another world. The language should be nothing like English, or whatever the character speaks.

This causes major story problems. Your character will have to spend enormous amounts of time just learning to communicate in order to get the story going. Unless your book is about exactly this problem, you probably don't want to deal with it. Fortunately, you have a number of solutions available to you. One is simple, long-standing tradition. Authors since Homer have ignored differences in language and just got on with the story. (It doesn't seem likely that citizens of Troy, situated on the western coast of what's now Turkey, spoke the exact same language as the Spartans in the middle of mainland Greece, but that doesn't stop Paris from falling in love with Helen, and Homer didn't bother to stick in a translator.)

You can also slip in a magical solution. A spell or magical object might allow for instant translation or understanding. Or the transition from one world to the next might create an automatic understanding of the new language. You *are* allowed to do a little hand-waving here—most readers want the story and characters to move along.

Some authors like to create bits of language—or even the entire thing. The gold standard for this, of course, is J.R.R. Tolkien, who created over a dozen languages for his books. Richard Adams created a language for rabbits for *Watership Down* (which has definite supernatural elements) so successfully that when Bigwig faces down General Woundwort and snarls, "*Silflay hraka, u embleer rah*" at the climax, the reader has no trouble understanding him.

If you don't want to go quite that far for your werewolves or pixies, you can create pieces of a language—words or phrases that the character can use now and then to remind the reader that the speaker thinks in a language other than English. Again, you'll want to look to other languages for inspiration. If you just throw together some vowels and consonants and substitute them for English word-for-word, it'll come across as stilted and silly. Different languages have different word order and rules for grammar, which should show up in a language you create.

On the other hand, you don't want to create eye-twisting, impossible words for your readers, either. Some African languages use a sort of clicking sound that English speakers can't re-create, not even to write—the official western character for it is an exclamation mark. Creating a language with words like *tqigl!maf* might be fun for the author, but it turns readers away. Balance creativity with the reader's ability to keep up.

....

STEVEN HARPER is the author of several science fiction books, including *In the Company of Mind, Corporate Mentality*, and The Silent Empire series. He's also written books based on *Star Trek, Battlestar Galactica*, and *The Ghost Whisperer*, as well as the movie novelization for *Identity*. He is the author of the Writer's Digest book *Writing the Paranormal Novel*. His numerous short stories have appeared, among other places, in Esther Friesner's *Chicks in Chainmail* anthologies.

PART IV

CHARACTERS & DIALOGUE

CHAPTER 13

WHAT DIALOGUE CAN DO FOR YOUR STORY

BY GLORIA KEMPTON

Believable dialogue doesn't just give your characters life. If done well, it can accomplish so many other goals in your story. Through dialogue, you give readers a very real sense of a story's setting. Dialogue can reveal your characters' motives and opposing agendas. It can even communicate your story's theme.

We fiction writers tend to stress out when we're trying to create believable dialogue for our characters. But by breaking down the process and following some simple dos and don'ts, writing dialogue can become a more natural process—as natural as talking.

DON'T WORRY ABOUT PERFECTION

Dialogue is the one element of fiction where you have to worry least about getting it "right." By that I mean grammar and sentence structure. You can get by with more in dialogue than you can in any other element of fiction, because you want characters to sound real. People talk in sentence fragments, phrases, slang, and dialects. Most of us don't care how we sound when we're just hanging out, and our characters shouldn't, either. It's only the writer who gets uptight about this stuff.

Letting go of your need to write perfect sentences allows you to create dialogue that's more authentic, because you'll let your characters be who they are.

DON'T LET DIALOGUE DRIVE THE SCENE

Dialogue is a vehicle for moving the plot forward, for characterization, for providing background information to the reader, for description of other characters, and for building tension. But dialogue is the means to an end, not an end in itself.

In a plot-driven story, events drive the tale forward, and in a character-driven story, the protagonist's internal transformation is the driving force. The dialogue is simply a means of engaging characters in a scene with each other so they can move—externally or internally, preferably both.

When you allow dialogue to drive a scene, your characters could end up talking all over the place about the story events and the other characters. The characters come off as shallow, and the action and narrative suffers.

You want your story to be three-dimensional, to include action, narrative, and dialogue. The challenge is to weave these three elements into each scene you write. In a three-dimensional scene, dialogue affects the narrative, and the narrative affects the action.

DON'T USE YOUR CHARACTERS TO PREACH

I feel strongly about the death penalty, child abuse, and chocolate. But what kind of writer would I be if, every chance I got, I was putting words into my characters' mouths about these subjects?

Okay, I'd be lying if I said I'm writing stories that don't include my personal pet peeves and issues I feel strongly about. I don't know of any writer who's so detached from his personal agenda that he isn't writing about it at all. We write about subjects that matter to us. But our characters will be authentic only if we allow them to have their personal issues, too, and to express their thoughts and feelings about those issues in their own voices.

For example, I do happen to be writing a novel about the death penalty. So when one of my characters makes a philosophical statement, I have to make sure it's her philosophical statement, not mine. One of the main characters has a lot of traits I don't respect, and sometimes I don't like writing her scenes. She says things that make me mad, yet I need her because she represents the opposing side of the death penalty. She's the catalyst for the discussions I want my characters to engage in on this subject.

DON'T TRY TO BE CUTE OR CLEVER

Writers who think that every time their characters open their mouths they have to say something entertaining, amusing, or clever are in the same league as actual people who are forever trying to make the rest of us laugh. After a while, they're just annoying. You really don't want your characters to annoy your readers.

Are your characters always laughing at one another? If you find yourself constantly writing, "he laughed," "she chuckled," and "he cracked up," you're probably guilty of this. It's better to underplay than overplay. Subtlety is always preferable to bowling the reader over with your characters' personalities.

DO KNOW YOUR CHARACTERS

It's only as you know your characters that you can write dialogue that rings true. Otherwise, it sounds like stick people talking, and all your characters will sound the same (which is to say, they'll sound like you). If the dialogue you create could be spoken by any of the characters in your story, then you don't really know your characters.

Damon Knight offers good advice on this subject in his book, *Creating Short Fiction*:

> Fictional dialogue should resemble real dialogue with the various hesitations, repetitions and other glitches edited out. Listen to people talk. No two are exactly alike. By the way they talk, their choice of words, the things they talk about and the attitudes they express, they tell you where they grew up, how they were educated, the work they do and their social class. When you know who your character is and where she comes from, you know instinctively what she'll say and how she'll say it.

Crafting Dynamic Dialogue

You may take special effort to do character sketches and charts on your protagonist, antagonist, and one or two minor characters, but you also need to know the rest of the cast so the entire story will ring true when your characters speak.

Several years ago, I started writing first-person profiles for all my characters. This allows them to tell me who they are in their own voices. This is actually pages and pages of dialogue when you think about it—because I'm letting them talk to me. It's opened my characters up to me like nothing else I've tried.

DO WRITE FROM YOUR GUT

Dialogue needs to do a lot of things for the story—convey important information, advance the plot, offer character insight—sometimes all at once. But if you're constantly worrying about all these elements, it puts a lot of pressure on you. Don't think so hard. You write dialogue from your gut—not your head.

Guess what happens when we try too hard to write dialogue? It shows. And because it shows, it doesn't work. When a writer's trying too hard, the dialogue often feels contrived and forced. To overcome this, simply try relaxing into your character to the point that the dialogue is coming out of the place deep inside you that is the character. You created these characters, and you should be able to speak out of the deepest part of who they are.

DO PACE YOUR DIALOGUE

Every story has a rhythm, and we need to try to get into our story's rhythm so it moves well. We can use dialogue to either speed up a scene or slow it down. When we're conscious of this process, our dialogue works in tandem with the action and narrative to create a flow that's organic to the story we want to tell.

For example, if that's an action/adventure story, the dialogue will move as quickly as the action and narrative—unless the action is over the top, and then you can use nondramatic dialogue to slow the scenes down.

When you've just come off a fast-paced action scene, you might want to create a scene of interaction between your characters for the purpose of reflecting on the events. Whatever your story needs, you want to be conscious of how dialogue works in pacing so you can accelerate or brake at will. This will make your dialogue more effective because it will contribute to the story's overall rhythm, making the entire story a smoother ride for your reader.

DO SEARCH FOR THE ESSENCE

In *How to Write Best Selling Fiction* (Writer's Digest Books), Dean Koontz writes:

> Many writers think—erroneously—that fiction should be a mirror of reality. Actually, it should act as a sifter to refine reality until only the essence is before the reader. This is nowhere more evident than in fictional dialogue. In real life, conversation is roundabout, filled with general commentary and polite rituals. In fiction, the characters must always get right to the point when they talk.

Every scene of dialogue has an essence, and that's what the writer is responsible for re-creating. The goal is to write authentic dialogue while writing only the dialogue that matters in the current scene as it connects to the overall story.

To get in the habit of searching for the essence in your dialogue, comb through your characters' words until you find the ones they *have* to say. You need the words that characterize, create suspense, and tighten the tension. To find the essence means to tie these words into the story's theme so every word in every scene connects in some way to the big picture.

You don't always know upfront what the dialogue's essence is, but if your intention is to find it and cut away everything around it so it can come forth, then this is what will happen. All it takes is a willingness to find it.

Crafting Dynamic Dialogue

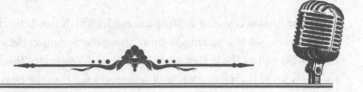

CHAPTER 14

MAKE YOUR CHARACTERS SOUND REAL

BY ELIZABETH SIMS

Now for the nuts and bolts of making your people sound real. I'm a big believer in stormwriting at every opportunity and especially when writing dialogue. Note: I don't like the word "brainstorming." It puts too much emphasis on thinking.

You need to use something deeper and more productive to write a good book: You need to engage your heartbrain, that is to say your whole, deepest self. When you tap into your heartbrain, you'll be writing up a storm, which is why I call this technique stormwriting. This is a results-driven tool.

Stormwriting is essentially a heartbrainstorm, a process by which you open your heartbrain and provoke it to not merely dump stuff out, but generate new questions and ideas that lead you to more good stuff: The stuff that becomes building blocks for your book.

If you're writing along and you feel you need some dialogue but you don't know what your characters should say, do some stormwriting.

FIRST STRESS-FREE GUIDELINE TO STORMWRITING DIALOGUE

Ask: What do I need in this scene?

Do they even need to talk here? If they do, what needs to come clear? What needs to happen?

Shed your author skin while writing dialogue.

If, for instance, you're writing a scene in which two little children are lost in the woods, you might think about the dynamics between the two—who will be the leader, who the follower? You might think about the logistics of their situation, and you might fall into the trap of making *them* think and talk that way.

TWO KIDS IN WOODS, VERSION I

Joyce looked at the sun and said, "It won't be light for long."

"How will we find our way home?" asked Terrell.

"I don't know. If I had a compass I bet we could find our way."

"Mom and Dad must be worried."

That's not all that realistic. The kids are gonna be kids. They're going to focus on themselves and their immediate feelings, their immediate surroundings, and in a time of stress they will likely engage in magical thinking.

TWO KIDS IN WOODS, VERSION II

Terrell said, "I'm hungry."

"Well, we don't have anything to eat," said Joyce, turning away from the tears in her little brother's eyes. "Let's walk this way."

Terrell squatted on the trail. "Look at this caterpillar! I think he's trying to show us which way to go."

Joyce thought that if she could close her eyes and stand still for long enough, she'd stop being lost.

Which brings us to the …

SECOND STRESS-FREE GUIDELINE TO STORMWRITING DIALOGUE

Become the character.

Open your heartbrain and write from there. Become the person you're writing about. What do you need, what do you want, what are you afraid of? What do you want to say, what do you want to avoid saying, what will you say instead?

Seek the heartbrain of your character. Go deep into your characters' fears. This works for both fiction and nonfiction. Even a how-to book can be made more interesting if you riff on fear, like "When I walked into the bank for my first business loan, I was so scared I thought I'd have a stroke."

Also remember that people talk *around* issues a lot. It's our job to cut through that. (As writers and as humans, I might add!)

> CHISEL IT IN STONE:
> THE THING THAT IS HARDEST TO SAY IS THE THING THAT MOST NEEDS TO BE SAID.

Fear is the most primal emotion there is, and a whole lot of behavior and thought springs from it. Sometimes people don't even know they're afraid, and that's a potent thing for a writer to realize—and exploit.

The third and last guideline is my favorite:

THIRD STRESS-FREE GUIDELINE TO STORMWRITING DIALOGUE

Be irrational.

I hope you smiled. Because you know exactly what I mean. Humans don't always act rationally, and neither should your characters. There's always a bit of randomness in the things we do every day, the decisions we make, the things we say.

Abandon literalism in your writing of dialogue. People talk in elliptical ways sometimes; that is, they try to get at something indirectly, maybe because they haven't formed a clear thought in their own mind yet. They trail off, they pause, they stop talking while they think, they feel dissatisfied with something they just said, they try to say it over, with better meaning. Show your characters doing this from time to time.

Sometimes we talk things out in order to think them out. Let your people do this, too.

Professionals constantly ask themselves while writing, "Do I even need dialogue here?" If you're uncertain whether dialogue is necessary at any point, try dropping it altogether and add some action instead.

For instance, two characters who are having a conflict could have a shouting match—or they could have a silent fistfight—or they could go through a whole weekend not talking! Imagine writing that. Now that's a challenge I could sink my teeth into.

Although I'm against hard-and-fast dos and don'ts, especially don'ts, here's one:

Do not permit your people to say what they're going to do and then show them doing it. Why? Because it's redundant.

Redundancy = Reader boredom!

Say you have a character who says, "I'm going to make a pan of lasagna and take it over to the house after the funeral." You don't have to show him cooking the pasta, draining the tomatoes, etc. Simply cut to the arrival with the lasagna. Or just cut the dialogue in the first place

On the other hand, when a character says one thing and does another, you have something to show.

> Zoe watched Jim zip his jacket. "Where are you going?"
>
> "To the police station. I'm going to turn myself in."
>
> Zoe let out her breath; she hadn't realized she'd been holding it. "They'll arrest you, of course."
>
> "I'm ready."
>
> Fifteen minutes later Jim stood at Lt. Halsey's desk. "I want to take that deal after all."
>
> "Yeah?" The detective sat back, waiting.
>
> "Immunity for the name, right?"
>
> "Right."
>
> "It was my sister Zoe who killed Senator Carson, and I can prove it."

Do you notice that in this sample, there are no tags like 'he said' or 'she muttered'? You don't need them all the time.

But sometimes you want them. What are some of these tags?

Common dialogue tags:

- said
- asked
- told
- answered
- replied
- remarked
- repeated

- insisted
- yelled
- barked
- snarled
- cried
- sneered
- droned

and many more.

You can never go wrong with plain old *said*, though I do like to use different tags once in a while, when appropriate. Be advised that way too many detectives *bark*, way too many villains *snarl*, and way too many second wives *pout* their words. I kind of like *droned*, which you don't see every day.

You can break a long sentence by putting your dialogue tag in the middle, like this:

> "When I was a boy," he began, "we never thought twice about jumping off that riverbank, especially during spring flood."

Mix it up by putting dialogue tags at the beginning of some sentences, at the ends of others, and in the middle of longer ones.

And as you observed in an earlier example, you don't need to use tags all the time, especially when you're combining dialogue with action. Which, by the way, is a great way to break up long passages of dialogue and make the conversation more interesting.

Two people sitting in a room talking is an unnecessarily boring setting. Why not put them in fencing outfits and make them have a go while they're talking? Obviously fencing would have to be part of the plot, but I'm just saying. At least make them take a walk or a drive. By having them interact with their environment, you can develop their characters. I always remember the opening of John Steinbeck's *The Grapes of Wrath*, where Tom Joad, fresh from prison, catches a ride with a trucker.

During their seemingly inconsequential conversation, a bee flies into the open window of the truck cab. The trucker carefully cups his hand around it and guides it out again. A few minutes later a grasshopper flies in, and Tom squashes it. We are to understand differences between the two men. The whole time they're talking, and the whole time we're learning about Tom from the dialogue and from the action.

So, when you have a lot of dialogue to deal with, i.e., you need the characters to reveal a lot of info in a short period of time, break it up with some action—any action—smoking a cigarette, planting shrubs, shooting practice—and you'll be fine.

ADVERBS AND THEIR CRUEL ABUSES

We've talked about dialogue tags, now we need to talk about adverbs— a.k.a. the -ly words:

- he said menacingly
- angrily
- coolly
- fearfully
- cheerfully
- ironically
- quickly
- slowly
- sorrowfully

…ad infinitumly.

New authors tend to abuse adverbs. Professionals, however, have learned that when it comes to adverbs, less is more. Some writing coaches advise not to use them at all, because they want you to *show* readers that the assailant is menacing. But I say, use adverbs only on occasion, because then when you *do* use them, they'll have more impact. Avoid using them as a way to hotfoot it over showing the reader what's going on.

Here's what I'm talking about. Which is better?

"You don't know me at all," he said angrily.

VERSUS

He slammed the table. "You don't know me at all."

The second example is better, because it *shows* you his anger. "You don't know me at all," is essentially a neutral sentence. Context is what brings it alive.

HOW TO PORTRAY EMOTION IN DIALOGUE

Smart professionals know that mixing dialogue with bits of action is an excellent way to portray emotion. Here's another example, with the narrator giving the clue:

> She groped for a response. "I—I'm sorry you feel that way."

The words themselves aren't so hot at portraying emotion; it's the business that comes before or after them that helps get the feeling across to the reader.

Swear words can get emotion across.

> "Who the hell do you think you are?"

We get a pretty good idea of just what emotion is on display here.

You can have a character betray impatience by being sarcastic.

> "Now, we'll never see Cleveland again."
> "I'm devastated."

So far, we've talked about developing your ear for dialogue, and we've talked about generating dialogue, and just now we talked about some basic techniques. Let's go further.

HOW TO GIVE EACH CHARACTER A DISTINCTIVE VOICE

This is the single most important goal for you as a writer of dialogue. Why? Because agents' and editors' most common criticism of amateur writing is—and you know what I'm going to say—"All the characters sound the same."

Kiss of death, right?

The main thing is to make your characters speak in individual ways. Which is a challenge, because you're writing all of your characters, and you're only one person.

It would sound fake if you made every character say *everything* in a different way from every other character. There's not a lot you can do with, "Turn left at the next light." But one thing you can do is to use dialogue markers.

DIALOGUE MARKERS

Quick little labels that help characterize how your people talk are dialogue markers.

The key is to place them intermittently, not constantly.

What are the basic dialogue markers?

Well, we want to give your people different and distinct *vocal characteristics*. What are their voices like? The way you describe a voice can go a long way.

> "But I love you," he said in his hoarse voice.
>
> Her voice lilting, she protested, "But I love you."
>
> His baritone voice broke as he murmured, "But I love you."

This works as a once-in-a-while thing. Obviously you're not going to write *his hoarse voice* every time the character speaks. But using it judiciously, once in a while, works.

Describe the pitch and timbre of a person's voice early on, shortly after we meet him or her. Then bring it up again, every now and then, to remind the reader of it, so the reader will supply that gravelly voice on her own as she reads.

> What are those words you just used, pitch and timbre?

They represent sonic characteristics.

PITCH is the frequency of a sound; that is, how low or high it sounds.

TIMBRE (pronounced 'tamber') is the distinctive tonal quality of the sound. For instance, I just described a voice as being *hoarse*. The timbre of a flute, for instance, could be described as smooth and airy compared to that of a *bassoon*, which could be described as throaty or dark, or even hoarse, come to think of it.

Human voices are just as varied. When you get close to a big, barrel-chested guy and he talks, you can almost feel the vibrations. A high-pitched voice, such as that of a nervous child or woman, can be like needles shooting into your eardrums. Notice these things. Let your people notice these things.

You can compare human voices to those of birds, animals, or nonanimate things. For instance, I write a character in my Lillian Byrd crime novels, a butchy female, whose voice the narrator, Lillian, describes as, "like rocks grinding along a fault line." She doesn't simply say, "Her voice was rough," or even gravelly, which I wanted to surpass.

Here's another example that shows how you can use just one word of narrative to characterize a voice:

> He addressed his elderly neighbor, as usual, in a deferential bellow. "Good morning, Mr. Rinaldi!"

He wouldn't just yell, "Hiya, Pops!" The descriptive word is *deferential*.

OTHER WAYS TO ILLUSTRATE A VOICE

A metaphor is a figure of speech that uses one object or concept in place of another, to suggest alikeness. A simile is also a figure of speech, but it compares one thing to another.

An example of the difference:

> **METAPHOR:** His voice was a jackhammer: "Do it, do it, do it!"

> **SIMILE:** His voice was as insistent as a jackhammer: "Do it, do it, do it!"

Metaphors tend to be more direct and, in my opinion, fresher. Why do I even mention the words metaphor and simile? Why do I distinguish between them? To build up your knowledge and make you aware of your options as a writer, and also so that you know what the hell literary professionals mean when they use the words.

Other examples, to get your juices flowing:

> Her whisper was like fine snow drifting down his neck. "I'll never tell..." (simile)

> He talked on, his voice silk and flowers. "I've never felt about a woman the way I feel about you." (metaphor)

> "Devin!" Her voice made him jump like a firecracker. "Don't touch that." (simile)

Did you notice that in that last one, the simile really refers to Devin rather than the voice? We need not be rigid about any of this stuff. Have fun and let your imagination loose!

Now, as to what your people *say.*

HOW TO GIVE YOUR PEOPLE DISTINCTIVE VERBAL MARKERS

Verbal markers (what they say) are different from vocal markers (how they sound when they say it).

Contractions

You can have a character use different habitual contractions, like:

> "I'm gonna watch in case they come back."

> "You guys'll take fifty percent."

When it comes to "Yeah" and "Yes," it rarely works to have a character say "Yeah" all the time; most of us use both, depending on the context. Like this:

> "Do you know where the remote is?"
> "Yeah, here."

> **VERSUS**

> "Would you like to go on a free cruise?"
> "Yes!"

Elisions

Characters might *elide* sounds or syllables, meaning eliminate them, like this:

> "We're gonna go swimmin' after school."

> "Prob'ly she'll divorce him."

Idiosyncrasies

A character can use a certain idiosyncratic construction habitually, like "Yessiree!" or "I'm obliged to you," instead of thank you and "Oh, you bet," instead of you're welcome.

Interjections

An interjection is a common dialogue marker. In speech, an interjection is an abrupt exclamation that conveys emotion.

> "Holy hell!"

> "Oh, my word!"

> "Mercy me!"

> "Dammit, Jim!"

> "Oh, no way!"

One of Dickens's characters in *David Copperfield* keeps saying, "Oh, my lungs and liver!" The White Rabbit in Lewis Carroll's *Alice's Adventures in Wonderland*, says, "Oh, my ears and whiskers!"

A contemporary character might say, for example, "Get outta here!" or "Well, I'll be a ..." Fill in the blank with something fun. The cliché is "Well, I'll be a monkey's uncle" or "I'll be damned," but you can think of something unique to your character. "Well, I'll be a barbecued barracuda." Something. Take liberties with common clichés and expressions, and make them into your characters' own.

Slang

Slang is nonstandard vocabulary.

> yeah
>
> megabucks
>
> reefer

Yeah, actually is slang. *Megabucks* is slang. *Reefer* is slang for a marijuana cigarette. I find habitual slang to be useful as a dialogue marker.

HABITUAL EMPHASIS is a cousin of slang, I feel, and can be a marker in itself. That is, a person can be shown to be intense, or overly dramatic, simply by using italics. Like this:

> "I *told* you, but you didn't *listen*. I can't *believe* they left us behind."

Of course any person can emphasize a word here and there, either out of irritation, as above, or another emotion, and you'll use italics to show it. But you can have a character who talks this way a lot, and that will distinguish that person as a drama queen or an especially intense personality.

Idioms

Idioms differ from slang in that they are expressions that are not understandable or don't make sense if taken literally:

- hit the ceiling
- totaled
- put all your eggs in one basket
- a piece of cake
- to make a silk purse out of a sow's ear

The phrase "to hit the ceiling" is an idiom. "When he found out I totaled the car, he hit the ceiling." Totaled used this way is slang for "declared a total loss by the insurance company." To literally hit the ceiling, you'd have to find a ladder or stand on a chair, make a fist, and pound on the plaster.

All languages have idioms, not just American English.

Crafting Dynamic Dialogue

Make up your own idioms. For example, in a scene from my novel *The Actress*, I needed a Japanese-American character to scold another character. I wanted him to use a Japanese idiom, but I didn't know any, so I made one up. The line goes: "I leave you on your own for one day, and you drop your whole fish box!" So far no one has said, "Where the hell'd you get that fish box thing?"

If an off-the-wall construction occurs to you as you're writing, don't cross it out just because you've never heard it before. Keep it and look at it again later.

You can distinguish a character by having her or him talk more formally than anyone else. Someone who makes a point of not using contractions might be trying to show their high class or esteemed education—this of course betrays insecurity and informs readers about the character. A perceptive reader will see this.

(Note here: *Always* write for a perceptive reader. Don't ever dumb your writing down, even if you're writing for children. *Especially* if you're writing for children.)

PROFANITY AND YOU

Since we've touched on profanity, we might as well discuss it.

You have four choices with profanity:

1. Don't allow it at all.
2. Allow some or all of your people to use it in a limited way, including mild swear words like *hell* and *damn* (this is what a lot of authors writing in the young adult genre use).
3. Allow some or all of your people to use it as far as they want to take it, including the f-word and whatever other vulgarities the characters might need to express themselves.
4. Or use fake profanity (which I will explain).

The fact that authors are divided on the subject of profanity is not surprising because *readers* are divided as well. Some really big tough-guy authors such as Lee Child, author of the Jack Reacher series, use no profanity in their books, and lots of readers don't even notice it. Why? Because Lee, for instance, doesn't even write *dammit* which would call attention to the fact that he's not using *god damn it*. And he's certainly not going to have his characters, who blow each other's brains out at the drop of a hat, say *darn it*, for the same reason. This is important to remember if you want to omit profanity entirely.

On the other hand, Tom Clancy, another tough-guy author, used lots of profanity, and he sold a lot of books. I use profanity in most of my books.

You can have a character who habitually uses profanity in contrast to others who don't. That in itself is a good *individualizer*.

What is fake profanity? Well, I really mean nonprofane words used in places where you'd expect to see profanity or a vulgarism. This can work if you want to call attention to the fact that the character's sensibilities are too refined to use profanity, even in an extreme situation. I referred to *darn it* earlier.

Here's another example: You have a police veteran who, in the midst of a shoot-out, gets hit. He yells, "Fiddlesticks!" If you want this to be funny, or to call attention to his unshakeable squareness, fine. Otherwise, use real profanity, or nothing at all. The police officer could simply scream, or he could yell, "I've been hit!"

KEEPING TRACK

In fiction, it's useful to keep a list of who uses what verbal and dialogue markers. You can expand on this list as you write, and refer to it when you need to refresh your mind.

Here's a sample. Can you guess which classic fictional character the following describes:

- Swears liberally, but no f-word
- "For Crissake!"
- "That kills me."
- "No kidding, I really do."

It's Holden Caulfield, from *The Catcher in the Rye* by J.D. Salinger. Salinger was fabulous at writing dialogue, and I believe it was because of his excellent ear. Study his books with an eye to dialogue and you'll see. No kidding.

Crafting Dynamic Dialogue

VOCABULARY AS SOCIAL MARKER

Educated people tend to have larger vocabularies than uneducated people, and of course an educated person will usually be comfortable enough with language to use contractions, elisions, and slang when appropriate.

If you study speech habits, you'll find that in general, people of lower socioeconomic levels talk more than the upper crust. And you can use this to help distinguish your characters from each other, as well as to develop each character.

In my experience, it boils down to self-esteem more than social rank. Of course, self-esteem often comes with social rank, which is why the generalization holds. But the poorest monk is often a man of great dignity and few words, while an insecure member of the nouveau riche might chatter nervously all over the place.

These are subtleties that you can use, once you're conscious of them.

THE ENGINE BENEATH THE WORDS: SUBTEXT

Writing compelling dialogue is about focusing on what's important. What is the kernel of this scene? What needs to be revealed, what needs to be concealed?

Who needs what?

This issue of what your characters need is one that professional authors go deeply into; they don't stop at the surface.

For instance, if a character is in need of support from another, that's one need. But what is beneath that need? Wanting support might mean the character is temporarily weak due to circumstances or it might mean the character is profoundly anxious and fearful, and has been for decades. Digging deep for your characters' motivations will help bring your dialogue to life—the dialogue will be about more than what shows on the surface.

In other words, you must have *subtext*.

Subtext is simply the real issues beneath the surface, the stuff people try to say without saying, the inner feelings that motivate their talking. Subtext is the bush people beat around.

The movies are great to study for subtext. "A scene should never be about what it's about," is advice every student in screenwriting classes hears again and again.

If it's about what it's about, it's dead.

The exception is sex. That's why so many authors and screenwriters have a hard time with sex scenes: Sex is about what it's about. Unless, that is, the story calls for conflict or ambiguity, because then you can do more.

If, for example, an argument crops up during foreplay, you have something more interesting going on. Will the couple get this resolved here and now so they can both wind up with some pleasure, or not?

SUBTEXT IN ACTION

If you're unsure what subtext is, this example will instantly make it clear:

> A thirty-year-old guy, who lives near his mother, comes over to see her.
>
> "Mom, I'm going to start college in the fall."
>
> "I thought you couldn't afford it." (Subtext: not happy for him)
>
> "Well, I've been saving from my job. I can take three classes: math, biology, and writing."
>
> "What are you going to do with that?" (Subtext: skeptical)
>
> "I want to be an ichthyologist and study sharks."
>
> "Well, there aren't many sharks around here." (Subtext: hints of fear, jealousy, and desire for control arise through a ridiculous objection)
>
> "Right, I'll have to leave Abilene eventually and transfer to a school with a marine studies program." (Subtext: this is the news he needs to deliver, and he sticks to the point)
>
> "I don't think that would be a good idea, honey. Why don't you study accounting? Then you could get a good job right here in Abilene."
>
> "Well ..." (Subtext: he doesn't agree but sees he may not get his feelings across)
>
> "What if fish fail to keep your interest? I mean, honestly, fish?" (Subtext: another objection, this one quite weak)
>
> "Fish are fascinating to me."
>
> "Well, what if something happens to you? It's dangerous to go diving and things in the ocean. I don't think you realize that." (Subtext: subtle threat through another objection)
>
> "I'll be OK. They have all these safety precautions." (Subtext: goals are researched, staying factual, sticking to the point)

Crafting Dynamic Dialogue

"What if you run out of money? Don't think I'll be able to help you. Ever since your father died, I don't have anything extra, you know." (Subtext: another objection by eliciting sympathy, as well as another threat)

"I'll be OK. I'm keeping my job. This time, I'm really serious about getting a science degree." (Subtext: he's caved in to her objections before, but he's changed)

"Ohhh…"

"Mom, what's the matter?"

"Suddenly I don't feel well. I think it's my heart." (Subtext: now we're really into passive-aggressive threat territory!)

On the surface, this conversation is about college.

But below the words, there is subtext. This conversation is not about college!

It's about the mother's fear of abandonment, it's about her attempts to manipulate her son, and it's about the son's growing independence. Will he give in to her? Will she step up her efforts to undermine him in an attempt to make him stay close to her? Will she segue into an outright guilt trip? ("Oh, honey, I can't believe you'd go away from me after all I've done for you.") That is the subtext. That is what's really going on.

If we wrote a scene about the guy talking to the college admissions officer about class availability, etc., that would be a scene that's *about what it's about*.

But we wouldn't put that scene in our story. Wouldn't need to. You understand this intuitively; I'm making it explicit to bring it to your conscious attention.

The above sample contains only dialogue and no other business, but you could make things even more interesting by highlighting the subtext. For instance, the son could be fixing the computer for his mom, or the two could be out on a shopping trip, or they could be robbing a bank together, or they could be at a cattle auction (their town being Abilene and all). And the things they do in between their speech can help show the reader the nature of their relationship and what's really going on with it.

Give it a go!

WRITING SUBTEXT

With dialogue there is often disagreement. That's good, because:

    Disagreement = Conflict = Reader Interest

    Gather your writing materials.

    Find a comfortable place.

    Enter garret mode. (Note: See chapter six.)

    Here's a scenario for you: A married couple are on vacation. They've rented a large motor home and they're driving it across the country. The subtext: *Their marriage is in trouble.* He's talked her into going on this trip, thinking maybe they can work on their relationship. But vacations can bring their own stresses! No matter what happens, they can't agree for long.

    Write it for ten minutes. Let 'er rip.

    Check in with your gut as you go along. Let your heartbrain loose. Use *Yes and—* and *What if?* a lot. Using these open-ended prompts will keep your writing flowing.

    Have fun! Take it to the max!

    Write for as long as you like.

    When you're ready to stop writing, stop.

    As you wrote, did you discover or invent more subtext? Like, the husband might be insecure about his job, the wife might want children. The husband is uncomfortable with the prospect of visiting her hometown because her childhood sweetheart still lives there. The situation escalates! I love writing stuff like this.

PHONE CONVERSATIONS

I get questions from aspiring authors about how to use phone conversations in their work. I actually try to avoid writing them in my fiction, but if there's no way around it, keep it brief and have your characters do their processing off the phone.

A phone conversation is a good thing to *summarize*.

> He told me he was breaking up with Clarice, which I'd expected, then he said they were going on one last Club Med vacation together. I gave him hell for that, but we hung up friends just the same. Let's see how much of a tan he comes home with.

That summary can be a phone conversation or an in-person one.

Another very effective technique is to intersperse summarized dialogue with real-time dialogue, especially if you have a long conversation going, with a lot of information to give to the reader. Like this:

> They discussed the kids for fifteen minutes, then Trent said, "I got another speeding ticket today from that same bastard cop."
>
> "Really? Was he in the same place?"
>
> "Yeah, behind those trees on Mill Road."
>
> "That so totally sucks."
>
> Trent changed the subject, but Leslie could tell he was going to stay steamed about that cop for at least a week.
>
> "So," he said, "would you like tickets for that Jets game?"

WRITING COMPLEX CONVERSATIONS THE EASY WAY

First of all, challenge yourself to see whether you need as many people in the scene as you think you do. If you have lots of characters who are there just for that scene, for instance, you might combine a couple into one. Leave out anyone who isn't essential.

Physically placing your characters can help the reader make a mental picture. Say you have a bunch of people in a drawing room discussing who the real murderer is. As soon as somebody talks or appears, make it clear where they are:

> "I think the butler did it," said Gen. Kassar from the window seat. Opposite him, at the door, the Fairchilds looked at each other and stayed where they were. Craig racked the billiard balls while Tyler got ready to break. Craig tossed the rack aside. "You can't be serious."

Mrs. Marten laid her head on the divan's velvet arm. "Will you stop that rackety-yack?" she asked drunkenly. The footman fed a chunk of maple to the fire and wished he'd taken his day off like he'd planned. The flames intensified and he flapped his armpits discreetly.

Make sure you use vocal tags:

In his sissy-boy voice Tyler said, "If I don't win, I don't play."

The footman picked up the errant coal with his bare hand, grunting an apology as he threw it into the hearth.

You can also leave several characters hanging until you need them to talk or act. If you've placed them well, the reader will remember them when they speak up.

And simply use their names.

Readers do appreciate being reminded of who is speaking a little more often when a scene involves three or more people. It's not an intrusion; it's a help.

One of my correspondents recommends the dinner scene from Frank Herbert's *Dune* as a great example of a complex scene with lots of characters talking.

As you write dialogue, use any or all of the techniques you've learned in these chapters. Give your characters distinct voices and individual dialogue markers, and give them some business to do, and you'll be golden. Speaking of gold, here's:

THE GOLDEN TEST FOR DIALOGUE

Read it aloud.

Simple.

How does it sound, how does it feel in your mouth and throat? Even better, read it into a recording device, then play it back and listen. Or give it to somebody else to read aloud to you. You'll instantly hear whether it sounds right. Your attention will be drawn to what *doesn't* sound right. Tinker until it's better.

I encourage you, going forward, to do what I do: Pay attention when you're reading the news or magazines whenever you come across an article that discusses a study about speech habits and patterns. You can learn a lot of little things that will help you. The same goes for material concerning body language and psychology, for that matter.

A good author is a student of people and the language they use. Watch, listen, write it down, search for context.

Simple: Live. Be aware. Go far.

CHAPTER 15
HOW YOUR CHARACTERS SPEAK

BY NANCY KRESS

Say what? Or, just as important, say how?

How your characters talk is just as important as what they actually say. In fact, good dialogue can be defined as the right speech content expressed in the right words. And good dialogue can do as much to create strong characterization as can description and exposition put together. Speech is a powerful expression of personality.

Consider, for example, this situation: Your character Harry has a car accident. Later that day, as the bashed-in car sits in Harry's driveway, the doorbell rings. Harry opens the door to his Uncle Jim. Jim's first words are one of the following:

> "Harry, what happened to your car?"
>
> "Jeeze, that car looks bad! Gonna set you back your whole deductible, boy ... oh, I just remembered, you didn't get collision, right?"
>
> "Harry! Your car! Are you all right? Was anybody hurt?"
>
> "Harry, my lad, that automobile looks like it met my last wife in a towering rage. Was Gloria here, by any chance?"
>
> "Harry, it looks like you may need a new car. Have I ever mentioned my friend Del Samler, who runs a car lot on Sycamore? Good prices, fair dealing. I could give him a call right now."

The first version of Uncle Jim is a straightforward, rational, reserving reaction until he has the facts. The second version is a gloating oaf; the third, an emotional person with concern for people's safety; the fourth, a wit who doesn't mind using other people's misfortunes to exercise his slightly patronizing brand of humor; the fifth, a pushy opportunist. All that characterization was conveyed solely by a few sentences of dialogue.

How can you do that for your character? By paying attention to four areas of speech: content, diction, grammar, and length.

CONTENT: SUBSTANCE IS STYLE

Obviously, the most important aspect of your character's speech is the content. Presumably, you wouldn't be giving him dialogue at all if you didn't have something you needed him to say. The detective asks questions because that's his job; the mother reprimands her teenage daughter because she doesn't like the girl's staying out past curfew; the doctor tells the patient's family that the patient has died because the doctor has no choice.

All these examples, however, are primary content, determined by plot or circumstance. Dialogue also can carry secondary content. This means information conveyed along with the primary content but not necessary to the actual story. Secondary content is like sauce on beef: not the main ingredient but definitely altering the taste of the dish.

For instance, look again at that last version of Uncle Jim's greeting to Harry. Jim urges Harry to call Jim's friend Del to buy a used car. In this story, Harry isn't going to call Del, and, in fact, Del will never be mentioned again. Jim will turn out to be essential to the plot, but Del is there solely to let us know what kind of person Jim is. That's secondary content, and it can be a gold mine of characterization.

Another example is this exchange of dialogue from Joanne Harris' novel *Chocolat*. Protagonist Vianne Rocher has just opened a chocolate shop in a French village. Her first customer, Guillaume, is amazed at how Vianne has cleaned up and decorated the ancient building:

> "It's quite a transformation," said Guillaume. "You know, I'm not sure why, but I'd just assumed it was going to be another bakery."
>
> "What, and ruin poor Monsieur Poitou's trade? I'm sure he'd thank me for that, with his lumbago playing up the way it is, and his poor wife an invalid and sleeping so badly."

Vianne could have answered simply, "No, Lansquenet already has a bakery." But, by including the secondary content of the baker's name and the troubles he already has without competition from Vianne, the author lets Vianne's dialogue characterize her. It shows Vianne to be perceptive about village economics, observant about her new neighbors, and sensitive to their needs and wishes. Secondary content reveals personality.

To characterize through secondary content, start by asking yourself, "What kind of person is saying this dialogue?" Then try to include small bits of extra—not extraneous—content that reflects that emotional quality. A mean-spirited person adds different details to her speech than a kind person. Reflect that in the content of your dialogue.

QUICK TIPS

Here are quick tips you can use to enhance characterization through dialogue:

- Use secondary content—information not necessary to the actual story—to add personality to your characters.
- Allow your character's choice of words—is he formal or informal, precise or vague—to imply his cultural, historical, or ethnic background.
- The use of slang or misspellings in an attempt to reproduce dialect can interrupt the flow of your dialogue.
- Use grammar to suggest the education and background of your character.
- Vary sentence length to convey your character's traits.

DICTION MATTERS

English is a rich and varied language, teeming with synonyms. Words indicating essentially the same concept may be formal or informal, precise or vague, familiar or obscure. Your character's choice of words—diction—will reveal a lot about him. Here are two ways of telling a stranger to control his dog:

"Please restrain your St. Bernard from invading my meal!"

"Hey, Bub, you wanna get your dog off my picnic?"

The first version suggests someone precise ("St. Bernard" rather than just "dog"), formal ("restrain," "meal"), even prissy and indignant ("invading"). The second speaker is informal, overly familiar ("Bub"), and not as upset.

In general, English words come from two sources: Latin and Anglo-Saxon. The Latin versions usually sound more educated, formal, and distancing than their Anglo-Saxon counterparts. Thus, "I detest the odor of manure" gives a much different impression from "I hate the smell of shit." Which is your character more likely to use: Latinate or Anglo-Saxon words? Exploit the difference.

Special cases of diction include slang and dialect. Both can be effective in implying cultural, historical, or ethnic background for your characters—if you avoid their many pitfalls. These include datedness (slang changes so quickly) and triteness.

Hackneyed, clichéd dialect, or slang implies stereotypes rather than characterization and may even be condescending. An Irishman who says "Faith and begorrah," a Chinese person who talks in pidgin, or a contemporary Englishman who says "Blimey" quickly will undermine your reader's faith in your knowledge of those cultures.

The main danger, however, is overuse. A little goes a long way. Don't misspell half the words in a sentence in an attempt to reproduce dialect, or load dialogue with so much slang that it becomes incomprehensible or satiric. It's far better to give the flavor of the region or historical period through the way familiar words are arranged in the sentence, spiced with just a few carefully chosen local expressions. Here are some effective examples:

> "Not that I don't love Mother, because I do. One gets fond of them, you know. But she's a bit dotty, and she's got a bit of a heart."
> —1930s English gentlewoman, in Angela Thirkell's *High Rising*

> "No kidding, now. Do that composition for me. Don't knock yourself out or anything, but just make it descriptive as hell. Okay?"
> —1950s teenager, in J.D. Salinger's *The Catcher in the Rye*

> "Ah now, ah now. 'Tisn't his fault if there's Presbyterians in his family."
> —Early-20th century Irishman, in Frank McCourt's *Angela's Ashes*

> "Mr. ... Mr. Maturin. Why, there you are, sir. I owe you a thousand apologies, I am afraid. I must have been a sad bore to you last night. We sailors

hear so little music—are so little used to genteel music—that we grow
carried away. I beg your pardon."

—19th century naval captain, in Patrick O'Brian's *Master and Commander*

If you are genuinely familiar with a culture, and if you can do it with a
light hand, then enhance your character's dialogue with slang and/or
dialect to suggest time, place, and background.

GRAMMAR: YOU SURE TALK GOOD

In every time and place, grammatically correct speech suggests
education. Either the character himself is educated, or he grew up
among educated people. Take this into account when you write dialogue
for a specific character. How educated is the character? Does his speech
reflect this background? What impressions, for instance, do you get
from these three characters' speech?

> "Yesterday I saw Jack with Sue, and the day before I saw him with a differ-
> ent girl. I'm not sure who she was."

> "Yesterday I seen Jack with Sue, and the day before I seen him with some
> other girl, don't know who."

> "Yesterday I saw Jack with Sue, and the day before I had seen him with
> someone else, whom I hadn't recognized."

The first speaks standard English (average education). The second is
very ungrammatical (either little education or deliberate affectation;
context will make clear which). The third speaks hypercorrectly (usually indicates a pedantic fussiness).

LENGTH: HE JUST GOES ON AND ON …

Terse, short speeches can suggest either strength of character (the
"strong, silent type") or an antisocial personality. In contrast, characters who ramble on and on will strike your readers as unfocused, inde-
cisive, or narcissistic. Context will determine the exact interpretation.
Which of these characters sounds more competent to you?

Crafting Dynamic Dialogue

"Please put the chair in the den."

"Put the chair in the ... no, wait, the color won't go there ... put it in the living room. No, just a sec, maybe the den would be better, after all ... Larry, do you think the chair should go in the den or the living room? The color isn't right for the den, but the living room ... Larry? Are you listening to me?"

Larry probably isn't. The speaker comes across as a ditz. If that's the effect you want, then repetition that interrupts itself is certainly one way to get it.

On the other hand, repetition that is shaped and formed can indicate a polished, forceful delivery backed by strong conviction. If your protagonist says, "I won't let you bully me. I won't let you scare me, not ever again," we believe her. The repetition is balanced, and so is she.

As with slang and dialect, a little repetition or extended speech goes a long way. Use judiciously.

A CAVEAT: IT'S NOT AS HARD AS IT LOOKS

If this discussion has left you feeling that dialogue is difficult to write or that you must agonize over every single word your character utters, take heart. You only need to be loosely aware of the possibilities as you write dialogue in your first draft, incorporating whichever techniques seem natural. Then, in later drafts, you can tinker with a word or sentence here and there, adding slang or repetition, sharpening diction, cutting for terseness.

With dialogue, minor adjustments can make quite a difference. It's worth the effort.

NANCY KRESS is the author of thirty-three books, including twenty-six novels, four collections of short stories, and three books on writing. Her work has won six Nebulas, two Hugos, a Sturgeon, and the John W. Campbell Memorial Award. Her most recent works are the Nebula-winning *Yesterday's Kin* (Tachyon, 2014) and *The Best of Nancy Kress* (Subterranean, 2015). In addition to writing, Kress often teaches at various venues around the country and abroad; in 2008, she was the Picador visiting lecturer at the University of Leipzig. Kress lives in Seattle with her husband, writer Jack Skillingstead, and Cosette, the world's most spoiled toy poodle.

CHAPTER 16

A VARIETY OF VOICES

BY CHRIS ROGERS

Who can forget Eliza's "Oawoo!" from *My Fair Lady* or Yoda's "stubborn you are" from *Return of the Jedi*? Distinctive characters not only come instantly alive and draw us deep into their fictional words, they also live on in our minds.

Viewpoint characters should sound the same in their thoughts as in their words. For this reason, if no other, I avoid strong dialect with its plethora of apostrophes. Instead, I devise a language for each character that consists of simple choices.

Like other novelists, I develop character profiles: Where is he from? What does she read? When did he marry? Who does she trust? When I advance that process a step further and create speech profiles, I find my characters more engaging and their dialogue free-flowing.

Individuals from widely different background are easy to distinguish. An educated person speaks more eloquently, for example, than does one with little schooling. But among characters of the same ethnic derivation, educational level, and socioeconomic scale, giving each a personal language, or idiolect, takes a bit of work. But it pays off.

Here are a few techniques to help you develop unique voices for your own characters.

WORD CHOICE

As you originate characters' speech patterns, consider their interests, vocations, hobbies, marital situation, family background. Do they come from a fast-paced city or from a country town? Did they graduate cum laude or drop out of high school? Would they use expletives? Repeat phrases?

PRACTICE MAKES PERFECT

Consider how two neighbors, similarly educated, might discuss erecting a fence between their yards. First, give each a specific vocabulary.

- Sara is a young wife with two dogs and a strong sense of décor. She recently moved from Texas, where ample space is taken for granted. A human resource recruiter at a bank, she is expecting her first child. Sara's vocabulary might include such words and phrases as romp, rambunctious, elbow room, spacious, cramped, enough room to spit, picket, rail, neighborly, as well as such job-related terms as offer, inclusive, expectations, needs assessment, opportunity.
- Britt, a divorced woman with two teenagers, takes pride in her burgeoning flower garden. She works as a CPA in a large firm and has lived in her Colorado home for two years. Her previous neighbor was elderly. Britt's vocabulary might include such words as schedules, busy, quality time, wind down, sunlight, fresh air, rocky, outdoor, color, odor, fertile, as well as such job-related words as money, balance, upside, increase, debit.

Sara needs the fence to keep her dogs in the yard. Britt enjoys her garden in its relation to the neighboring yards. Choosing words from their respective vocabulary lists, how would each woman express her views?

SENSORY PREFERENCES

A rich source of word choice comes from our sensory preference. Like being right- or left-handed, each of us is either visual, auditory, or kinesthetic (feeling). Although we each use all the senses—just as we use both hands—we tend to strongly favor one sense over the others. By determining which sense your characters prefer, you'll add depth and distinction to your chorus of voices.

VISUAL. These characters might use such words as clear, colorful, imagine, bright, show me, cloudy, view, envision, pale, vivid, picture, outlook, spectacle.

AUDITORY. These characters might use resonate, listen, tell me, talk, noisy, lyrical, sound, tone, dulcet, timbre, musical, loud, clamorous.

KINESTHETIC. Such characters may use touch words, such as open, soft, hard, cool, warm, fuzzy, rough, give it to me, get a handle on, approach, angle, standpoint, smooth, unruffled.

By choosing a sensory preference, you can establish an entire vocabulary for each character. But remember, you only need to sprinkle such sensory words like pepper. Build your characters without considering whether they are auditory, visual, or kinesthetic, however, and their language will likely reflect your own sensory style. Worse still, they might all sound alike.

INTERESTS AND HOBBIES

Characters' interests and hobbies are another rich source for language. For example, an avid fisherman might use such terms as hooking into, catching up, reeling in, sinking feelings, baiting a sucker, floating a loan, netting results, waiting for a boat to come in, trawling for leads, holy mackerel, dumb as a gull, smelly as fish bait. A seamstress, on the other hand, might speak in sewing terms, such as button your lip, cut the strings, thread your way, tight as a bobbin, stitch it up, snip it, line his pockets, spool it, coat of another color, dress it up, seamless, wash-and-wear, take the starch out.

Again, if you build a straightjacket of colorful words, you'll create a caricature instead of a character. A good way to work is to design an idiolect made up of all the background, interests, and sensory material in the character profile. Then, keep this word list handy while you write and edit. Get into the character's head. Imagine yourself a Texas fisherman, retired, arthritic, cranky. How would you answer a simple question like, "How are you doing?" differently from a disabled coach who still turns out to cheer the high school football team to glory?

CADENCE

The rhythm in which your characters speak is also a reflection of who they are and where they've been. By altering inflection and/or sentence length, you can show your characters in a whole new light.

PHRASES. A person who riddles his speech or internal narrative with prepositional or parenthetical phrases will speak in a completely different rhythm from someone who uses few or none:

- Simple: The table legs splayed, causing a tilt that sent dishes crashing.
- Complex: The legs of the table, obviously improperly attached, splayed, which caused a tilt in the surface of the table; the dishes, a legacy from my grandmother, crashed to the floor.

ADVERBS. These create a different cadence than adjectives modifying nouns or pronouns:

- Adjectives: Fine wine after an excellent program put Chelsea in a warm and generous mood.
- Adverbs: After the program, wine flowed lavishly, turning Chelsea's mood warmly generous.

MULTISYLLABIC WORDS. A character who uses multisyllabic words will have a slightly more lyrical cadence than someone who primarily uses words of one syllable:

- Single syllable: Bees flit from bloom to bloom.
- Multisyllable: Bumblebees flutter among the blossoms.

ARTICLES. Dropped articles (the, a, an) or incomplete sentences also will affect rhythm:

- Complete: "The car won't start. A new battery might fix it."
- Casual: "Car won't start. New batter might fix it."
- Complete: "You have no chance of making it to first base."
- Casual: "No chance. Won't get to first base."

Fashion a character's voice as you similarly invent clothing style, body type, mannerisms, social structure, education, psychology, and attitude. Allow speech to spring from the character as a whole. Create a profile that includes words and phrases only that person is allowed to use. The result will be characters who come alive on the page and linger in a reader's mind long after the story ends.

....

CHRIS ROGERS is the author of fourteen books in diverse genres, fiction and nonfiction, including *Emissary*, a science-fiction thriller, and *Here Lies a Wicked Man*, the first in her Booker Krane mystery series. Rogers is also a painter with works in private and corporate collections.

PART V

·············

DIALOGUE SETS THE STAGE

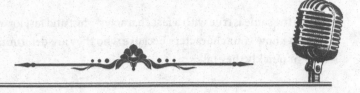

CHAPTER 17

DIALOGUE AS A MEANS OF PACING

BY GLORIA KEMPTON

"Let's see," the small-town, slow-talking cop said as he stood outside my window.

It doesn't matter if he was slow talking, fast-talking, or a deaf mute—cops intimidate me.

"Looks like you were doing about sixty-seven in a fifty-five mile-per-hour zone. Well, I suppose I'll have to write you up."

Whatever. Just hurry up so I can get back on the road and out of this humiliating moment sitting here in my car hanging out with you.

I can't believe it, I grumbled to myself as he returned to his patrol car to write me up. Almost twenty years without a ticket and here I am. I mean, really, I would have hit the twenty-year mark in another year or so.

"Okay, I'm just gonna make it sixty-five instead of sixty-seven so it'll bring your fee down a bit."

"I haven't had a ticket in almost twenty years," I told the cop, thinking this bit of trivia might make him swell with pride for me, resulting in a torn-up ticket. "Isn't that something?"

"That's something, all right," he said as he handed me the ticket. "You gotta be careful around here because, you know, us small-town cops don't have nothing else to do but sit out here and catch folks like you hightailing it through our town like you got somewhere to go."

This is a true story; I'm still feeling the pain of the seventy-five dollar ticket. The point? I might have been speeding, but the minute I ran into Mr. Small-Town Cop, my true story slowed right down. We weren't going anywhere fast. And that's simply because he wasn't in a hurry. You can't speed up a slow character; he moves in two speeds—slow and reverse. The same is true with a fast character—fast and fast forward. So it pays to know your characters because who they are determines how slowly or quickly they talk.

PACING YOUR STORY

Every story has its own pace. Most literary and many mainstream stories move slowly, easily, from opening to conclusion. Such a story may ramble on about the characters' philosophies and life strategies, and on occasion the author will even use dialogue to achieve the slow pace—if the author knows what he's doing. Reading slow-moving dialogue is preferable to reading lengthy passages of philosophical narrative.

Genre stories generally move quickly, employing more dialogue and action and less slow-paced narrative, because they are generally plot-driven rather than character-driven, like literary and mainstream stories. The emphasis is on the action that keeps the plot moving rather than the narrative that keeps the character growing.

Whatever kind of story you're writing, you want to be conscious of the pacing. It makes sense that a character-driven literary story will move more contemplatively than an action-suspense story. Dialogue generally speeds things up, but of course there are exceptions, as there are exceptions to everything in fiction. For example, you might have a slow talker who, every time he appears in a scene, causes the action and other characters to just kind of come to a stop. But that's the exception, and we want to look at the general rule—that dialogue normally speeds everything up. A story is woven, using both fast and slow-paced scenes, to achieve a rhythm that works for the kind of story you're writing.

Let's say you're writing a suspense thriller and you need to keep things moving. The focus of your story will be on your fast-paced dialogue and action scenes, and the narrative will be woven in only if and when you need it. The characters in a suspense thriller don't do a lot of thinking other than moments of wondering how to get out of the scrapes in which they find themselves. These nondramatic scenes are placed strategically every so often so the viewpoint character can catch

Crafting Dynamic Dialogue

up with himself. Other than that, the story keeps moving. And dialogue makes up the bulk of a fast-paced story.

What you want to learn is how to control the pace of your story through dialogue. Without knowing how to do this, you have no sense of whether you're putting your reader to sleep or keeping her wide awake and turning pages as fast as she can. By the way, you can keep your reader quickly turning pages in a literary or mainstream story, too, if you can learn to write dialogue that has some substance.

The only thing standing in the way of our being able to pace our stories is plain and simple unconsciousness. We're just not thinking about pacing as we're writing, so my challenge to you in this chapter is to start to think about it. Not after you've completed the story and you notice your critique group's yawns and blank stares. Most stories are paced not too fast, but too slow. The time to think about pacing is while you're writing your first draft.

EXERCISE

PACING YOUR STORY. Focus on just one scene in a story you're writing. Now answer the following questions as honestly as you can:

- Is this a slow-paced or a fast-paced scene? Or neither?
- In relation to the entire story, what kind of pace do I want this scene to have?
- What is making this scene move so slowly (or quickly)?
- How much dialogue have I used in this scene, as compared to action and narrative?
- Using more or less dialogue, how can I adjust the pacing of the scene?
- Are the scenes on either side of this one slow or fast-paced?
- How much dialogue have I used in the scenes on either side of this one? Do either one of them need more or less dialogue to make them move better, so they're in rhythm with this one?

Now rewrite the scene so it moves at the pace you want it to.

CREATING MOMENTUM

A story gathers momentum as it moves. That's not to say we should start our stories out slowly, hoping things will pick up as we write. We can't afford that luxury. We situate our characters in the scene's setting, introduce the conflict, create some emotion, all while the characters are moving into dialogue with one another. In real life, conversation can take many twists and turns, and sometimes you're left wondering how you even got into a particular conversation. Dialogue has its own momentum and is driven by—guess who—the characters. We have to trust our characters enough to let them talk to each other about what they need to talk about. This isn't always easy because as writers we have agendas, and it's so easy to impose our agendas on our characters. When we do that, the characters start making speeches and going off on all kinds of tangents that aren't theirs but ours.

In the following scene from John Kennedy Toole's comedic novel *A Confederacy of Dunces*, the protagonist, Ignatius Reilly, is visiting a ladies' art show trying to sell some of his hot dogs. The scene starts off slowly as Ignatius approaches some of the paintings, then gathers steam as he starts to comment quite candidly on the artwork.

> The Alley was filled with well-dressed ladies in large hats. Ignatius pointed the prow of the wagon into the throng and pushed forwards. A woman read the Big Chief statement and screamed, summoning her companions to draw aside from the ghastly apparition that had appeared at their art show.
>
> "Hot dog, ladies?" Ignatius asked pleasantly.
>
> The ladies' eyes studied the sign, the earring, the scarf, the cutlass, and pleaded for him to move along. Rain for their hanging would have been bad enough. But *this*.
>
> "Hot dogs, hot dogs," Ignatius said a little angrily "Savories from the hygienic Paradise kitchens."
>
> He belched violently during the silence that followed. The ladies pretended to study the sky and the little garden behind the Cathedral.

The author now inserts a narrative paragraph where Ignatius abandons his cart for a moment to scrutinize the ladies' paintings of flowers—critically.

"Oh, my God!" Ignatius bellowed after he had promenaded up and down along the fence. "How dare you present such abortions to the public."

"Please move along, sir," a bold lady said.

"Magnolias don't look like that." Ignatius said, thrusting his cutlass at the offending pastel magnolia. "You ladies need a course in botany. And perhaps geometry, too."

"You don't *have* to look at our work," an offended voice said from the group, the voice of the lady who had drawn the magnolia in question.

"Yes, I do!" Ignatius screamed. "You ladies need a critic with some taste and decency. Good heavens! Which one of you did this camellia? Speak up. The water in this bowl looks like motor oil."

"Let us alone," a shrill voice said.

"You women had better stop giving teas and brunches and settle down to the business of learning how to draw," Ignatius thundered.

What causes a dialogue scene to gather momentum and really begin to move is when one or more characters begin to express emotion or strong opinions. It happens when your characters' agendas begin to collide, when one character can't get what he wants from the other characters. In the above scene, Ignatius, in rare form, is actually minding his own business, but then true to his nature, he can't keep his mouth shut and his opinions to himself. Of course, the scene speeds up the minute he opens his mouth and begins to express just how appalled he is at the atrocities he sees in front of him in the name of art. And of course, the ladies just want him to leave and stop attracting so much negative attention to their artwork.

You want your story to go somewhere. You know you need to pick up the pace a bit so that it does. Dialogue does this because, of all of the fiction tools at your disposal, dialogue is the one that most quickly puts your characters and your reader in the present moment.

EXERCISE

CREATING MOMENTUM. Choose one or all three of the following scenarios. Start the scene out slowly and then, through dialogue, gather momentum as you write. You also may want to do this with a scene or scenes in your own story.

• A father and his daughter are stuck in rush hour traffic. She's fiddling with the radio, and he's talking on his cell phone. Suddenly the phone

---

goes dead and the girl's favorite radio station won't come in. They have to talk. Write this scene from either the father's or the daughter's viewpoint, or try one of each.

• A man and woman are having an affair, but up until now, it's been only physical. One of the two decides the relationship needs to be taken to the next level. Write a sex scene that turns out to be more about talk than sex.

• Two homeless men, strangers to each other, end up under the same freeway overpass for the night. They ignore each other at first, but then one of them starts to talk and can't seem to quit.

SPEEDING UP

Letting a scene drag is one of the worst mistakes a writer can make. There is no excuse for this. Bringing two or more characters together and letting them chat on and on about nothing is inexcusable. The problem is many writers aren't even aware that their characters are doing this, even when it's in front of their noses. They're sitting right there writing the story and fail to see that they're boring their reader to death with going-nowhere-fast dialogue.

There are many reasons dialogue scenes bog down. The main one is that we clutter them with so much added narrative and action that the reader has to muddle his way through and the going becomes a little clunky. Sometimes, the scene is weak when it comes to tension and suspense, and the reader is yawning big time. Our characters are just talking about nothing. For a very long time. Like this:

"Hi Mom," Dolores spoke loudly into the phone. Her mother was hard of hearing.

"Dolores, is that you?"

"It's me, Mom, how are you?"

"Fine, I'm fine, my back's been acting up again."

"Have you been to the doctor?"

"Oh, yes, he can't do anything, just writes out more prescriptions. I'm so drugged up now, I can hardly even stay awake."

"How have you been sleeping?"

"Oh, fine, just fine."

"Do you need anything?"

> "Need anything? You mean, like milk or eggs or—"
> "Anything at all. Do you need me to bring you anything?"
> "Oh, no, I'm fine. How's the boys?"
> "They're fine, growing like weeds."
> "How's Bill?"
> "He's fine. He got laid off his job."
> "That's nice, dear, well, thanks for calling."
> "Bye, Mom."
> "Bye, Dolores."

I see scenes written like this all of the time, more often than I care to admit. Long and slow and boring. No tension. No drama. No suspense.

As I mentioned above, dialogue by its very nature is an accelerator, metaphorically speaking. When a story or scene needs to move, get people talking. The faster you get them talking, the faster the scene moves. Cutting out any extra narrative or action sequences causes your story to speed along. You can even cut out descriptive tags so your dialogue comes down to the bare bones. Also, the more emotion you put into a scene, the faster it moves.

The reason emotion speeds things up is because it heightens the tension and suspense. Characters expressing emotion are unpredictable and often out of control. Anything can happen, so the stakes are up.

Do you ever notice how, when you're watching a fast-paced movie and the stalker is closing in on his victim, you start shoveling your popcorn into your mouth at breakneck speed?

That's where your reader is when you include the kinds of emotional dialogue scenes that move so fast that the characters are stumbling over their own words. Whether the emotion is fear or anger (closely connected) or sadness, it gives the dialogue a power surge and propels the scene forward. In this scene from Anne Tyler's *Ladder of Years*, the protagonist, Delia, a wife and mother, has run away from home. Her sister, Eliza, has come to visit her, possibly to talk some sense into her.

> "Sit down," she told Eliza. "Could I offer you some tea?"
> "Oh, I … no thanks." Eliza took a tighter grip on her purse. She seemed out of place in these surroundings—somebody from home, with that

humble, faded look that home people always have. "Let me make sure I'm understanding this," she said.

"I could heat up the water in no time. Just have a seat on the bed."

"You are telling me you're leaving us forever," Eliza said, not moving. "You plan to stay on permanently in Bay Borough. You're leaving your husband, and you're leaving all three of your children, one of whom is still in high school."

"In high school, yes, and fifteen years old, and able to manage without me fine and dandy," Delia said. To her horror, she felt tears beginning to war her eyelids. "Better than with me, in fact," she continued firmly. "How are the kids, by the way?"

"They're bewildered; what would you expect?" Eliza said.

"But are they doing all right otherwise?"

"Do you care?" Eliza asked.

"Of course I care!"

Things start out slowly with long sentences and paragraphs as Eliza is getting settled in the room. But when she starts to accuse Delia, things start to speed up. Delia feels the tears warming her eyelids, and the scene surges forward with short sentences and paragraphs. We're in the emotion now and everything feels more urgent.

Pumping up the emotion doesn't necessarily mean using a lot of exclamation points. It could mean shortening sentences and paragraphs or cutting out any and all narrative and action sentences. It could mean having your characters shooting short phrases of dialogue back and forth at a rapid pace. This can be very effective when done well and not overdone.

JUST FOR FUN

A married couple, Marilyn and Robert, are going to garage sales, one of their favorite pastimes. Well, until recently. Marilyn has been tiring of this twenty-year hobby and has recently taken up gardening. They are presently going through someone's junk at a garage sale, and a conflict ensues when Marilyn decides she's ready to go home. Using either Marilyn's or Robert's viewpoint, write a two-page, fast-paced scene and then a one-page, slow-paced scene taking these two through their conflict.

Crafting Dynamic Dialogue

SLOWING DOWN

As I mentioned earlier, often the problem with our stories is that that they move too slowly. But if they move too quickly, the reader can't catch her breath and the story often feels fragmented, kind of like it's running away with the characters. Both characters and scenes feel undeveloped, causing the whole story to kind of derail. While too much dialogue is usually not the problem in a story that's not working, every once in a while, someone gives me a story to evaluate where the write has decided that the characters will just talk away. And away. And away. Just as we can learn how to use dialogue to gather momentum in a scene, we can also learn how to control our scenes by slowing them down.

But if dialogue is a device used to speed stories up, then how can dialogue be used to slow them down?

It's true that to use dialogue is most often to step on the accelerator. But if the story is running away with you in the middle of a dialogue scene and you need to put the brakes on, there are a few ways you can do it.

You can weigh the scene down with narrative, description, and background, or you can bring slow-talking Harry onstage and everything will come to a screeching halt. Harry just isn't in a hurry.

When everyone in the scene is running on at the mouth and things are heating up but the point has been made and now you want to slow things down, a slow-talking character can bring the other characters, as well as the reader, back into the moment. Use some hems and haws and uhs along with long, rambling sentences to show the slow pace. You can add bits of action—slow action—to show Harry kind of moseying his way through the conversation. Picture an old guy on a porch sitting next to his friend talking about fishing. That's Harry.

Another way to slow the scene and/or story down using dialogue is to move your characters into a rational conversation where there's less action and emotion and more cerebral logic concerning their situation. Note I said less action and emotion, not less tension. Tension is something that needs to be present in every scene of dialogue no matter how slow or fast. But dialogue that focuses on the intellectual side of a conflict or problem simply moves more slowly and methodically than dialogue where the characters are emoting and arguing.

Following is an example of this from John Steinbeck's novel *East of Eden*. The younger brother, Charles, is insanely jealous of his father's love for his older brother, Adam. In this scene, Charles has just unleashed his rage on Adam and beaten him into a bloody pulp. The scene moves at high speed through the fight, slows down just a bit as Adam makes his way home, then speeds up again as the boys' father demands to know why Charles beat up his older brother.

> Cyrus stumped over to him and grasped him by the arm so fiercely that he winced and tried to pull away. "Don't lie to me! Why did he do it? Did you have an argument?"
>
> "No."
>
> Cyrus wrenched at him. "Tell me! I want to know. Tell me! You'll have to tell me. I'll make you tell me! Goddam it, you're always protecting him! Don't you think I know that? Did you think you were fooling me? Now tell me, or by God I'll keep you standing there all night!"
>
> Adam cast about for an answer. "He doesn't think you love him."

The father's heightened emotion keeps the scene moving quickly because people in a heightened state of emotion are unpredictable. You never know what they're going to do next. But once Adam tells his father this, his father immediately turns away, walks out the door without another word, and the boys' mother begins to rationally explain away her younger son's behavior, slowing the scene down.

> "He doesn't think his father loves him. But you love him—you always have."
>
> Adam did not answer him.
>
> She went on quietly, "He's a strange boy. You have to know him—all rough shell, all anger until you know." She paused to cough, leaned down and coughed, and when the spell was over her cheeks were flushed and she was exhausted. "You have to know him," she repeated. "For a long time he has given me little presents, pretty things you wouldn't think he'd

Crafting Dynamic Dialogue

even notice. But he doesn't give them right out. He hides them where he knows I'll find them. And you can look at him for hours and he won't ever give the slightest sign he did it. You have to know him."

I did mention that you could slow a scene down by adding bits of narrative, description, and background to your dialogue scene. In the next chapter, we see Adam again, after spending four days in bed recovering from his brother's beating. This scene is very brief but shows how you can use narrative, description, and background to make a scene move more slowly, even though there's dialogue in the scene.

> Into the house, into Adam's bedroom, came a captain of cavalry and two sergeants in dress uniform of blue. In the dooryard their horses were held by two privates. Lying in his bed, Adam was enlisted in the army as a private in the cavalry. He signed the Articles of War and took the oath while his father and Alice looked on. And his father's eyes glistened with tears.
>
> After the soldiers had gone his father sat with him a long time. "I've put you in the cavalry for a reason," he said. "Barrack life is not a good life for long. But the cavalry has work to do. I made sure of that. You'll like going for the Indian country. There's action coming I can't tell you how I know. There's fighting on the way."

Can you see how just a little bit of narrative, background, and description can make a scene of dialogue move more slowly? There's little emotion in the above scene, only the glistening of Adam's father's tears. But his words are matter-of-fact. We get the background first, then his father simply offers a half-baked explanation for why he's doing what he's doing, and the scene is over.

EXERCISE

SLOWING DOWN. Steve and Jennifer are a happily married couple, well, most of the time. Jennifer is a little uptight and anal, always needing to be on time wherever they go. Steve is just the opposite. He really doesn't get why everyone is in such a hurry all of the time, especially his wife. In the following scene, you'll find only the bare dialogue between Steve and Jennifer. When a scene includes only dialogue, it moves quickly. Your task is to slow this scene down by adding narrative, description, background, and bits of action here and there.

> "I'm ready to go, Steve."
>   "Coming."
>   "When?"
>   "Right now, right now. I'll be right down."
>   "It's 4:15, Steve."
>   "Yeah, it sure is. I just looked at the clock."
>   "Mom is going to be so upset if we're late to pick her up."
>   "Yeah, she gets like that, all right."
>   "Steve!"
>   "Huh?"
>   "C'mon!"
>   "I'm coming, honey, just putting on my socks."
>   "I'm going out to start the car."
>   "Don't forget to open the garage door—don't want to asphyxiate yourself."
>   "Are you coming?"
>   "I'll be right down."

GAINING CONTROL

Pacing your dialogue is about gaining control of your scenes so they don't run away from you or drag to the point that even you can't stay awake while writing them.

What exactly causes us to lose control of our stories and therefore the pace of our dialogue?

Losing control happens for a number of reasons and again, when we're conscious of this, it's easier to stay in control. Of course, the very act of losing control is an unconscious one. By definition, that's what losing control is, whether in real life or in storytelling. To lose control is to lose consciousness. During the act of writing a story, what causes us to lose consciousness so the dialogue suddenly begins to speed out of control or painfully drag along?

I think we often underestimate the personal connection we have to the stories we write. We think we're writing about characters we've made up. After all, this is fiction, isn't it?

Yes and no.

When our dialogue begins to take our characters to places we hadn't intended faster than we intended to go there, we need to pay attention. Most writing books will tell you that when this happens, you need to go back to where you began to lose your way and fix the dialogue right there, to pick up the thread where you lost it and start over.

This isn't necessarily true. Losing control of our dialogue at certain points simply means we're finally feeling the freedom to say those things we've always wanted to say to whomever we've wanted to say them. They're our words rather than our characters' words, and at this point, if we recognize what's going on, the story may turn out to be about something we hadn't intended at all. You may think you're writing about a young man landing his first job and then discover you're really writing about a young man thrust into adulthood before he feels ready. Maybe this is your story, after all, one you've never told. When you realize this, you have a choice. You can keep following the real story or you can go back to where you lost your way and get the dialogue back on track with the story you started out to tell. If you choose the second option, that's fine, but at some point you should consider writing the real story as well, because you can count on it being the most authentic one. The one that's inside of you crying to get out.

A sudden change in pace when we're writing dialogue can signal to us that we need to pay closer attention to what the scene is bringing up for us personally. Sometimes the dialogue will speed up and we'll lose control because, yes, we've touched on a theme in our real life. But instead of going ahead and writing authentic dialogue, we become uncomfortable with the *feelings* connected to the dialogue and so quickly, go off on some tangent to get away from them. Again, awareness is what gets us back on track.

When a dialogue scene slows way down so that it drags, and this doesn't happen as often, the reasons for it are the same as when it speeds up too fast. When our characters start talking to each other again, it can happen that we come upon a personal theme that we unconsciously decide to explore, and we have to slow down in order to fully follow where it seems to be leading us. We may start weighing it down with actions of the other characters or too many of the protagonist's thoughts. We're really into this before we realize it has nothing to do with the original topic of dialogue.

We always have a choice. We can follow the tangent and see where it leads us or we can arrest the dialogue we're writing, set the real story aside for later, and continue.

We always hear about how being a control freak is such a negative thing. But maybe, in the world of writing, our efforts to gain control of our dialogue, and therefore our stories, means that we're control freaks in a good way because we're trying to write the most authentic story possible.

IS IT WORKING?

How do you know if your dialogue is paced well? This is often something you can't know until you've finished the story. When reading through the entire story, you'll be able to see where you need to speed a scene up here, slow a scene down there, add a bit of setting here to keep things steady, and a bit of narrative there to momentarily let the reader breathe again.

You want a combination of slow and fast-paced scenes, alternating them so you don't either wear the reader out or put her to sleep. In Jack Bickham's book *Scene & Structure*, he instructs us to write both scenes and sequels. The scenes move more quickly while the sequels are often more nondramatic moments in the story where both character and reader catch up with themselves. There are no hard and fast rules. Certainly there will be times where you'll need two or three fast-paced scenes in a row to move your plot along. But just be conscious of when you're doing what so you stay in control of your story.

FIXING YOUR OWN STORY

When you realize you've lost control of a scene of dialogue, ask yourself the following questions to help know whether you want to gain control of the original story or tell another, possibly more authentic, story.

1. Where did I begin to lose my way in this dialogue scene?
2. Why did I speed the dialogue up faster than it needed to go? Or why did I slow the dialogue down, making it suddenly drag?
3. Is the original direction the way I still want to take this story?
4. Should I be listening to the new direction these characters seem to be leading me through their dialogue, and where do I think they might be taking me?

Crafting Dynamic Dialogue

5. Do I trust these characters enough to follow them into the kind of dialogue discussion I hadn't originally planned for them?
6. Which direction—the original or the new—is the most authentic dialogue and therefore the most authentic story?
7. Can I give up control of the dialogue that I think I want to write so in the end I will gain control of my most authentic story?

Go through your novel or short story and find the scenes that move either too slowly or too quickly and rewrite them, adding bits and pieces of narrative and action, or taking it away, so that every scene is in balance with the rest of the story and effectively pulls its weight.

Don't worry too much about pacing while you're writing. Just get the story down. Then put on your editor's hat and with a purple or green pen (it's a new day—no red pens anymore), go through the story and mark the places where you want to speed things up or slow them down. Following are some questions you can ask about your viewpoint character to try to discover if a dialogue scene is moving too slowly or too quickly.

- Is he talking too fast, not giving the other characters time to answer?
- Is he avoiding the subject and rambling on about nothing that has anything to do with what the story's been about so far?
- Is he thinking too much and not talking enough? Or is it the other way around?
- Are there too many tags and other identifying actions so his words become lost in the clutter?
- Is he making speeches instead of interacting with the other character(s)? (You may want him to make speeches in order to slow things down; just be aware that you're doing it and make sure that the speeches further the plot.)
- Is he too focused on observing the other characters in great detail or describing the setting to himself, sacrificing the kind of dialogue that would create tension and suspense in the scene?
- Do you, as the author, keep intruding on the scene with your own observations and descriptions that interrupt the flow of dialogue between the viewpoint and the other characters?

You can never completely know when you're going over a hair into dialogue that moves too slowly or hanging back a hair with dialogue that doesn't move quite fast enough, but the above questions will get you close enough. As always, awareness of pacing your dialogue is what will eventually get and keep you on track.

Seeing dialogue as either brakes or accelerator will help you stay in control of your story so it doesn't leave you in the dust like a runaway stagecoach or move at a snail's pace. You're the one who can press hard on the gas to propel the dialogue into motion or hard on the brakes to slow it way down. Every story has its own rhythm and motion, and pacing your dialogue to pace your story will give your reader an easy and smooth ride.

Crafting Dynamic Dialogue

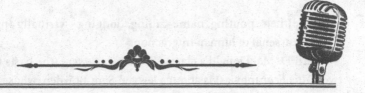

CHAPTER 18

CREATING ACTIVE DIALOGUE

BY JAMES SCOTT BELL

Whoever said "Sticks and stones may break my bones but words can never hurt me" was full of beans. I still remember the insults fired at me in the schoolyard. And I regret what my own words have done to some of my loved ones through the years. Words can hurt so bad they cling to your soul forever.

Thankfully, words also heal. And uplift. In short, words do things.

That's important to keep in mind when writing dialogue. The words uttered by your characters are a form of action, used to help them get their way.

Speaking is a physical act, after all. John Howard Lawson, the respected—and later blacklisted—screenwriter, wrote that fictional speech should be viewed as a way for characters to expand their activities. "It serves, as it does in life, to broaden the scope of action; it organizes and extends what people do."

The one thing dialogue must never be is pointless. Every word a character speaks should emerge for a reason.

That's not to say each word must be weighty. A character who says "oh" may be expressing surprise or stalling. The important thing is to know the *why* behind your characters' words.

WIELDING VERBAL WEAPONS

Verbal weapons are employed by characters who are trying to outmaneuver each other. There is a whole range of weaponry to choose from—

anger, epithets, pouting, name-calling, dodging—virtually anything from the arsenal of human interaction.

John D. MacDonald's classic *The Executioners* (the basis for the two *Cape Fear* movies) is about a lawyer, Sam Bowden, whose family is stalked by the sadistic rapist Max Cady. Cady's first act is poisoning the family dog, Marilyn. Sam has not been totally upfront with his wife, Carol. She challenges him:

> "I'm not a child and I'm not a fool and I resent being ... overprotected."

Her volley is direct, telling him she resents the coddling. Sam responds:

> "I should have told you. I'm sorry."

Sam's apology is meant to diminish his wife's anger. But his words ring hollow to her, and she continues to advance:

> "So now this Cady can roam around at will and poison our dog and work his way up to the children. Which do you think he'll start on first? The oldest or the youngest?"
>
> "Carol, honey. Please."
>
> "I'm a hysterical woman? You are so damn right. I am a hysterical woman."

Here, Carol uses sarcasm; Sam tries again to soften her up; and she responds with a bitter observation and a curse word. Then, Sam the lawyer tries another trick:

> "We haven't any proof it was Cady."
>
> She threw a towel into the sink. "Listen to me. I have proof it was Cady. I've got that proof. It's not the kind of proof you would like. No evidence. No testimony. Nothing legalistic. I just know."

Seeing that this has no effect on her husband, Carol quickly shifts and brings out her heavy artillery:

> "What kind of a man are you? This is your family. Marilyn was part of your family. Are you going to look up all the precedents and prepare a brief?"

She has attacked both his manhood and his profession. Sam attempts an answer but Carol cuts him off (interruptions are good weapons, too):

> "You don't know how—"
>> "I don't know anything. This is happening because of something you did a long time ago."
>> "Something I had to do."
>> "I'm not saying you shouldn't have. You tell me the man hates you. You don't think he's sane. So do something about him!"

Carol wants instant action, and Sam knows he can't provide it. The stress of the situation brings out weapon-like dialogue.

Don't forget that silence can be a weapon as well. In William E. Barrett's *The Lilies of the Field*, a German nun wants wandering handyman Homer Smith to stay and build a chapel for her modest order. He just wants to get paid for a small job and move on. He confronts Mother Maria Marthe:

> "I want to talk to you," he said.
>> "I've been doing work for you. Good work. I want pay for what I do."
>> She sat silent, with her hands clasped in front of her. Her small eyes looked at him out of the wrinkled mask of her face but there was no light in them. He did not know whether she understood him or not.

If one great character knows what holds great importance for another character, he can often turn that into his strongest weapon. After the silent treatment, Homer decides to play hardball. He directs the nun to a Bible verse:

> "The labourer is worthy of his hire," and explains, "I'm a poor man. I work for wages."

Not to be outdone, and using the same weapon, Mother Maria Marthe shows Homer another passage:

> "And why take ye thought for raiment? Consider the lilies of the field, how they grow; they toil not, neither do they spin. And yet I say unto you that even Solomon in all his glory was not arrayed like one of these."

Homer realizes he is dealing with one crafty nun who has won the initial tussle.

Not every scene, of course, is going to involve stark conflict. Some scenes are preludes to conflict. But even then characters can use dialogue to position themselves for the battles yet to come.

FINDING THE RIGHT WORDS

How do you know what verbal weapons a character should use? And when? How can you anticipate the various moves opposing characters should make?

It's easier if, before writing a scene, you have a few things in mind.

First, what are the characters like? If a character is the charge-ahead type, he'll speak that way. His words will be forceful, direct. Sam Spade in Dashiell Hammett's *The Maltese Falcon* is like that. Here he confronts an odd little intruder, Joel Cairo:

> "I've got you by the neck, Cairo. You've walked in and tied yourself up, plenty strong enough to suit the police, with last night's killing. Well, now you'll have to play with me or else."

But the dandy Cairo, smelling faintly of gardenia, uses fancier verbiage:

> "I made somewhat extensive inquiries about you before taking any action, and was assured that you were far too reasonable to allow other considerations to interfere with profitable business relations."

We know, simply from the words, that these are two very different characters.

Next, be sure to assign objectives to your characters in every scene. Without conflicting objectives—be they overt or subtle—your scene is in danger of falling flat. Knowing what each character wants allows you to choreograph the dance—the ups and downs, the feints and jabs.

The chapter in *The Maltese Falcon*, from which the above dialogue was lifted, begins with Cairo pointing a pistol at Spade. The dynamic changes radically when Spade elbows Cairo in the face and takes the gun.

Cairo must now convince Spade to take the case of the missing black bird. Spade finally accepts and returns Cairo's gun—which Cairo promptly points at him again. Another shift.

Finally, you may find it helpful to create a list of synonyms for fighting words like "punch," "dodge," or "thrust." Go wild. Refer to this list when developing characters and conflicts in a scene. One of those words may suggest the perfect verbal weapon for a character to use.

USING THE ACTION TAG

Because dialogue is a form of action, we can use the physical to assist the verbal. This is called the action tag.

The use of tags has long been a challenge for novelists. In the old days, novelists were freer with speech tags, applying verbs and adverbs with abandon. For example, a random page in Thorne Smith's 1929 novel, *The Stray Lamb*, reveals the following:

> "Off again, major," Sandra said resignedly. ...
>
> "Not a scrap of evidence left behind," Mr. Long optimistically informed the party. ...
>
> "It's a shame we haven't a camera," she observed. ...
>
> "That depends," answered Thomas consideringly. ...

Needless to say (I write disapprovingly), such effulgent grammar is frowned upon today.

Recently there has been a favoring of the simple "said"—and the occasional "asked" for questions—as the only appropriate tags. I think this errs too much in the other direction. I've read stretches of dialogue peppered only with "said" and found it repetitive in a woodpecker sort of way.

I still lean toward "said" as the default tag. But the action tag is often the better choice, because it offers a character's physical movements, such as in Lisa Samson's *Women's Intuition*:

Marsha shoved her music into a satchel. "She's on a no-sugar kick now anyway, Father."

He turned to me with surprise. "You don't say? How come?"

Marsha jumped right in, thank you very much. "She saw a special on one of those health news spots on WJZ that sugar is actually a poison."

I shook my head. "Marsha, come on."

This is not to be done every time, of course. Variety is called for, and often the best choice is no tag at all. If the reader knows who is speaking—because of alternating lines or a distinct manner of speech—that's often enough.

Look for ways to let your tag add to the dynamics of a scene. You will be giving the reader more bang for the written buck.

In life, talk may be cheap. Not so in fiction. Make every word count by writing a character's speech as an expansion of his actions.

....

JAMES SCOTT BELL is the author of the number one bestseller for writers, *Plot & Structure*, and numerous thrillers, including, *Romeo's Rules*, *Try Dying*, and *Don't Leave Me*. In addition to his traditional novels, Jim has self-published in a variety of forms. His novella *One More Lie* was the first self-published work to be nominated for an International Thriller Writers Award. He served as the fiction columnist for *Writer's Digest* magazine and has written highly popular craft books including: *Write Your Novel From the Middle*, *Super Structure*, *The Art of War for Writers*, *Conflict & Suspense*, and *Dazzling Dialogue*. Jim has taught writing at Pepperdine University and at numerous writers conferences in the United States, Canada, Great Britain, Australia, and New Zealand. He attended the University of California, Santa Barbara where he studied writing with Raymond Carver, and graduated with honors from the University of Southern California Law Center.

CHAPTER 19

USING DIALOGUE TO REVEAL STORY SETTING & BACKGROUND

BY GLORIA KEMPTON

Of all of the elements of fiction, setting has always been the most difficult for me to incorporate into my stories because, while I'm an observer of human nature, I forget to notice my environment. I take walks with a certain friend on occasion and she is forever stopping because she hears the chattering of a flicker (what's that?) and wants to interact with it. Or she might pass a certain tree or bush and stop to touch it. Without her by my side, I notice none of these things.

What I do love is to listen to people talk. To eavesdrop. Dialogue is my favorite element of telling stories. When I learned—I can't remember how—that I could use dialogue to reveal setting in my stories, I was thrilled. No more long narrative descriptions where I was trying to describe things I never "saw" in the first place. All I had to do from now on in the way of setting was notice what my characters noticed. That was easy enough because the characters I was used to creating weren't all that different from myself.

This may not be your problem. You may love to describe your story's setting and can easily go on for pages doing so. But that's a problem of another kind. Unless you're writing literary fiction, pages of description aren't usually what a reader is looking for, and he will often skip over it. It depends on the kind of story you're writing, of course. Literary and mainstream fiction are sometimes setting driven, but in the other genres, setting is most often simply the story's background. And dialogue is a useful tool for revealing it.

In order to reveal it through dialogue, of course, you have to first know your characters.

KNOW YOUR CHARACTERS

Just as we want our characters to speak authentically out of who they are, we also want our settings to be authentic, so that when we plunk our stories down somewhere we can bring our readers in and know that all of our props and background characters are for real. The very first thing we can do to ensure that this happens is to know our characters. It's only when we know our characters and how they feel and relate to the settings in which they find themselves that we can create authenticity in a scene. We have to know them so well that when we create dialogue for them that's connected with their setting, we're not surprised at how they feel about where they are.

For example, if your character, John, finds himself in the middle of a crowded street fair on a blind date and he's claustrophobic, he isn't going to take his time at a booth admiring the leather belts. You might want to mention the leather belts, though, to show that John is a biker. This is your story setting, and you have an opportunity here. Rather than let the need to establish setting drive the scene, go for authenticity and let John's claustrophobic, biker self drive the scene through dialogue.

> "Yeah, cool belts," John said, nodding at the owner of the booth and nudging Lori along. "I only have ten belts now." An older man bumped into him and John swore. "It's sure hot, isn't it?" He pulled his kerchief out of his back pocket and tied it around his head. "I bet it's twenty degrees hotter in this crowd than it is out there." He looked longingly through the crowd to the empty sidewalk a few feet away.

You get the idea. You want to weave the setting details into the dialogue, integrating action and narrative. You're looking for a three-dimensional feel.

It's important to know your character. Would a character who lives in Seattle even notice the Space Needle on his way to work in the morning? I live in Seattle, and I can tell you that I see it sometimes because it stands by itself and it's so tall, but most of the time I don't really *see* it. Oh, except on New Year's Eve and the Fourth of July when fireworks are shooting out the top of it—then everyone in Seattle notices it, if they're outside.

When you're on vacation, how often do you and your family and friends sit around and have a lively discussion about the hotel room you've rented for the weekend?

When at work, do you and your co-workers have regular animated discussions about your office building, the color of the walls, the way the desks are arranged, the drab carpet, etc.?

When taking your kids or grandkids to the park, are your eyes on the elm trees or your kids? On the ducks in the pond or your grandkids? If you were to strike up a conversation with a stranger, also with kids, would you most likely talk about the playground equipment or your kids?

You can see where this is going. Getting setting details into a scene is a little tricky because people/characters don't sit around discussing place.

However, setting isn't just about concrete place details. Setting isn't just a house or a beauty salon or a park. Setting can be an industry, a profession, or an organization. Whether or not your characters are sitting around discussing place, there are many opportunities to get setting details into scenes of dialogue if you are fully confident of your setting and you know your character.

Let's go back to John for a moment. You want to give the dialogue scene a three-dimensional feeling, so you have John saying, *"Wow, look at these cool garden decorations. Oh, and hey, here's a booth with homemade kitchen towels."*

John the biker? I don't think so. I hate to stereotype any group of people, but if this biker is into garden decorations and homemade kitchen towels, you better set this up before we get to the street fair so we'll believe you. And there better be a good reason, too.

No, John is more likely to say, *"Hey, babe, there's the beer garden,"* grab his old lady's hand and pass right by all of the booths full of garden decorations and homemade kitchen towels.

Know your character so you'll know what he might notice at a street fair, a circus, or the grocery store. Know what he might notice and what he might say about what he notices. What he would notice and not say anything about. Know him very well so your dialogue scenes will ring true, which is always more important than anything else.

EXERCISE

KNOW YOUR CHARACTERS. Jerry is a computer geek who is accompanying his wife to her company picnic at a large park near a reservoir. She works for the Sanitation Department. Write a two-page dialogue scene that focuses on setting. What would Jerry notice about the setting and what would he say out loud?

ESTABLISHING SETTING

A written story is like a movie, where we see the characters on a screen acting out their scenes. As writers, we don't want our readers to have to work hard at *seeing* our characters, at visualizing the setting where the characters are in dialogue with each other. This means we need to make sure to establish the setting in the beginning of each scene of dialogue. If you open a scene with dialogue, integrate some setting details as quickly as you can so the reader can begin to picture the characters and the atmosphere in which the dialogue takes place. This is one way to make the scene three-dimensional so your characters aren't talking to each other in a vacuum.

Use only those details that will further the story situation, your theme, or your character's conflict. Once the setting is established for the dialogue, you can relax a bit, but continue to feed setting details into the scene so the reader can continue to visualize where the characters are in relation to their physical surroundings.

TOO MUCH TOO SOON

When writing dialogue, there's something we can keep in mind that will help us immensely. The story's dialogue shouldn't be that different from real-life conversation. With that in mind, when was the last time you or another person engaged in conversation that focused on setting to the exclusion of just about anything else?

"Oh and here we are at the circus. Just smell that popcorn, would you, and well, my favorite is the cotton candy, but I can't wait to see the clowns. As a child, they were my favorite part, and the sawdust on the ground feels so crunchy."

"I know what you mean. Here comes the elephants with their pretty riders in pink outfits matching the elephants' neck ruffles. Don't you love how the trapeze artists are always in such good shape? They must work out for hours every day."

"Okay, I'm counting eleven clowns that have climbed out of that Volkswagen now. How do they do that?"

In case you haven't noticed, this isn't working. The author (that would be me, hate to say it) is trying to acclimate us to the setting by throwing all kinds of setting details into the dialogue. While dialogue is a great way to introduce the setting, it's not effective to dump it all on the reader at once. The above is called an "info dump," and it never works. It's contrived and unnatural, not the way people really talk. So let's say you want to give the reader the authentic feeling of being at the circus, but in a natural way, weaving it into the dialogue. Everything depends on the story situation you're developing in the scene. No matter what your agenda as the author, you can't let *your* agenda drive a scene. The characters' needs should always drive the scene. So, let's say a married couple on the verge of divorce has arrived at the circus for one last date together with their four-year-old son. Let's use the mother's first-person voice. The action is your primary focus, but you want the setting to feel authentic. You *don't* want an info dump.

"Cotton candy, Mom?" Jason turned to me, his eyes wide with wonder at everything around him.

"Sure, honey." She stepped up to the cotton candy man and gave him two dollars. "One, thanks."

"I want one, too." Aaron looked at me, and I remembered how much he loved cotton candy.

The sawdust crunched under our footsteps as we made our way to the auditorium. "Remember when circuses were under a tent?" Aaron said as he led the way past the cages of tigers and lions.

He said that every time we'd gone to a circus for the last ten years.

A clown on stilts passed us, smiling down at Jason and stopping to shake his hand.

"Tall man, Mom," he said.

I'd never understood why he directed all of his comments to me rather than Aaron. Was it because Aaron seldom interacted with his son?

I think it's clear why this circus scene works better than the previous one. The setting details in the first scene feel contrived, like the author's goal is to make sure the setting comes through. In the second scene, the setting is the scene's backdrop and the details are integrated into the story situation. It feels much more natural this way.

There's nothing wrong with wanting to get the details into a scene as soon as possible. This is good because when characters start talking, the reader needs to know where to picture them.

EXERCISE

TOO MUCH TOO SOON. Your characters are entering a winter wonderland. It's their first date and they've decided to leave the city behind and drive up to the slopes for the day to go skiing. One of the characters is from California and has only seen snow once before, as a small child. Describe the setting from her point of view as she describes it to her male partner in the car. The goal is not to info dump but to let it gradually emerge—not too much too soon.

IT'S ALL IN THE DETAILS

Whether you're writing dialogue, action, or narrative, vivid details are what cause a reader to be able to see, hear, touch, taste, and smell—in short, to be able to experience your story on a sensory level.

Now, in dialogue, we have to remember that characters don't necessarily talk using rich details to describe another character's appearance, a building, or anything else. Most of us are actually quite uncreative when it comes to using sensory details. So above all, you want your characters to sound real.

Everything depends on the kind of story you're writing and the characters that inhabit it. Anne Rice, because of the voice she uses in her vampire novels, can get away with some pretty heavy descriptive details in her dialogue passages. Let's look at one in *Interview With the Vampire*. The vampire, Louis, is telling a boy about a journey he took with his daughter, Claudia. In this particular passage, he describes their approach to a monastery. *Listen* to the richness of the detail in this short paragraph, which is only a small part of the setting.

> "In moments we had found the gap that would admit us, the great opening that was blacker still than the walls around it, the vines encrusting its edges as if to hold the stones in place. High above, through the open room, the damp smell of the stones strong in my nostrils, I saw, beyond the streaks of clouds a faint sprinkling of stars. A great staircase moved upward, from corner to corner, all the way to the narrow windows that looked out upon the valley. And beneath the first rise of the star, out of the gloom emerged the vast, dark opening to the monastery's remaining rooms."

This passage appeals to the reader's sense of sight and smell. The reader can see the *great black opening*, *the vines encrusting the edges*, and the *sprinkling of stars*. Can't you *smell* the damp stones?

Rice doesn't stop there. She continues with the sensory details, putting them into Louis' mouth as he goes on with his story. She appeals next to the reader's sense of hearing.

> "There was only the low backdrop of the wind ... I could see a flat stone there, and it sounded hollow as she gently tapped it with her heel."

Claudia stops to listen and asks Louis if he can hear what she hears.

> "It was so low no mortal could have heard it ... Just a rustling now, a scraping, but it was steady; and then slowly the round tramping of a foot began to distinguish itself ... The tramp of the feet grew louder, and I began to sense that one step preceded the other very sharply, the second dragging slowly across the earth."

In the middle of all of this emphasis on sensory sound, the author throws in the sense of touch, as well.

> "Claudia's hand tightened on mine, and with a gentle pressure she moved me silently beneath the slope of the stairway ... I could feel the fabric of my shirt against me, the stiff cut of the collar, the very scraping of the buttons against my cape."

Crafting Dynamic Dialogue

Would that we could all tell stories that were so suspenseful and employ the kinds of sensory detail that causes the reader to hold her breath and intensely feel every moment of the scene.

Again, the author can get away with this because of the voice she uses in her vampire novels. You probably wouldn't be able to reveal this level of detail in the dialogue of a character who's a gangster or a plumber. The level of detail might be the same, but the way it's expressed would be different.

When creating setting details for your character to express through dialogue, you don't want to go overboard and clutter the dialogue with a lot of unnecessary minutia. Include only those details that enhance the mood you're trying to create, get across the emotion the character is feeling, or move the plot forward in some way. Actually, the fewer the details, the more each one will stand out. And the sharper the detail, the more the setting will come into focus.

Setting contrasts are another way to make details stand out. In the previous passage, one reason the *streaks of clouds* and *sprinkling of stars* stands out is because the author already established in our minds the *black* walls and opening into the room.

If you find that the dialogue in your story suffers form a lack of detail when you're trying to establish your story's setting, try a visualization exercise. Imagine yourself as your character in the story setting:

- What do you see before you?
- What do you smell in this particular setting?
- What can you reach out and touch?
- What do you hear all around you?
- Can you taste anything? What?
- How are some of the sensory details contrasted?

EXERCISE

IT'S ALL IN THE DETAILS. In the heart of downtown Seattle, we have a place called Pike's Place Market. It's an outside array of food booths and shops full of tables of homemade clothing, jewelry, leather goods, and anything else you could think of. In one area, the vendors throw fish

---

back and forth to entertain the customers. You can buy any kind of fish imaginable here. It's a place full of life and energy, a sensory heaven. Create a one- or two-page scene of dialogue between two characters who are visiting from out of town. Use all five senses in your descriptive dialogue of this setting.

DIALOGUE DESCRIPTION

Writers use a variety of techniques to describe their story settings:

1. omniscient narrative description as a character appears in a particular setting
2. a character's thoughts about the setting in which he finds himself
3. moving the character into action and throwing in setting details as the characters are chasing each other and interacting in every way possible
4. dialogue

Setting details can often feel static in narrative descriptions (1), and many readers can easily get bored after a few paragraphs that describe a house's furnishing or a town's main street. The same thing happens if a character stands in the middle of a setting looking around and thinking, *Ugh* (2). Yet this is what seems to come to us to do first when considering how we might present setting. Action (3) works well because the writer is dispensing details as the characters move, so it's just a few here and there.

But what about using dialogue to get your settings across to your reader? If you do it in a lively and intriguing style, putting words in the mouths of characters the readers care about, this can work nicely.

In Terry Goodkind's novel *Wizard's First Rule*, one of the characters, Kahlan, is explaining the setting to another character, Richard, in such a way that even includes suspense for the future, because this is a setting they're going to have to understand if they're going to navigate it and get where they want to go in the story.

> Kahlan stared into the fire. "The boundaries are part of the underworld: the dominion of the dead. They were conjured into our world by magic,

to separate the three lands. They are like a curtain drawn across our world. A rift in the world of the living."

"You mean that going into the boundary is, what, like falling through a crack into another world? Into the underworld?"

She shook her head. "No. Our world is still here. The underworld is there in the same place at the same time. It is about a two-day walk across the land where the boundary, the underworld, lies. But while you are walking the land where the boundary is, you are also walking through the underworld. It is a wasteland. Any life that touches the underworld, or is touched by it, is touching death. That is why no one can cross the boundary. If you enter it, you enter the land of the dead. No one can return from the dead."

"Then how did you?"

She swallowed as she watched the fire. "With magic. The boundary was brought here with magic, so the wizards reasoned they could get me safely through with the aid and protection of magic. It was frightfully difficult for them to cast the spells. They were dealing in things they didn't fully understand, dangerous things, and they weren't the ones who conjured the boundary into this world, so they weren't sure it would work. None of us knew what to expect." Her voice was weak, distant. "Even though I came through, I fear I will never be able to entirely leave it."

Using words like *the underworld*, *death*, *curtain*, *rift*, *wasteland*, *magic*, *spells*, and *dangerous*, the author brings this setting to life even though we're not quite there. We anticipate getting there because now we know it's an exciting place fraught with all kinds of scary things.

The use of dialogue to convey setting is effective here because we trust Kahlan. She speaks with authority and confidence and we know that she knows what she's talking about. We believe her. We're actually in Richard's point of view in this scene, and one reason we believe her is because Richard believes her, and he's a trustworthy character.

Once again, when using dialogue to describe, you have to know your characters so you know what kinds of details they would mention in their description of a place. As you can see, Kahlan is the kind of character who goes psychologically deeper when describing place than many characters would. She doesn't just describe the physical appearance of the boundary or the underworld. She goes into the wizards casting spells and what it all means, which is much more interesting than just physical details.

STAY IN VOICE

Sometimes I see fiction manuscripts from my students who use dialogue to describe setting and the characters begin to sound like those time-share salespeople: "And over here in this corner we have a gas fireplace with a marble hearth and mantle and strobe lights on the ceiling above." What you want to remember when using dialogue to describe setting is to stay in your character's voice. If you have a character in your novel who's into hip-hop, then, "Hey, man, it's yo mama's blue rag on the floor there," and well, you know what I mean. Joyce Carol Oates handles this pretty well in her novel *Middle Age*. Roger and his fifteen-year-old daughter, Robin, are in the car together discussing a dead uncle. While the setting they're discussing doesn't play a huge part in the story, it's important for the characterization of Uncle Adam.

> She said hesitantly, "Mom was telling me, she'd heard from some friends there, Mr. Berendt had—some things?—people were surprised to find?—in his house?"
> "What things?"
> "Oh, I don't know."
> "What kind of things?"
> "It's just gossip, you know Mom. She'll say anything people tell her."
> "Honey, what kind of things? I'm Adam's estate executor, and I know."
> "Mom was saying she'd heard Mr. Berendt had, like, lots of money hidden away? In boxes? Like, buried in the cellar of his house? Millions

of dollars?" Robin was watching him closely. Seeing his grimace, she said, "I never believe it, why'd Uncle Adam hide money like that, if he had it? If, like, anybody had it? You'd put it in a bank, right? I told Mom that. She's so credulous."

They discuss the ridiculousness of this idea for a moment, and then Robin continues:

> "I was in Uncle Adam's cellar, a few times. When we were there visiting. I must've been, like, ten. A long time ago."
> "Were you?"
> "The cellar was old. It was sort of creepy. Uncle Adam said maybe there'd been dead people buried there, a really long time ago? Like, if they'd been murdered in the tavern, that the house used to be, they were buried in the cellar. Was that so?"

Oates uses the setting details to show the eccentricity of Robin's Uncle Adam. We learn that he may have hid money in the old house and told his niece stories about possible dead people buried in the cellar. Robin talks about her uncle and his creepy house and cellar. But note how she phrases so many of her remarks as questions. This is how she talks throughout the story and how so many teens typically speak, raising their voices at the end of their sentences in a question.

When your character is describing place, be sure to remember who's talking and stay in voice.

EXERCISE

STAY IN VOICE. Write a one-page scene of dialogue describing a Harley-Davidson convention from any or all of the following characters:

- a Buddhist monk
- a Ninja motorcycle enthusiast
- a small child
- a mental hospital escapee
- a political candidate

DIFFERENT STORIES, DIFFERENT SETTINGS

There are all kinds of stories, settings, and characters, and when certain characters in certain kinds of stories talk about certain settings, they mention certain things that other characters in other kinds of stories would never think of mentioning. The following are three very different characters from three very different kinds of novels speaking about three very different kinds of settings.

In this first excerpt from J.K. Rowling's *Harry Potter and the Sorcerer's Stone*, Mr. Dursley, Harry's uncle, is listening to the news. This is how the local newscaster and weatherman describe one aspect of the story's setting on this particular day in Britain:

> When Dudley had been put to bed, he went into the living room in time to catch the last report on the evening news:
>
> "And finally, bird-watchers everywhere have reported that the nation's owls have been behaving very unusually today. Although owls normally hunt at night and are hardly ever seen in daylight, there have been hundreds of sightings of these birds flying in every direction since sunrise. Experts are unable to explain why the owls have suddenly changed their sleeping patterns."

The newscaster passes to the weatherman and the dialogue continues:

> "Well, Ted," said the weatherman. "I don't know about that, but it's not only the owls that have been acting oddly today. Viewers as far apart as Kent, Yorkshire, and Dundee have been phoning in to tell me that instead of the rain I promised yesterday, they've had a downpour of shooting stars!"

Owls and shooting stars mark Harry Potter's arrival at the Dursley's. And J.K. Rowling came up with a rather creative way to describe the setting in this fantasy novel, through the evening news.

The next excerpt is taken from *The Lords of Discipline*, a mainstream novel by Pat Conroy. The protagonist, Will, is telling Abigail, an old friend, how he feels about the Corps, which is the story's primary setting, comparing it to how she feels about her roses.

> "I used to think that the Corps represented sameness. We all dress the same, we look the same, we live by the same rules, everything. But each one of us is different. When I walk into this garden each rose looks about the same to me, and you go to a parade at the Institute and all two thousand cadets look exactly the same to you. But if you look at them carefully, Abigail, the same thing happens to those cadets as to your roses. Each one is different, with his own surprises, his own miracles."

Keep in mind that this is a mainstream novel so the dialogue, the description, and even the action should make some kind of universal statement to the reader that connects ultimately to the story's theme. Will is describing the setting as he speaks, but he's doing it in such a way as to also make a statement about what he believes to be true about human beings. As you can see, the voice is very different than the newscaster's in the Harry Potter novel.

Finally, the following is an excerpt from *Fried Green Tomatoes at the Whistle Stop Café* by Fannie Flag. This is a literary novel, and in this scene Evelyn Couch and elderly Mrs. Threadgoode are sitting in the visitor's lounge at Rose Terrace where Mrs. Threadgoode, now that she has an ear she can bend, is going on and on and on about her life. Understandably, her voice is very different from the newscaster's in *Harry Potter and the Sorcerer's Stone* and Will's in *The Lords of Discipline*.

> "The railroad tracks ran right across the backyard, and on summer nights that yard would be just full of lightening bugs and the smell of honeysuckle that grew wild, right alongside the tracks. Poppa had the back planted with fig trees and apple trees, and he had built Momma the most beautiful white lattice grape arbor that was full of wisteria vines ... and little pink sweetheart roses grew all over the back of the house. Oh, I wish you could have seen it."

Since most of the story is in a flashback, this is a creative way to introduce the setting to us before we even get there ourselves. We begin to get a feel for the town of Whistle Stop through the aged voice of one of its most prominent citizens.

WEAVING NARRATIVE SETTING INTO DIALOGUE

If done right, we can keep unfolding the setting throughout the scene as it moves. This is how weaving narrative setting into dialogue should be done—otherwise, the action and dialogue will begin to feel like it's taking place in a vacuum. We want our scenes to be visual. We don't want to create a bunch of talking heads; the reader needs to be able to picture our characters somewhere. Weaving also gets us away from the tendency to create info dumps, those large paragraphs full of background, characterization, and setting details that are boring to write—we know they don't feel quite right—and worse yet, boring to read. So as much as you can, try to throw setting details into the actual dialogue as the scene moves forward. The following example from Lorna Landvik's novel *Your Oasis on Flame Lake* will give you a small example of how this is done.

> Darcy *was boogying around to "Love the One You're With," playing air* guitar like the maestro she is, and I was laughing, *trying to screw a fixture into its socket,* when *Sergio blasted through the door* like a gas explosion.
>
> "It looks fantastic," he said, *twirling around like the little plastic ballerina inside a jewel box* I once bought Lin. Even if *I hadn't been high up on the ladder,* I wouldn't have been able to watch him—he just made me too damn dizzy.
>
> "Wow," said Franny, who had followed Sergio in. *She plopped down on the couch and hugged a pillow to her chest.* "It looks just like a nightclub."
>
> Darcy's air guitar vanished *and she flung herself on the couch* next to Franny.

Obviously, the words in italic are the lines I want you to pay special attention to. This isn't heavy on setting, and you could do a lot more if you had to. For example, if you wanted to show that the characters were affluent, instead of just screwing a fixture into a socket, the viewpoint character could be changing the lightbulb in a crystal candelabra. You could describe the couch as a *mammoth black leather sofa with a mink afghan hung over the back.* You could go the other way and describe a *25-watt bulb hanging from the ceiling* and a *ratty red futon with an old blanket that smelled like a dog bunched up in one corner.* How you use a dialogue scene to describe the setting always depends on what you're trying to get across about the characters or the story.

EXERCISE

WEAVING NARRATIVE SETTING INTO DIALOGUE. Write a one-page dialogue scene for the following settings, weaving narrative details into the characters' dialogue:

- a dingy bar on the edge of town
- a candy store in a beach town
- a vacant lot

- a cross-dresser's closet
- a zoo

INTEGRATING YOUR SETTING

The most effective way to integrate setting into a story is to use all three of the fiction elements at your disposal: dialogue, action, and narrative. This causes setting to simply form a background for the story. It's always there, almost like another character. It takes a gifted writer to be able to pull this off and make it feel natural.

Katherine Dunn is such a writer. In her shocking novel *Geek Love* (and I do mean shocking—and it takes a lot to shock me), Dunn is able to pull of just about everything in one scene. This is a story about a family of carnies. The main characters are the parents and their five children: Arturo, better known as Aqua Boy because he has flippers for arms and legs; Electra/Iphigenia, Siamese twins joined at the hips; Olympia, the hunchbacked protagonist; and Fortunato, who can move objects around rooms. Lil Binewski, the mother, ingested drugs—insecticides, arsenic, radioisotopes, anything to make her babies more "special"—so she and her husband could make a living with them in the carnival, which was their home. In this scene, the father is telling his children the by now very familiar story about how he came by the idea of creating the Binewski freak show using his own children as the stars of the show. The story is told in Olympia's first-person voice.

> "It was in Oregon, up in Portland, which they call the Rose City, though I never got in gear to do anything about it until a year or so later when we were stuck in Fort Lauderdale."
>
> He had been restless one day, troubled by business boondoggies. He drove up into a park on a hillside and got out for a walk. "You could see for miles from up there. And there was a big rose garden with arbors and trellises and fountains. The paths were brick and wound in and out." He sat on a step leading from one terrace to another and stared listlessly at the experimental roses. "It was a test garden, and the colors were ... designed. Striped and layered. One color inside the petal and another color outside ..."

... The roses started him thinking, how the oddity of them was beautiful and how that oddity was contrived to give them value. "It just struck me—clear and complete all at once—no long figuring about it." He realized that children could be designed. "And I thought to myself, now that would be a rose garden worthy of a man's interest!"

We children would smile and hug him and he would grin around at us and send the twins for a pot of cocoa from the drink wagon and me for a bag of popcorn because the red-haired girls would just throw it out when they finished closing the concession anyway. And we could all be cozy in the warm booth of the van, eating popcorn and drinking cocoa and feeling like Papa's roses.

I love the way the author moves between dialogue, narrative, and action as well as between the past and the present to give a sense of the story's setting, while at the same time turning the key to unlock the door to the story's theme. Brilliant. If you can ever pull this off, you, too, will fall into the category of brilliant.

EXERCISE

INTEGRATING YOUR SETTING. A father has taken his ten-year-old son on a vacation to his childhood hometown. Using his thoughts, words, and actions, write a two-page scene of descriptive dialogue.

CHAPTER 20

PUTTING DIALOGUE TO WORK

BY JAMES SCOTT BELL

> "Are you ready to go, Pookums?"
> "Yes, Darling."
> "That's grand."
> "Yes, it is."
> "Such an interesting life we lead."

Oh, really? Not if this dialogue is any indication. Characters can declare their feelings all they want, but it's the reader who must be touched for your tale to work—and dull, two-dimensional dialogue is an instant story killer.

One of the fastest ways to improve your fiction is to sharpen your characters' discourse. You can do this effectively by considering mood, pace, and meaning.

SUPPORTING THE MOOD

Dialogue that's consistent with the mood of a novel can help pull readers into emotional moments and deepen the reading experience. In Robert B. Parker's *Double Play*, World War II vet Joseph Burke meets another ex-Marine, Anthony, in a bar:

> "You're a strong guy," Anthony said. "How 'bout you be a fighter. My brother Angelo could fix you up with some easy fights."
> "How easy?"
> "Easy enough to win," Anthony said.
> "These guys going in the tank?"
> "Sure."
> "And?"

"And we build you a rep," Anthony said.

"And?"

"And we get you a couple big money fights, and maybe me and Angelo bet some side money and ..."

The terse conversation fits the mood of two tough ex-Marines hatching a boxing scheme. Notice how the single word sentences are like jabs, and the last line resembles a small flurry of punches.

Compare Parker's dialogue to Robin Lee Hatcher's in *The Victory Club*, a story that takes place on the home front during World War II. Grocer Howard Baxter befriends Lucy Anderson, whose husband is fighting overseas:

"A penny for your thoughts, Mrs. Anderson."

A flush of embarrassment warmed her cheeks. "I was just feeling envious. Of Mrs. Wright and her car. It's been so long since I've gone anywhere except on foot or by bus. I'd love to just get into a car and take a drive."

"That's understandable." He raised an eyebrow. "I don't suppose you'd care to drive to McCall with me next Saturday. There's plenty of snow in the mountains and the lake may still be frozen over, but the roads should be in good shape. We could go up, have lunch at the lodge, then drive back before dark."

"You own a car?"

The tone here is lush, dotted with emotion and detail—just right for two needy people making contact during trying times. It's right for the mood Hatcher establishes throughout her novel.

To discover how careful dialogue can add to the atmosphere in your novel, try writing a scene using only characters' discussion, with no action beats or description. Let the words flow and see what mood starts to surface. Now revise the scene, putting in appropriate action that complements the tone. Finally, rewrite the scene while listening to a "mood tune"—any music that helps you create. By the end, you'll have lots of material from which to shape the effect you desire.

CONTROLLING THE PACE

At certain times in your novel, dialogue can help you speed up or slow down the pace. Look for scenes that drag or those exchanges that seem to fly by—these are opportunities to insert a discussion or tête-à-tête and adjust the pace accordingly.

If you need to speed up a space, use short verbal exchanges with few action beats. This will leave plenty of white space on the page and create a feeling of fast motion. In the Lawrence Block story "A Candle for the Bag Lady," a waitress tells P.I. Matt Scudder that someone was looking for him, ending her description by saying he looked "underslung":

> "Perfectly good word."
> "I said you'd probably get here sooner or later."
> "I always do. Sooner or later."
> "Uh-huh. You okay, Matt?"
> "The Mets lost a close one."
> "I heard it was 13 to four."
> "That's close for them these days. Did he say what it was about?"

Block uses fast dialogue to characterize and set up the crucial end of the exchange, where Scudder finally flashes his uneasiness. It's a nice change-up, too, from what has transpired in the story to this point.

To slow the pace of a scene, try adding the following:

- Action beats: "Get out!" Barry pulled his gun. He stared into the man's eyes and calculated how long it would take for the stranger to bolt.
- Thoughts: "Get out!" *Why isn't he moving? Maybe a look down the barrel of a gun will get his attention.*
- Description: "Get out!" Barry pulled his gun and stared into the man's bloodshot eyes. The smell of whiskey and fear thickened the air.

Of course, you can also expand the dialogue itself. In Block's story, a man confesses to Scudder about killing the bag lady. Scudder asks why he did it:

> "Same as bourbon and coffee. Had to see. Had to taste it and find out what it was like." His eyes met mine. His were very large, hollow, empty. I fancied I could see right through them to the blackness at the back of his skull.
>
> "I couldn't get my mind away from murder ... I just couldn't do it. It was on my mind all the time and I was afraid of what I might do. I couldn't function, I couldn't think, I just saw blood and death all the time. I was afraid to close my eyes for fear of what I might see. I would just stay up, days it seemed, and then I'd be tired enough to pass out the minute I closed my eyes. I stopped eating. I used to be fairly heavy and the weight just fell off of me."

Crafting Dynamic Dialogue

Speeches like this should be rare in your fiction, but don't be afraid to write one when appropriate. And be sure that what's said has a purpose true to the character.

GOING DEEPER

In "A Candle for the Bag Lady," Scudder interviews the manager of the low-rent tenement where the victim, Mary Alice Redfield, lived. The manager, an older woman, reflects:

> "I got used to having her about. I might say Hello and Good morning and Isn't it a nice day and not get a look in reply, but even on those days she was someone familiar to say something to. And she's gone now and we're all of us older, aren't we?"
>
> "We are."
>
> "The poor old thing. How could anyone do it, will you tell me that? How could anyone murder her?"
>
> I don't think she expected an answer. Just as well. I didn't have one.

This dialogue is consistent with the characters while also reflecting the theme of inexplicable loss in the city. Notice that Block uses another powerful dialogue device—silence—to emphasize a point at the end.

When done well, and briefly, thematic dialogue has a powerful deepening effect. Here are some tips:

- When you're well into your novel, stop and ask what theme is taking shape. Theme should emerge naturally from the story you're telling, rather than being forced into it.
- Give several characters a chance to engage in dialogue that reflects the theme. Let it flow and write more dialogue than you'll need.
- Edit these exchanges and compress the language so characters explore and touch on the theme peripherally, rather than discussing thematic elements "on the nose." This will keep the dialogue from sounding preachy.

With continued practice, dialogue will become one of your strongest fiction tools, adding meaningful layers to your story. Now that's something worth talking about.

CHAPTER 21

USING DIALOGUE TO SET THE MOOD & FACILITATE EMOTION

BY GLORIA KEMPTON

"I'd rather be working at Taco Bell!" I told my friend as I climbed out of her car after a heated discussion about my current editorial job. Nothing wrong with Taco Bell, you understand—that's not the point. The point is I was over-the-top tired, angry, frustrated, disappointed, and done with my job. I spoke those words with so much emotion that they haunted me for days and I eventually quit my job.

The words that you say, scream, or whisper to others with the most emotion are the ones that you remember. The words that others say, scream, or whisper to you with the most emotion are the ones you remember.

We want our stories to be memorable for our readers. We want to create characters who are unforgettable. In order to do this, we must write dialogue that is full of emotion. It doesn't matter whether the emotion is fear, sadness, joy, or anger. What matters is that our characters are emotionally engaged with the situations and the conflicts we've created for them, and that they're conveying their feelings to one another through dialogue that is charged with emotion. Charged and super-charged. Turbo-charged. The more emotion, the better.

I didn't say melodrama, I said emotion. There's a difference. We're not writing soap operas. The emotion in a scene of dialogue is what draws your reader into your characters' situational conflict and makes her care about the problems facing the character. Every bit of dialogue in your story must convey some kind of emotion. What you have to decide is what kind. This is determined by the kind of story you're writing and what is going on for the characters in any one particular scene.

I see new writers make a lot of mistakes when it comes to writing emotional dialogue. This usually comes from trying too hard:

- characters cracking jokes and laughing uproariously when the jokes aren't funny
- characters crying and sobbing all over each other to the point that the reader is watching, going, "Yeah, yeah, get on with it."
- characters who are full of fury when the situation amounts to something like a stubbed toe or a broken fingernail

We create characters that go over the top and are inappropriate in the expression of their emotions because we (1) are not able to access our own emotions and therefore act inappropriately ourselves, or (2) we're trying to make a point in our story and think extreme emotion is the way to do it.

More often, I see the other extreme. Writers that underplay the emotion:

- A character loses her husband, whether to an affair or death, and goes to her Bridge Club the next night, the main concern on her mind getting the recipe for the cranberry cucumber salad.
- A female character hears a noise, and with no fear, grabs a baseball bat and runs down the dark basement stairs to confront the burglar.
- A character loses his job only to tell his wife when he gets home that he knows he deserved to be fired—no anger, just acceptance.

We create characters who deny and repress their emotions because we deny and repress our own.

As a writing coach, I'm often frustrated that I can't help writers with this aspect of their storytelling. I joke that writers need therapy to be able to write well, but somewhere down deep, I think I really believe that.

Whether or not you get therapy is up to you. In the meantime, there are some practical things you can do to make sure your dialogue is full of the kind of emotion that grabs readers and makes your characters memorable. In this chapter, we'll take a few common emotions and see how dialogue can be used to show these emotions through your characters. But first, let's talk about how the use of emotion can establish your story's mood.

SETTING THE MOOD

"I hate you!"

"I don't want to live ..."

"I won!"

"Don't you dare move—"

These are strong statements. When we, as real-life people, are emoting, we express ourselves in a variety of physical ways. We may punch a wall, grit our teeth, or clap our hands—any number of physical movements. But at some point, we talk. To ourselves or someone else. One of the most effective ways to reveal our characters' emotions is to let them talk. Out loud, whether whispering or yelling. Interwoven with action and narrative.

Cartoonists have it made. They can simply draw a mad, sad, happy, or scared face on their cartoon figures and we know immediately what's going on with the characters in the present moment. Likewise, scriptwriters have real actors to work with. The audience will see the frowns, the tears, the smiles, and the eyes wide with fear.

Writers don't have these luxuries. Our only tool is words and we must put those words in our characters' mouths so our reader will know what our characters' emotional states are at each present moment. The only way to connect with our reader on an emotional level is to first connect with our characters. The way we do this is to make sure our characters connect with themselves.

This isn't a self-help book on the psychology of human emotions, but many of us don't slow down enough to feel our feelings on a moment-by-moment basis. However, whether or not we know how we feel, we are continually giving off signals to others. The same is true of our characters. While they may not be able to tell you how they feel unless another character asks them, their behavior and words will give them

Crafting Dynamic Dialogue

away. You'll know, no matter how they try to hide their feelings. We can only hide our real feelings for so long.

The feelings of anger, sadness, joy, and fear are primary, although we might have a range of other more minor feelings that come and go: jealousy, confusion, frustration, etc. These other minor feelings are most states of being, so in this chapter we'll deal with the primary feelings and learn how we can use dialogue to set a mood in our story.

JUST FOR FUN

Do you want your reader to know what your character is feeling? Use dialogue. When your character opens her mouth and speaks, she immediately reveals her emotional state of being, which is very powerful and very effective. You can use the following exercises to practice using dialogue to show your character expressing emotion. They all involve at least two characters so you can use dialogue as the primary vehicle to show the specific emotion. Write a one-page scene of dialogue for each scenario. Feel free to modify any of the scenes to fit your own needs.

1. Your character and his best friend are driving down the freeway minding their own business when an older vehicle sideswipes your character's brand-new SUV and then keeps driving. What are the first angry words out of his mouth?

2. Your character and her boyfriend are out to dinner at an upscale restaurant. The boyfriend has just told your viewpoint character that he wants to break up, that he doesn't love her anymore. Without using tears, let your character express her shock and sadness through dialogue.

3. Your character has just landed his dream job. He will be doing work he loves and getting paid more than he ever imagined. He's sitting in the office of his future employer. He can hardly contain himself, he's so excited. He blurts out how he feels.

4. Your character and her boyfriend have been hiking since early in the morning. It's now dusk and they realize they are hopelessly lost. Your viewpoint character is growing increasingly anxious on the inside. Suddenly she's terrified and expresses it out loud.

5. Your character has just learned that his emotionally unavailable father has died. He's in his therapist's office, and feeling numb. When he asks him what he'll miss most about his father, suddenly he's no longer numb and has a lot to say.

Love

Regardless of what you think of *The Bridges of Madison County* (some readers loved it, many hated it; personally, I'm a sucker for mushy love stories), there's an effective bit of dialogue in the middle of a love scene between Francesca Johnson and Robert Kincaid. I even heard Oprah read this bit of dialogue on her show when the author, Robert James Waller, was her guest.

The story is about a man who waltzes into a woman's life for four days and waltzes back out again, taking her heart with him and leaving behind a part of his own. That's basically it. Well, I doubt that's the synopsis Waller turned into his agent or editor, but it's pretty close. The following line of dialogue was spoken as Francesca tried to get Robert to understand why she couldn't just leave her husband and kids to follow him across the backcountry roads of Iowa and off into the sunset. It was about responsibility.

> Robert Kincaid was silent. He knew what she was saying about the road and responsibilities and how the guilt could transform her. He knew she was right, in a way. Looking out the window, he fought within himself, fought to understand her feelings. She began to cry.
>
> Then they held each other for a long time. And he whispered to her: "I have one thing to say, one thing only, I'll never say it another time, to anyone, and I ask you to remember it. In a universe of ambiguity, this kind of certainty comes only once, and never again, no matter how many lifetimes you live."

Women readers swooned over this line in the book. Is there a woman anywhere in the world who wouldn't give anything to hear that special someone say those words to her? To be thought of as that special?

But what specifically makes these words connect with readers so effectively? And how can you create the kind of emotional dialogue that can convey a character's feelings of love in a tone that's both genuine and authentic?

You might be writing a love scene or coming to that point in your story where your character is full of feelings of love—for another character, an animal, a setting. How can she express herself without sounding corny, melodramatic, or like a character in a novel, which, of course, is exactly what she is?

One reason the passage works so well is because it contains both conflict and resolution. These two people want what they can't have, what they can't make happen. So they're both torn, even though deep down they both know that Francesca will do the *right* thing because that's who she is. It's all right there in those two paragraphs. And we can identify with the certainty that Robert is talking about. We've felt that way.

As human beings, we are afraid of intimacy with other human beings. And love is very intimate. So what's important to remember when creating a love scene between two characters, whether it leads to sex or not, is that your character is simultaneously feeling both fear and love. To make the scene feel authentic, you have to capture both feelings at once in the same character—sometimes in both characters, since it takes two to tango, or tangle, as the case may be in a love scene that leads to sex.

How is this done? By practicing. The more comfortable you are with real love scenes, the more comfortable your characters will be. You may have to put your characters in a number of love scenes and various settings to come up with one that works. Keep in mind that a love scene doesn't always mean a sex scene. What we're after is a feeling of love. That could be between parent and child or between friends just as easily as it could be a romantic feeling between a man and a woman. Sometimes jumping to sex between a man and woman actually short circuits the feeling of love that is surfacing for the couple. If you really want to develop a love relationship between two characters, take your time and reveal it gradually through the dialogue as they grow closer.

EXERCISE

LOVE. Following are some scenarios in which characters find themselves wanting to express their love for someone but are scared of their intense feelings. Not just scared of expressing the feeling but scared of the feeling itself. Put the words in their mouths, halting though they might be, in a one-page scene of dialogue.

- Sixteen-year-old Carl's father has terminal cancer. Carl knows his father's days are numbered. He's watching him waste away before his eyes. On a rare occasion, his mother is out for dinner with friends and has left Carl alone in the house with his father. Carl is looking for something in the attic and comes across a box full of childhood items: his first baseball mitt, an old tackle box, a bunch of snapshots of him and his father—wrestling in the backyard, climbing a tree, taking the boat out. Carl is overcome with feelings of love and gratitude for his father. He was a good dad. Always. He runs upstairs to tell his father. Something. Anything what?

• The nurse has just placed Susan's newborn daughter in her arms. Her first baby. Susan isn't prepared for the feelings that wash over her. She begins to talk to her baby.

• Twenty-year-old Eli has been going out with Marisa for over a year. Recently, he has been feeling an unusual warmth in his heart whenever he's with her. And he can't seem to get enough of her. He's never been in love before, so has no frame of reference. One night as they're sitting on her front porch, he's overcome with that warm feeling again, and it's too much for him. He turns to her.

Anger

The emotion of anger expresses itself in many different ways. Watch what makes you angry so you can access your anger and authentically use it in your dialogue scenes. You also want to watch what makes others angry and how they express it, which will often be very different than how you do.

Let's look at a passage from Michael Dorris' novel *A Yellow Raft in Blue Water*. Here we have a character whose mother abandoned her ten years before, leaving her with her grandmother. She's just a little upset about that. Her mother, who doesn't quite have her head on straight, is also angry. When people are angry, they blame, defend, say things they don't mean, and say things they do mean. The words usually rush out without much thought given to them. Here, the viewpoint character, Rayona, is finally taking advantage of the opportunity to blast her mother for abandoning her so many years before.

> I'm so used to being Mom's daughter, I defend myself.
> "I meant to get in touch," I say.
> "You meant to, you meant to!" Mom pulls the sash of her robe tight and ties it in a knot. "That's just great. Here I am, sick as a dog, and you're off ..."
> "I was working at Bearpaw Lake State Park."

Crafting Dynamic Dialogue

"Having fun!" Mom shouts. "At some park."

"But you left first."

"That's right, blame me." Mom turns to Dayton. "It's my fault she walked out on her grandmother. Of course."

"Now don't get yourself all upset," he says. "When you calm down, you're going to be glad to see Ray."

"I thought something happened to you!" Mom screams at me. It's the worst thing yet she's said.

"A lot you cared." I've got my second wind. "You could come for your box of pills from Charlene, but not for me."

That stops her. "How did you know it was pills?"

"And all that time, here you are, not ten miles away. Don't tell me about leaving."

"She has no heart!" Mom appeals to Dayton. "She wants to hurt me, sick as I am."

"You tried that on Dad and it didn't work." I'm mad beyond the bounds of what's fair. "You're not sick."

But of course she is. I see it the minute the words are out of my mouth. In some part of my brain it has been registering every since the car stopped. She's ragged, pale. There are new wrinkles in the skin of her forehead, thin lines that stretch like threads above her eyebrows. Her cheeks are hollow but her waist has thickened.

"You're just like him," she says to me in a voice tied to a rock. "In every way."

What makes this dialogue scene work so well is that it feels so real. Angry people in conversation don't often make a lot of sense, and the train of thought in a conversation can't often be followed because there really isn't one. They're just throwing out whatever they can to hurt each other and to defend their own position, all the while not wanting the other to see their raw underbelly.

Most often, when your characters become engaged in anger, you want to speed up the scene. Use shorter sentences and paragraphs, less narrative. An angry slower-paced scene works, too, and is often even scarier because it could mean an explosion is on the horizon. See the second head next, the slow burn. Carie is holding it together, but if this scene was to continue, and Matt was to keep arguing with her, this character would inevitably erupt in angry threats and accusations.

For example, the words "I hate you" may be spoken loudly and with one's body shaking. The words "I hate you" may also be spoken softly and coldly and with one's body tense. Hatred is not a feeling—it's a state of being. Anger is the feeling. And we get angry for a myriad of reasons, less often as we grow older, I've been pleased to discover. How much anger we hold inside of us depends on how much we work on ourselves during our lives, expressing that anger and dealing with the root causes. This is one reason it's important to create a character chart before writing your story so you know your character well enough to know what will make her angry. As I mentioned before, the same things do not make people angry. You know how we tell each other not to talk about religion or politics because of the strong feelings these subjects evoke in us. Well, the truth is, you can talk politics all you want, and I won't even feel one tense muscle. But if you start in on religion, you'll be taking your life in your hands talking to me. This is the kind of thing you want to know about your character. What causes her anger—at every level? What frustrates her? What peeves her? What can create the kind of internal rage that causes her to lose control of herself in a matter of moments? Do you know?

This is one step forward knowing your character from the inside out. But you must also know your character from the outside in. Once feeling that anger, how does she express it physically and verbally? Some of us become unnaturally quiet. Others immediately vent our anger on whoever happens to be nearby. Few of us, it seems, understand how to be angry and take responsibility for that anger without blaming someone for the cause of the anger. Many of us try to deny we're even angry because we're not comfortable with this feeling. Which is it for your character? You'll want to know this about her before putting her in a situation in which her buttons are pushed. Let's look at three different ways a fictional character might express his anger in the exact same situation. As a young couple, Matt and Carie are saving for their first home so they can start a family, and Carie has just learned that Matt has gambled away their savings.

Denial

"We have that appointment with the mortgage broker tomorrow, remember." Carie spooned some mashed potatoes on her plate.

"Why bother? The money's gone." Matt's voice was flat.

"You couldn't possibly gamble away that much money—that was more than $20,000. You wouldn't do that. We've been saving for five years." Matt wouldn't do that. He must have been drinking and it felt like he was spending it all. How could he even get access to all of their savings in one night? "It's just not possible, that's all." Carie shook her head. "It can't be gone, not all of it. We've been saving. All of these years we've been putting away money every single week—out of our paychecks. Going without things we really needed. No, I know you like to gamble, but you must have figured wrong."

Matt just sat there staring at his plate. The silence in the room was deafening.

The Slow Burn

"You what? Carie spooned some mashed potatoes on her plate. "You didn't say what I just thought you said."

"You heard right." He ducked his head. "The money's gone. That weekend I went to Vegas for that business trip? I was winning ... I started off the night winning and well, before I knew it—"

"Get out." Carie stared at her plate. "Get out right now before I throw you out."

"Huh? What do you mean get out? This is my home, too—"

"Not any more it's not." Her voice sounded far away, even to her. "This is the last time. I'm filing for divorce tomorrow. You'll never do this to me again."

The Explosion

"We have that appointment with the mortgage broker tomorrow, honey. This is it. We're finally going to be able to do it. After all these years of saving. I'm so excited—"

"It's gone ..."

"What?" Carie stared at Matt, her forkful of mashed potatoes halfway to her mouth. She let it clatter to her plate. "What did you say? What's gone?"

"The money. That night in Vegas—that business trip I took. I started out winning. I don't know what happened. Before I knew it—"

"What?" she cried. "You're telling me all of our money, twenty thousand dollars, is gone?"

"That's what I'm saying. You catch on quick."

"No! Omigod! Are you out of your mind? How could you do that?" She was standing now, towering over him, grabbing her fork, raising it above her head.

He looked up at her with that sheepish grin she used to love. "This is how it's going to end? Our marriage? You're going to stab me with a fork?"

She looked up at her fork, then slumped back into her chair and dissolved into tears.

Matt rose and stood beside her, putting a hand on her shoulder. "Honey—"

"Don't touch me!" she said, shaking off his hand. "I hate you! I can't believe I married such a loser. You've always been a loser, I just couldn't see it." She was screaming now. "Leave! Now!" She stood to face him, his face inches from hers. "Get out of this house and out of my life!"

EXERCISE

ANGER. Have you ever felt betrayed? Or betrayed someone? Write a dialogue scene where one confronts the other about the betrayal. Write two pages of dialogue from the betrayer's point of view and then rewrite the same scene from the viewpoint of the character who was betrayed.

Fear

Showing the emotion of fear in a character is again a matter of knowing your character so you know what she'll do and say when scared. I remember standing in the airport with a bunch of my friends on the day of my very first airplane ride. I couldn't even talk, I was that scared. It's funny because other times when I'm scared, I chatter on endlessly. So it also depends on the situation. One thing for sure in a passage of dialogue where you want to indicate a character's fear—there's tension. Fear creates tension, not just in the person who's afraid, but also in everyone in that person's energy field.

Mystery and suspense thriller writers must become masters of revealing this emotion in their characters because that's what readers of this kind of story are looking for. Mary Higgins Clark has written a large number of novels with the emotion of fear at the core of each story. Following is a passage from *While My Pretty One Sleeps*. Note especially the pace of the scene.

> The door to Sal's showroom was open. She ran in and closed it behind her. The room was empty. "Sal!" she called, almost panicked. "Uncle Sal!"
>
> He hurried from his private office. "Neeve, what's the matter?"
>
> "Sal, I think someone is following me." Neeve grasped his arm. "Lock the door, please."
>
> Sal stared at her. "Neeve, are you sure?"
>
> "Yes. I've seen him three or four times."
>
> Those dark deep-set eyes, the sallow skin. Neeve felt the color run from her face. "Sal," she whispered, "I know who it is. He works in the coffee shop."
>
> "Why would he be following you?"
>
> "I don't know." Neeve stared at Sal. "Unless Myles was right all along. Is it possible Nicky Sepetti wanted me dead?"

The author weaves the dialogue and action so you get a picture of a scared character. Read the scene again and pull out the actions: She's running into the room, grasping his arm, and the color is draining from her face. She uses short sentences, which always make a scene speed up:

> "I think someone is following me."
> "Lock the door, please."
> "I know who it is."
> "Is it possible Nicholas Sepetti wanted me dead?"

The emotion of fear speeds everything up and makes it all stand still at the same time. The protagonist's thoughts, words, and actions are accelerated while the story stops for just a moment as the reader assimilates what's going on in the scene and feels the danger, whatever it is.

FIXING YOUR OWN STORY

Choose the character in your story that seems the most flat and one-dimensional. You've tried to get to know him, but he's not coming through the way you'd like him to. The problem could be that the emotions he needs to express in the story are ones you yourself are uncomfortable with.

Decide that you're going to let go of this character for just one scene. Let 'er rip. Undo the leash and let him say anything he wants. If that

---

means screaming, throwing things, crying, even killing someone, let him do it. Give him full reign and see if he comes to life for you. If you need a little help, here are three possible scenarios you could use to bring out his emotion:

- He's at a Little League game with his ten-year-old son when the umpire makes a bad call. (anger)
- He has just realized he's in love with the heroine in your story. They're in bed together, and he wants to tell her. He's overcome by emotion. (love)
- The phone is ringing and he picks it up to hear a representative from the IRS identifying herself, telling him they're planning an audit. He cheated on his income tax this year. (fear)

EXERCISE

FEAR. Write a two-page scene of dialogue that shows a viewpoint character whose fear is accelerating as the action progresses. This could mean the other character giving the protagonist new information or making immediate threats against the protagonist.

Joy

For a new writer, getting something published is a big deal. I know of no writer who would dispute that. Over the years I've seen a variety of joyful responses. One writer might happen to mention to a friend, "Oh, my story came out in *The Atlantic Monthly* last week," while another might make twenty-five phone calls and carry her published story around in her purse to show everyone. I spotted my very first published article in a magazine on the newsstand, grabbed it and ran around to all the store clerks, holding it up and shrieking like a crazy woman.

Joy, like fear and anger, shows itself in a variety of ways. A character who's normally introverted and quiet may simply share her joy in a few brief sentences of peaceful contentment, while the more extroverted character may shriek and cry out her excitement while jumping up and down, eyes lighting up and hands flailing—like I did when I saw my article in the magazine. What do you do when feeling joy?

Crafting Dynamic Dialogue

In the following passage from Iris Ranier Dart's novel *Beaches*, you'll find a combination of emotions. It's especially effective when you can combine positive and painful emotions in the same passage of dialogue, giving the reader one wild emotional roller coaster ride. The author does this so well in this passage as Cee Cee and Bertie, two best friends, are sharing an incredible moment—a very happy event for Bertie while the same event is destroying Cee Cee.

> They walked silently again for a long time until Bertie broke the silence again.
> "Cee Cee," she said. "I did it."
> Later, when she thought about the conversation, Cee Cee remembered that the minute Bertie said those words, she knew exactly what Bertie had done and with whom, but she was hoping (God, are you listening?) she was wrong.
> "Did what?" Cee Cee asked, and she stopped walking.
> "Got laid. By John."
> Cee Cee couldn't speak. It was a joke. Now Bertie would say, "It's a joke, Cee. You didn't believe me, did you?"
> "Oh, boy, I didn't mean to blurt it out like that," she said instead. "To say I got laid—which is really an awful way to put it, because it wasn't like that. We made love. I mean, we really made love, and it was so neat, Cee Cee, not like it would probably be with someone my own age. He was so gentle and sweet. And you want to know the funny thing?"
> "Yes," Cee Cee managed to say. Oh, God, yes, she wanted to know the funny thing. Let the funny thing be that this was a lie, and that everything she was picturing now that was making her feel weak wasn't true.
> "The funny thing is that I don't feel guilty, and I don't feel dirty, and I'm not the least bit in love with him. You know the old myth about the man you give your virginity to being the first man you fall in love with. Well, I'm not. And I think that's really great."
> But I am! Cee Cee screamed inside. Outside, she just stood there, looking at the ocean, unable to look at Bertie. Beautiful Bertie. With John Perry.
> "I'd never tell another soul, Cee," Bertie said hastily. "I mean, I'm not embarrassed or ashamed, because he's a wonderful person and everything, and I'm glad it could be with him my first time, but I had to tell you."
> A chill came over Cee Cee and she wished she'd brought a shawl.

Because we're in Cee Cee's point of view, this passage may feel like it's more about sadness and jealousy than it is about joy. But Bertie's pretty thrilled about what just happened. She's excitedly telling her friend about something that she's been wanting for a long time. When showing a character's happiness or excitement through dialogue, you don't want to rely on the exclamation point to convey the emotion. You'll notice there are no exclamation points in the above passage. The dialogue is worded in such a way that we can feel Bertie's thrill about her news as well as Cee Cee's sadness. This scene would have been interesting in Bertie's point of view, too, but there's more suspense with Cee Cee's viewpoint as she's thinking a lot of sad thoughts she can't possibly say out loud.

What makes this scene work so well is the way the author alternated Bertie's words and Cee Cee's thoughts so we get the feeling of both happiness and sadness simultaneously.

Sadness

The emotion of sadness is often the most difficult to show in a scene of dialogue only because it's so easy to slip into melodrama. I once read that "if your character cries, your reader doesn't have to," and it seems to be true. Once characters start shedding tears, for some reason the reader seems to want to resist the emotion. So you want to try to show your characters' sorrow using something besides tears. Dialogue is good just because a character can talk about what's going on in his life in a way that moves the reader, but without melodrama, because the truth is, when it comes time for most of us real folks (as compared to fictional characters) to emote about our lives, we tend to hold back rather than to break forth with tears or angry words or even admit that we're scared of something. We just don't want to make ourselves that vulnerable to others.

In the following scene from the novel *Terms of Endearment* by Larry McMurtry, the prevailing emotion is sadness. These two little boys, Tommy and Teddy, are losing their mother, who is dying of cancer. Everyone is trying to remain strong, and they all have their own way of doing so. But we can feel the intense sadness in the way they talk to each other.

Teddy had meant to be reserved, but he couldn't manage. His feelings rushed up, became words. "Oh, I really don't want you to die," he said. He had a husky little voice. "I want you to come home."

Tommy said nothing.

...

"Well, both of you better make some friends," Emma said. "I'm sorry about this, but I can't help it. I can't talk to you too much longer either, or I'll get too upset. Fortunately we had ten or twelve years and we did a lot of talking, and that's more than a lot of people get. Make some friends and be good to them. Don't be afraid of girls, either."

"We're not afraid of girls," Tommy said. "What makes you think that?"

"You might get to be later," Emma said.

"I doubt it," Tommy said, very tense.

When they came to hug her Teddy fell apart and Tommy remained stiff.

"Tommy, be sweet," Emma said. "Be sweet, please. Don't keep pretending you dislike me. That's silly."

"I like you," Tommy said, shrugging tightly.

"I know that, but for the last year or two you've been pretending you hate me," Emma said. "I know I love you more than anybody in the world except your brother and sister, and I'm not going to be around long enough to change my mind about you. But you're going to live a long time, and in a year or two when I'm not around to irritate you you're going to change your mind and remember that I read you a lot of stories and made you a lot of milkshakes and allowed you to goof off a lot when I could have been forcing you to mow the lawn."

Both boys looked away, shocked that their mother's voice was so weak.

"In other words, you're going to remember that you love me," Emma said. "I imagine you'll wish you could tell me that you've changed your mind, but you won't be able to, so I'm telling you now I already know you love me, just so you won't be in doubt about that later. Okay?"

"Okay," Tommy said quickly, a little gratefully.

Nobody's crying in this scene, and there's even some anger being expressed. But it's incredibly sad because this mother is dying and trying to redeem in this one last encounter with her sons every moment she's been a less than perfect mom. When your dialogue is poignant and honest enough, you don't need to get your characters crying to indicate just how sad they are. I remember how moved I was when I first read these words from a mother to her son: "... *I'm telling you now I already know you love me, just so you won't be in doubt about that later."* What incredible love—that she would contain her son's love for her when he couldn't speak the words himself. This would protect him from later guilt and shame over not being able to say the words himself when he had the opportunity. In that sense there is both amazing love and incredible sorrow in the same passage of dialogue. What an emotional ride for the reader.

EXERCISE

JOY AND SADNESS. Write a three-page scene that contrasts joy and sadness. First, write from the sad character's point of view, then rewrite the same scene from the happy character's point of view. This can be two characters breaking up, one character being offered another character's job, or a brother and sister learning what's in their recently deceased parent's will. You get the idea.

Peace

Showing a character at peace with himself is to show a state of being, but it's also to show an emotion in that it's a calmness exhibited by a character who has resolved or is resolving the issues in his life that have caused him so much confusion and stress. The challenge is to put him in a scene of dialogue that includes tension, because a character at peace isn't often a character with much drama. And drama is what readers require.

In the following scene from *The Prince of Tides* by Pat Conroy, Tom Wingo is telling his mistress (and therapist, but that's beside the point), Susan Lowenstein, that he's finally decided to go back to his wife. He's at peace with his decision, but you can imagine how she feels.

> Over wine I asked, "What do you feel like eating tonight, Lowenstein?"
> In silence, she watched me for a moment, then said, "I plan to order a perfectly lousy meal. I don't want to have anything like a wonderful meal on the night you say goodbye to me forever."
> "I'm going back to South Carolina, Lowenstein," I said, reaching over and squeezing her hand. "That's where I belong."
>
> ...

Crafting Dynamic Dialogue

"What happened?"

"My character rose to the surface," I said. "I didn't have the courage to leave my wife and children to make a new life with you. It's just not in me. You'll have to forgive me, Lowenstein. One part of me wants you more than anything else in the world. The other part of me is terrified of any major change in my life. That's the strongest part."

"But you love me, Tom," she said.

"I didn't know it was possible to be in love with two women at the same time."

"Yet you chose Sallie."

"I chose to honor my own history," I said. "If I were a braver man, I could do it."

...

"I've got to try to make something out of the ruins, Lowenstein," I said, looking into her eyes. "I don't know if I'll succeed, but I've got to try."

...

Have you told Sallie about us, Tom?"

"Yes," I said.

"Then you used me, Tom," she said.

"Yes," I said. "I used you, Susan, but not before I started loving you."

"If you liked me enough, Tom ..."

"No, Lowenstein. I adore you. You've changed my life. I've felt like a whole man again. An attractive man. A sensual one. You've made me face it all and you made me think I was doing it to help my sister."

"So this is how the story ends," she said.

"I believe so, Lowenstein," I answered.

"Then let's make our last night perfect," she said, kissing my hand, then slowly kissing each one of my fingers as the building swayed in a strong wind from the north.

Some of the tension in this scene comes from Tom and Susan being in two different places. He's going back to his wife and she's having a difficult time letting go of him.

The other part of the tension is Tom's admission that he's torn. He cares about Susan and wants her, but he also wants his wife. And he knows he's a man of character and so he could never leave his wife and kids without tremendous guilt, which would be toxic to his relationship with Susan anyway.

In this scene, Lowenstein continues, making sure that he's sure:

> "... on the night you say good-bye to me forever."
> "But you love me, Tom."
> "Yet you chose Sallie."
> "Then you used me, Tom."
> "If you liked me enough, Tom."

He continues to answer her, confident in his decision, although he's still able to acknowledge what he's losing:

> "That's where I belong."
> "My character rose to the surface."
> "I chose to honor my own history."
> "I've got to make something out of the ruins."

The above lines of dialogue reveal where both of these characters are. As the protagonist, Tom is at peace about his decision, but the other emotion that comes through here is sadness, although no one ever uses the word, and Conroy himself doesn't use it in the narrative. But the dialogue creates the sad feeling in us because we're watching two people who love each other but can't be together.

EXERCISE

PEACE. Write one passage of dialogue that reveals a character at peace but still includes tension. Some possible scenarios:

- a character who has accepted her doctor's cancer diagnosis, but whose family members are going nuts
- a character on death row being led to his execution
- a character facing off with a bear in the wild

Compassion

Like peace, the emotion of compassion, sympathy, or empathy is often a fairly nondramatic one, so it's your job to find a way to bring some drama to it. I honestly had a difficult time finding a published passage where compassion was the prevalent emotion, leading me to believe that maybe compassion doesn't make good drama.

Anne Tyler is one of my favorite writers because she's so good at creating all kinds of emotion in her characters, but in a subtle, matter-of-fact kind of way, it kind of hits you in the gut. The following is a scene from her novel *Breathing Lessons*. The protagonist, Maggie, is sitting in a hospital waiting room with two strangers—another woman and a man in overalls. Suddenly, from a nearby room comes a nurse's voice as she talks to a patient.

> "Now, Mr. Plum, I'm giving you this jar for urine."
> "My what?"
> "Urine."
> "How's that?"
> "It's for urine."
> "Speak up—I can't hear you."
> "*Urine*, I said. You take this jar home! You collect all your urine! For twenty-four hours! You bring the jar back!"
> In the chair across from Maggie, the wife gave an embarrassed titter. "He's deaf as a doorknob," she told Maggie. "Has to have everything shouted for all and sundry to hear."
> Maggie smiled and shook her head, not knowing how else to respond. Then the man in coveralls stirred. He placed his great, furry fist on his knees. He cleared his throat. "You know," he said, "It's the funniest thing. I can catch that nurse's voice all right but I don't understand a single word she's saying."
> Maggie's eyes filled with tears. She dropped her magazine and groped in her purse for a Kleenex, and the man said, "Lady? You okay?"
> She couldn't tell him it was his kindness that had undone her—such delicacy, in such an unlikely looking person ...

Maggie is so moved by this man's compassion as he pretends not to hear what the nurse is saying, in order to save a complete stranger, the patient's wife, from humiliation. Now, the man in coveralls isn't the viewpoint character so we can't feel the compassion from inside of the character speaking, but we can certainly feel it through his dialogue and Maggie's tearful response. One line:

"I can catch that nurse's voice all right but I don't understand a single word she's saying."

Sometimes it doesn't take much. One line.

Setting a mood and conveying a character's emotions through dialogue is one of the most effective ways to bring your story to life on the page. Creating tense dialogue is one thing, but creating tense dialogue that is also full of a character's fear, or sorrow, or joy is another. This is the stuff that moves readers so that they engage with your characters on an emotional level. And once you are able to accomplish that, you're home free. The reader will stay with you until the last page.

EXERCISE

COMPASSION. Create a scenario between two characters who are arguing and trying to get their points across. They're conflictive and defensive, but one finally makes a statement that causes the protagonist to feel compassion. Go inside of the protagonist for the emotion and then carefully craft his response.

Crafting Dynamic Dialogue

PART VI

DIALOGUE DRIVES THE PLOT

CHAPTER 22

CONSTRUCTING SCENES WITH DIALOGUE

BY JORDAN ROSENFELD

Dialogue is one of the most versatile elements of fiction writing because it can achieve multiple effects. When done well, dialogue can even be a scene-stealer. Most of the great lines in literature were *spoken* by characters, not narrated. This chapter will focus on scenes that are composed primarily of dialogue—not scenes with the occasional line of dialogue tossed in.

Dialogue scenes find their way into narratives of all genre types because of the versatility of conversation, so undoubtedly you'll wind up using these scenes. When dialogue is done right, it tends to feel fast, and therefore can be used to pick up the pace and propel your plot and characters forward. Dialogue is a great conflict builder too, as characters can argue, fight, and profess sentiments in words. It's also a wonderful medium for building tension, as characters jockey for power, love, and understanding.

OPENING A DIALOGUE SCENE

Before you start the scene, you'll want to decide if you're going to use dialogue to convey action, or to reveal character, plot, or backstory information. One of the most common errors is the use of dialogue as filler, with characters discussing the time or the weather. Don't make the assumption that dialogue scenes need to open in the middle of a conversation, either—in fact, this is often a confusing way to open a scene. A dialogue scene can open with one of the following elements—a scenic launch, or a narrative, action, or character launch—but then move quickly into dialogue. Here are some essential guidelines for opening this type of scene:

- Ground the reader in the setting before the conversation begins.
- Let the conversation begin within the first couple of paragraphs.
- Involve your protagonist in the conversation.
- Make it clear who is speaking to whom.
- Infuse conflict or opposition into the dialogue.

In J.D. Salinger's classic novel, *The Catcher in the Rye*, there are many dialogue scenes between protagonist Holden Caulfield and the minor characters who populate the story, and these serve many of the functions of dialogue as described later in this chapter. Salinger is good at setting up dialogue scenes so that they reveal character without being confusing. Here's an example of one such scene, in which Holden has come back to the dorm late and wants to talk to his roommate, Ackley:

> A tiny bit of light came through the shower curtains and all from our room, and I could see him lying in bed. I knew damn well he was wide awake. "Ackley?" I said. "Y'awake?"
>
> "Yeah."
>
> It was pretty dark and I stepped on somebody's shoe on the floor and damn near fell on my head. Ackley sort of sat up in bed and leaned on his arm. He had a lot of white stuff on his face, for his pimples. He looked sort of spooky in the dark. "What the hellya doing anyway?" I said.
>
> "Wuddya mean what the hell am I doing? I was tryna *sleep* before you guys started making all that noise. What the hell was the fight about, anyhow?"

Notice how the scene meets all the criteria laid out above—we're grounded through the setting, we can see that it takes place in the dorm room. The protagonist, Holden, is the one coming into the room. We know it's him because we're in his point of view, and we know he's talking to Ackley because he calls him by name. The dialogue then begins almost immediately after we know where we are, and it's full of conflict—he's ticked off his roommate by waking him up, so there's potential for the conversation to be fraught with further complication.

Though you want to get into the dialogue fairly quickly, you don't necessarily have to do so in the first sentence—it may even start a few paragraphs in. Remember, grounding the reader in physical details is important so she doesn't get confused, but the details should also reinforce qualities about the protagonist. This is a coming-of-age story, after all, so Salinger invites us in to the dorm-life experience through his choice of details.

DIALOGUE AND BIG REVEALS

Dialogue is a wonderfully versatile technique for giving the reader information necessary to drive the plot forward or deepen character understanding, without resorting to exposition. Through dialogue you can show the reader who your protagonist is, reveal the effect the protagonist has on other characters, and introduce new plot information that drives the narrative forward.

Revealing Character

One of the best ways to express your protagonist's personality, feelings, and perceptions is through his own words, rather than in exposition. Doing so allows the reader to feel as though he is right there in the same place as the character, getting to know him through direct experience. When the purpose of a dialogue scene is to reveal character, you want to:

- Show the character speaking under pressure or in conflict. Always avoid mundane conversation.
- Let your protagonist's true nature come through in words. Is he brave? Then show him speaking words of hope and courage. Is he seductive? Let him pull out all verbal stops to seduce every woman he meets.
- Show him expressing his feelings or thoughts about the significant situation or the most recent plot events. Through the character's internal dialogue and external action, you can show his personality.

In Truman Capote's brilliant novella *Breakfast at Tiffany's*, his main character, Holly Golightly, is revealed to the reader through memorable dialogue. Holly is rash and bold and sexy and girlish all at once, and this is conveyed every time she opens her mouth or appears in a scene.

The first time the narrator meets Holly, it's via an exchange she has with a neighbor:

> The voice that came back, welling up from the bottom of the stairs, was silly-young and self-amused. "Oh darling, I am sorry. I lost the goddamn key."
>
> "You cannot go on ringing my bell. You must please, please have yourself a key made."
>
> "But I lose them all."
>
> "I work. I have to sleep." Mr. Yunioshi shouted. "But always you are ringing my bell. ..."
>
> "Oh, *don't* be angry, you *dear* little man: I won't do it again. And if you promise not to be angry"—her voice was coming nearer, she was climbing the stairs—"I might let you take those pictures we mentioned."

Though the phrase "silly-young and self-amused" tells us about Holly's tone, her words speak for themselves. If she is sorry, as she claims, then why does she refer to it as the "goddamn key"? Clearly, in her worldview, the key is at fault, not she. She calls her neighbor *darling* and *dear* to soften him up, and then promises him a few lines later that if he lets her off the hook she will in turn let him "take those pictures we mentioned."

We suspect that Holly is used to manipulating with her charm and beauty to get her way. Just a few paragraphs into the scene, Holly Golightly makes an impression and demonstrates her personality.

When you use dialogue to reveal character, the dialogue should be stylized and suited specifically to the character. An educated person speaks differently from someone who has never learned grammar. A rude person will say rude things and insult people with her words.

Revealing Plot Information

One of the most important uses of dialogue—and the most necessary in a plot-driven narrative—is to reveal pertinent information that moves the plot forward, changes your protagonist, creates conflict, or leads the protagonist toward an epiphany. I like to think of this as the "Luke, I am your father" technique. The moment at which Darth Vader tells Luke he is not only his sworn nemesis, but also his father, is a huge turning point in the movie's plot and in the development of Luke's character. It forces Luke to choose between good and evil, and tests his ability to resist his own destruction. Now, not all reveals are this epic, but dialogue is one of the best ways to drop these emotional bombs and drive the plot forward.

When using dialogue to reveal plot information, consider the following:

- The information must be earned. Avoid *deus ex machina* techniques. (This term comes from the Greek and referred originally to when a god dropped into a play to solve difficult entanglements. In fiction it refers to any overly simple or convenient technique or device that solves difficult problems without any actual effort on the part of the characters.)
- You need to show your protagonist's emotional reaction to the new information. The reader needs to see the character exclaim, gasp, shout, speak a word of surprise.
- You must place the information drop in the middle of the scene or at the end to achieve the greatest emotional impact. This helps to create a sense of urgency in the reader.

Here's an example of a big revelation from Maryanne Stahl's novel *Forgive the Moon* that both reveals character and drives the plot forward. Amanda Kincaid comes to a Long Island beach resort for an annual family vacation. Her oldest daughter has left for college; her husband is involved with another woman, and their twenty-year marriage is crumbling; and her mother, who suffered from schizophrenia, has recently died in an accident. The scene opens with Amanda's new lover coming to the door while her father is visiting her cottage. Her father doesn't know who the man is, but from the opening of the scene there's discord, a feeling that something is going to come to a head. And it does, but not in one fell swoop—the scene builds slowly and plausibly toward the revelation.

In the exchange of dialogue below, which falls in the middle of the scene, Amanda and her father—who have never been close— begin talking about mundane details, like Amanda's childhood fear of lightning, and segue to more serious topics of the past, such as her mother's illness, then Amanda's accusation that her father retreated not only from his ill wife, but his children. At first her father is shocked, but then he asks her a question that begins the process of his revelation about her piano teacher:

"Were you angry, Amanda, about my relationship with Gloria?"

"What?" Gloria Price had taught me to play the piano, redirecting my adolescent pain and fueling the fire of my nascent passion for music. Eventually, she'd moved away, but not before she'd made me promise to pursue my talent.

Gloria's voice was the first auditory hallucination my mother had ever described to me.

"Gloria," I repeated.

Suddenly, as though I'd been physically struck, I realized what my father was saying. "What do you mean?"

His fingers rubbed the bridge of his nose beneath his glasses, lifting them till I thought they would fall off, but they stayed. He dropped his hands to his lap.

"Gloria and I," he said softly.

My stomach quivered, as though the low, rolling thunder outside had slipped in through the screen and become particles of air. My mouth grew watery, a sign I was going to vomit. I moved to lean toward the sink and as I did, sugar spilled out of the torn packet, pouring across one of my father's shoes. ...

"Amanda," he began, reaching his hand around to my forehead. I slipped away from him.

"It's the tea," I said without looking at him. "The acid."

My father retreated toward the table and sat back in his chair. He began again. "Your mother and I never discussed Gloria," he said, picking up his spoon and dropping it into his empty mug. "Not in any rational way."

I recalled my mother's accusations. Gloria was her enemy, trying to harm her, trying to steal her children: all said to be hallucinations, all dismissed as evidence of illness. Now it turned out my mother had been right after all. She'd been right and she'd been ill, both at the same time.

No one had believed her.

The revelation of her father's affair is doubly devastating as Amanda realizes that, due to her mother's illness, they thought she was just being paranoid. There are a number of elements in this revelation scene that any writer can learn from. First, Stahl starts the scene with her protagonist caught in an unbalanced situation: Amanda is reluctantly spending time with her father, when her lover comes to the door. She uses subtext to create foreshadowing: The lover's appearance points toward the other affair—her father's—that the scene reveals. Then, she uses segues, small transitions between related topics, to create a sense of conversation and a realistically measured pace. The conversation feels natural, like how people really talk. She uses her setting very well too: Two family members jammed into a small space creates a sense of tension, of something waiting to explode. And then there is the weather. In the opening pages of the scene, Amanda's lover says to her, "Feels like a storm," and the author continues to pepper in details about the weather. (Of course, the real storm coming is an emotional one.) Then there's the element of opposition: Amanda has a feeling that her father wants to talk, but she doesn't want to, so she tries a few unsuccessful strategies to urge her father to go to bed so they won't have to, building a tense atmosphere. And then—yes, there's more—the author shows how this information affects the protagonist: Not only does Amanda become physically ill, she curses at her father and then walks down the hallway, where she kicks his shoe in anger.

Revelations are best when they are complex and slowly built toward—so that they are not just two people standing in a room shouting words at each other. Use as many of the core scene elements as you can. Once the revelation comes, it should alter your protagonist in some way; whether her plot changes, or just her feelings, revelations should lead to some kind of shift.

INFUSING YOUR DIALOGUE SCENES WITH TENSION AND SUBTEXT

Now that we've looked at how to use a dialogue scene to reveal important character and plot information, let's look at how to build tension through opposition in an exchange and how to use subtext to keep even your most heated exchanges from turning into meaningless shouting matches. No matter what you want to reveal through your dialogue, infusing it with additional elements ensures a richer, more layered scene.

Creating Tension Through Tug-of-War Exchanges

In a strong fiction narrative, characters should want things from each other—information, affection, favors, material goods, and so on. The act of wanting powers both conflict and drama. When there's something desired, there is the potential for loss and gain—the essence of good drama. Dialogue should be, on some level, an act of bartering in order to keep tension alive during the course of the dialogue. I call this technique tug-of-war. To use this approach in dialogue, it works best to think of each character as both asking for something and withholding something at the same time. Use dialogue tug-of-war when you need to demonstrate differing points of view or illustrate the dynamics of a relationship. This approach also works when your characters are:

- exchanging insults or arguing over something
- trying to manipulate another character
- trying to seduce another character, or resist seduction themselves
- attempting to convince another character of a painful truth
- fending off untrue or unjust accusations

Here's an example from Alice Hoffman's novel *The Ice Queen*, in which the unnamed narrator is weighing whether or not to tell her brother Ned a shocking secret she has turned up about his wife. What the conversation reveals is that Ned has a secret too, but in order to learn each other's secrets, they would have to give up their own first, and neither character is willing to do that yet:

> "So are you sure you don't want to know any secrets?"
> "Do you?"
> "You have secrets?" I was surprised. ...
> "Unknown truths," my brother joked. "At least to you. Known to me, of course. At least in theory. What I know and what I don't know, I'm not sure I can be the judge of that."
> "Oh forget it." I was annoyed.

The tug-of-war style of conversation delays the reader's access to Ned's secret (a piece of plot information, incidentally), thus building tension. Then the tension mounts even more when the narrator keeps *her* secret a little longer. The scene shows the reader that both characters have an investment in keeping secrets, but the reader has to keep going to find out how these secrets will converge, and what effect they'll have when brought to light.

Here's another tug-of-war example, from J.M. Coetzee's Nobel Prize–winning novel, *Disgrace*. In apartheid-fueled South Africa, white professor David Lurie has come to stay with his slightly estranged daughter Lucy to flee scrutiny after a scandal involving an affair with one of his college students. In trying to escape one terrible event, he becomes a part of another, when his daughter and he are attacked by black men in her home as a territorial act. David is badly burned, and Lucy is ostensibly raped—but David doesn't know for sure, since he was not in the room with her and she won't tell him what happened. However, he quickly urges Lucy to press charges against the boy. Lucy has her own political and personal reasons for not wanting to do so. And there is the other, unspoken subtext, that if not for his own bad deeds, he wouldn't even have been there for her at all. Notice the feeling of tug-of-war between them—how they both want something and are resisting something at the same time:

> Sitting across the table from him, Lucy draws a deep breath, gathers herself, then breathes out again and shakes her head.
>
> "Can I guess?" he says. "Are you trying to remind me of something?"
>
> "Am I trying to remind you of what?"
>
> "Of what women undergo at the hands of men?"
>
> "Nothing could be farther from my thoughts. This has nothing to do with you, David. You want to know why I have not laid a particular charge with the police? I will tell you, as long as you agree not to raise the subject again. The reason is that, as far as I am concerned, what happened to me is a purely private matter. In another time, in another place it might be held to a public matter. But in this place, at this time, it is not. It is my business, mine alone."
>
> "This place being what?"
>
> "This place being South Africa."

"I don't agree. I don't agree with what you are doing. Do you think that by meekly accepting what happened to you, you can set yourself apart from farmers like Ettinger? Do you think what happened here was an exam: if you come through, you get a diploma and safe conduct into the future, or a sign to paint on the door lintel that will make the plague pass you by? That is not how vengeance works, Lucy. Vengeance is like a fire. The more it devours, the hungrier it gets."

"Stop it, David! I don't want to hear this talk of plagues and fires. I am not just trying to save my skin. If that is what you think, you miss the point entirely."

Notice in both of the previous examples, there's a sense of movement, of action, even though the authors don't provide the reader with any actual physical movements. This has to do with the pace of conversations—the tug-of-war approach gives the exchanges a quality of movement by infusing them with emotional energy. The respective conversations bounce back and forth between characters, and carry with them a sense of change.

Playing Up Subtext

While the tug-of-war technique is excellent for increasing the tension in a dialogue scene, you don't want your exchanges to become a meaningless volley of words. The key to keeping that from happening? Subtext. People don't always say what they really mean; they withhold information and feelings, use language to manipulate and barter and hint at things. Because of this, you have a lot of opportunity to play with your subtext.

Here's an example of a powerful subtext at work in a conversation from David Guterson's novel *Snow Falling on Cedars*. Ishmael Chambers grew up on San Piedro Island, Washington, and as a young teenager had a brief love affair with a Japanese girl named Hatsue. Their relationship was cut short, however, when Hatsue and her family and many more Japanese residents of the island were moved to the internment camp Manzanar after the attack on Pearl Harbor.

Now, years later, Ishmael is back in town to write about a trial in which Hatsue's husband is accused of murdering a local fisherman.

Hatsue and Ishmael have not spoken in all these years, and there is lingering resentment and desire between them. In this instance, the subtext comes from their history, which is shown in flashback scenes throughout the book. That history informs every scene in the present moment:

> "It's all unfair," she told him bitterly. "Kabuo didn't kill anyone. It isn't in his heart to kill anyone. They brought in that sergeant to say he's a killer—that was just prejudice. Did you hear the things that man was saying? How Kabuo had it in his heart to kill? How horrible he is, a killer? Put it in your paper, about that man's testimony, how all of it was unfair. How the whole trial is unfair."
>
> "I understand what you mean," answered Ishmael. "But I'm not a legal expert. I don't know if the judge should have suppressed Sergeant Maples' testimony. But I hope the jury comes in with the right verdict. I could write a column about that, maybe. How we all hope the justice system does its job. How we hope for an honest result."
>
> "There shouldn't even be a trial," said Hatsue. "The whole thing is wrong, it's wrong."
>
> "I'm bothered, too, when things are unfair," Ishmael said to her. "But sometimes I wonder if unfairness isn't ... part of things. I wonder if we should even expect fairness, if we should assume we have some sort of right to it. Or if—"
>
> "I'm not talking about the whole universe," cut in Hatsue. "I'm talking about people—the sheriff, that prosecutor, that judge, you. People who can do things because they run newspapers or arrest people or convict them or decide about their lives."

There is no way to talk about unfairness without conjuring the fact that Ishmael—who is white—has had a much easier life than Hatsue, who was punished merely for being Japanese. Yet Ishmael suffered too, because he lost her love, and so both characters feel that they have been unfairly treated. This subtext makes their dialogue that much more charged and interesting than it would otherwise be.

When trying to play up subtext in your dialogue scene, you can draw upon historical events as in the example we just saw, or you might try one of these techniques:

- Use body language to say what isn't being spoken in words.

- Use setting details and objects to elicit references to past events.
- Zoom in on symbolic or suggestive objects in the setting.
- Let the conversation dance around an unspoken topic.

To the last point, let's look at an example from Ernest Hemingway's story "Hills Like White Elephants." The story takes place in a bar and features two characters who don't ever leave their seats. Through the course of the conversation, the reader develops a slow, painful realization of what the couple is discussing. Without the dialogue, the story has almost no action.

Hemingway opens with a quick brush of setting describing the hills of the valley, as well as the American and the girl sitting at the bar. Then, within a few more lines, the dialogue begins. Notice how the conversation feels like action because it moves quickly back and forth between these two characters:

> "And if I do it you'll be happy and things will be like they were and you'll love me?"
> "I love you now. You know I love you."
> "I know. But if I do it, then it will be nice again if I say things are like white elephants, and you'll like it?"
> "I'll love it. I love it now but I just can't think about it. You know how I get when I worry."
> "If I do it you won't ever worry?"
> "I won't worry about that because it's perfectly simple."

Even though 99 percent of this story is dialogue, the subtext-laden nature of this tug-of-war exchange creates a sense of movement, of action throughout, allowing the reader to feel as though he is experiencing the events of a narrative himself, while the swiftness of the exchanges allows for emotional distance from the heavy topic of abortion. And even though the characters aren't engaged in a loud argument, even though there is no hot emotional intensity, the tension is palpable. There's real energy here as the reader sees the dynamics of the couple through their strained dance around a topic neither wishes to say outright.

ENDING A DIALOGUE SCENE

A strong dialogue scene includes information that either deepens the reader's understanding of the characters or explains a plot element (thus the big reveals we talked about earlier). In one way or another, dialogue scenes should offer characters a chance to reveal things. These revelations must be well timed. If you give away too much information at the beginning of the scene—say one character tells her married boyfriend that she's pregnant—in the rest of the scene you will use the dialogue to work out their feelings, motivations, fears, and reactions to that information.

But a particularly effective technique is to drop a revelation toward the end of the chapter. This will either force the reader to keep going on to the next chapter, or it will leave the reader with a powerful experience to mull over.

Here's an example of a revelation that comes at the end of a dialogue scene from Richard Russo's novel *Empire Falls*. In this exchange between protagonist Miles and his curmudgeonly screw-up of a father, Max, a piece of information is revealed that tells the reader a lot about the characters and affects the plot.

Miles has never understood why his father never protested his mother's affair with one of the town's wealthy founders, Charlie Whiting—whose family Miles is still in service to as a result. Max has gone missing, disappearing from town with a mentally addled priest and some church funds, and he calls his son on the phone from Florida to let him know he's okay. Max and Miles quickly get into one of their customary arguments, but this time, the argument comes with a revelation:

> Why shouldn't he have a little fun? was what Max wanted to know, since they were asking questions. "Old men like to have fun too, you know. Down here, people like old men."
> "Why?"
> "They don't say," Max admitted. "Tom hears confessions every afternoon at the end of the bar. You should see it."
> "That's terrible, Dad."

"Why? Think about it."

"It's sacrilegious."

"Your mother really messed you up, you know that?"

And that was all it took, just the one mention of Grace, and suddenly the question was out before Miles could consider the wisdom of asking it. "How come you never told me about Mom and Charlie Whiting, Dad?"

Max reacted as if he'd been expecting the question for years. "How come you never told *me*, son?"

The spoken revelation here is that not only did Max know about his wife's affair, he knew that Miles also knew. The implications, however, are far greater than a simple revelation of information. Miles has always blamed his father and held a grudge against him for being gone more than he was around. Yet here the reader learns that Miles took his mother's side against his father all those years ago, even knowing his mother was cheating. This exchange helps Miles realize that he has blamed the wrong parent, in essence, thus consigning himself to his fate: running the Empire Grill under the iron fist of Mrs. Whiting.

By letting this come at the end of the scene, not only does Russo catch the reader off-guard, he creates a powerful resting place. The next scene picks up in another character's point of view (the novel is co-narrated by multiple protagonists), so the reader is left mulling over how this information is going to sink in for Miles, and if it will help him to change his behavior and stop the cycle of guilt his mother started, binding her family to the Whiting family.

Some dialogue scenes will end just like that, on a *kerplunk*, with the final spoken word in the scene. If the revelation came earlier, however, such as at the beginning or middle of the scene, then the ending should reflect whatever took place in the scene: The revelation should have a visible, dramatic impact on the character.

In the scene from *Disgrace*, the tug-of-war conversation reveals that Lucy, despite being raped, doesn't see herself as a victim; and yet David—who *elected* to have an affair with his student—*does* see himself as a victim. Coetzee ends the scene with one reflective line of David's thoughts:

Never yet have they been so far and so bitterly apart. He is shaken.

This is a good, destabilized place to leave David in. Since David hasn't been terribly shaken by anything he's done yet, this signals to the reader that he may be able to change after all.

When it comes time to end a dialogue scene, you'll want to leave your protagonist in one of the following places:

- on the final words of a spoken revelation
- emotionally, mentally, or spiritually destabilized in some way
- taking an action based on what was revealed
- caught in a reflective space to muse on what came in the scene

Remember that dialogue should never be used to discuss mundane or quotidian topics, but always to reveal new information about plot and character. Dialogue can be stylized to match the personality of a character, and should sound realistic.

Finally, be careful with too many back-to-back dialogue scenes. Remember that dialogue feels like action to the reader, so you can break up action by following a dialogue-heavy scene with a suspenseful scene, a contemplative scene, or an epiphany scene. Even within a single scene, a lot of dialogue can start to feel rushed after a while, and should be grounded with physical gestures, setting details, or other brief snippets of exposition.

JORDAN E. ROSENFELD is the author of eight books, most recently *Writing Deep Scenes* and the forthcoming *Writing the Intimate Character* (Writer's Digest Books). Her work has been published in *The Atlantic*, *GOOD* magazine, *mental_floss*, *The New York Times*, *Pacific Standard*, *Publishers Weekly*, *Salon*, *The San Francisco Chronicle*, *The Washington Post*, *Writer's Digest* magazine, *The Writer*, and many more.

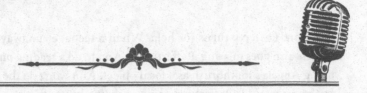

CHAPTER 23

TIGHTEN YOUR SCENES
WITH DIALOGUE

BY DONALD MAASS

A common downfall of many scenes is dialogue. The characters talk, talk, talk, but scenes spin in circles and don't travel much of anywhere. Plenty of dialogue in manuscripts also is hard to follow. Choked with incidental action, broken into fragments, and strewn over the length of a page, it can take almost archaeological skill to piece together an exchange.

Dialogue not only needs to do its own work, it also can bring clarity to middle scenes that would otherwise be muddy and inactive. Dialogue is strong (or can be). The process of stripping it down and finding the tension in it can be revealing. It can help define the purpose of a scene.

Brunonia Barry's best-selling debut novel, *The Lace Reader*, spins a story of the present-day denizens of Salem, Massachusetts, in particular the eccentric clan of Whitney women, who have the ability to "read" people by holding pieces of lace in front of their faces. The novel initially is narrated by Towner Whitney, another in the army of unreliable narrators who crowd the pages of contemporary fiction. Towner is called home to Salem when her mother, Eva, an often-arrested rescuer of battered and abused women, goes missing and later is found dead.

Deeper in, *The Lace Reader* switches to other points of view, principally John Rafferty, another in contemporary fiction's army of wounded big city cops who've retreated to small towns. It falls to Rafferty to investigate Eva's death, and thereby dig up Salem's dirt. Salem has a bona fide witch in Ann Chase, a contemporary of Towner's, to whom Rafferty turns for help. When a teenage runaway named Angela also goes missing, Rafferty asks Ann to do a reading on Angela using Angela's toothbrush as a focal object. Ann won't do the reading but offers to guide Rafferty in doing a reading himself.

Now, how would you handle this middle scene? Would you portray Rafferty's first eerie experience of seeing with second sight? Would you work from Ann's knowing point of view? Barry does neither. She portrays the reading and its aftermath in dialogue:

> "When you're ready, open your eyes."
>
> He opened them.
>
> He felt embarrassed, and completely inept. He'd totally failed.
>
> "Describe what you saw," Ann said.
>
> Rafferty didn't speak.
>
> "Go ahead," she said. "You can't make a mistake."
>
> "Well, first of all, I didn't go up, I went down."
>
> "All right, maybe *you* can make a mistake."
>
> "It was a ranch house," he said, trying to explain. He expected her to end the exercise right there. Or tell him to stop wasting her time. Instead she took a breath and continued.
>
> "What did you see when you went down the stairs?"
>
> "I didn't see anything," he said. "Nothing at all."
>
> "What did this nothing at all look like?"
>
> "What kind of question is that?"
>
> "Humor me," she said.
>
> "It was black. No, not black, but blank. Yeah. Dark and blank," Rafferty said.
>
> "What did you hear?"
>
> "What do you mean, what did I hear?"
>
> "Where there any sounds? Or smells?"
>
> "No. ... No sounds. No smells."
>
> He could feel her eyes on him.
>
> "I didn't see anything. I didn't hear anything. I kept trying to go back up the stairs. I failed Psychic 101," Rafferty said.
>
> "Maybe," Ann said. "Maybe not."
>
> "What's that supposed to mean?"
>
> "I went into the room with you," Ann said. "At least I thought I did."
>
> "And what did you see?"
>
> "Nothing. It was too dark."
>
> "I told you," Rafferty said.

"I heard something, though ... a word."

"What word?"

"Underground."

"Underground as in hiding? Or underground as in dead?"

Ann didn't answer. She had no idea.

Notice that Barry keeps her dialogue short. The exchange is not rat-a-tat, but even so it's quick. There's tension between Rafferty and Ann, however rudimentary it may be. Consider, too, what this snippet of the novel has to accomplish: It has to show that Ann is a true parasensitive, while Rafferty is not, and reveal a morsel of information about the missing Angela.

Dialogue lets Barry accomplish all that with immediacy and tension. We also do not have to believe in second sight. Barry doesn't force us to accept whether it's real or not. By remaining objective, with dialogue, she leaves the choice to us, which in a way preserves the mystery of it. More to the point, a sloggy and potentially off-putting middle scene has become taut and dramatic. Wouldn't you like all of your middle scenes to have that effect?

We can pretty much count on thriller writer Harlan Coben for crackling dialogue. Coben never wastes words and is particularly good at speeding his middles along with tension-filled talk. In *The Woods*, he spins another of his patented stories in which a past secret haunts his protagonist and someone who was presumed dead returns to stir things up.

Paul "Cope" Copeland is a county prosecutor in New Jersey. His past is clouded by a summer camp tragedy in which he and a girlfriend snuck into the woods along with four others, including Paul's sister. While Paul and his girlfriend were fooling around, the four others were slashed to death. Two bodies were found; the two others (including Paul's sister) were not. Guess what happens? Yup, the dead return. Or do they? And why is suspicion now directed at Paul?

Meanwhile, Paul is prosecuting a college frat house rape case. Thrillers (hopefully all fiction) are built on the axiom *make it worse for the protagonist*. This, Coben does. One obstacle he throws in Cope's way is EJ Jenrette, the father of one of the frat boys. He's rich. His friends support a cancer charity that Cope established in memory of his dead wife. Jenrette convinces these friends to back out of their commitments. There are a number of ways in which Coben could have handled this stakes-building step in his story, but he chooses a late-night phone call from Cope's brother-in-law, Bob, who runs the charity:

"What's the matter?" I asked.

"Your rape case is costing us big-time. Edward Jenrette's father has gotten several of his friends to back out of their commitments."

I closed my eyes. "Classy."

"Worse, he's making noises that we've embezzled funds. EJ Jenrette is a well-connected son of a bitch. I'm already getting calls."

"So we open our books," I said. "They won't find anything."

"Don't be naive, Cope. We compete with other charities for the giving dollar. If there is even a whiff of a scandal, we're finished."

"Not much we can do about it, Bob."

"I know. It's just that ... we're doing a lot of good here, Cope."

"I know."

"But funding is always tough."

"So what are you suggesting?"

"Nothing." Bob hesitated and I could tell he had more to say. So I waited. "But come on, Cope, you guys plea-bargain all the time, right?"

"We do."

"You let a lesser injustice slide so you can nail someone for a bigger one."

"When we have to."

"These two boys. I hear they're good kids."

"You hear wrong."

"Look, I'm not saying that they don't deserve to be punished, but sometimes you have to trade. The greater good. JaneCare is making big strides. It might be the greater good. That's all I'm saying."

"Good night, Bob."

"No offense, Cope. I'm just trying to help."

"I know. Good night, Bob."

Dialogue allows Coben to introduce this obstacle with brisk efficiency. In less than a page, and with plenty of tension, he raises Cope's stakes. The passage is easy to read. Bing, bam, boom, it makes its point. No slogging here.

Crafting Dynamic Dialogue

How many of your dragging middle scenes could be tightened and torqued up with dialogue? How tight is your dialogue generally? Is it lean and mean or is it choked up with incidental action and lengthy attributives? Strip it down. Pump it up. Taut dialogue is one of the secrets of making sure that middle scenes are not candidates for cutting.

....

DONALD MAASS heads the Donald Maass Literary Agency in New York City, which represents more than 150 novelists and sells more than 150 novels every year to publishers in America and overseas. He is a past president of the Association of Authors' Representatives, Inc., and is the author of several Writer's Digest books, including *Writing the Breakout Novel, The Fire in Fiction, The Breakout Novelist,* and *Writing 21st Century Fiction.*

CHAPTER 24

UNDERSTANDING INTERNAL DIALOGUE

BY ELIZABETH SIMS

Not long ago, one of my elderly neighbors lost several thousand dollars to a con artist. A stranger phoned with a convincing sob story that ended in a plea for money. My neighbor actually filled a paper lunch sack with twenty-dollar bills, drove to a nearby grocery store, stashed the bag behind a vegetable bin as directed, and left. Even when a friend explained that it was a trick, my neighbor was serene, believing he had done a service for someone in need.

The best con artists don't begin by asking for your confidence—they give you theirs first. *Here's my story. I want you, you especially, to hear this.* The request for help comes later. There's the short con—one quick deception and out—and the long con, which takes time and patience to execute. But before either compassion or greed can be exploited, the mark must feel something for the con artist.

When you think about it, what is fiction but one beautiful long con? The reader—the mark—opens a book craving a good story, thirsting to be part of something special. We, as writers, do everything possible to gain the trust of our readers so we can entertain, shock, delight, and amuse them all the way to the end. And the greatest tool for gaining reader confidence is internal dialogue.

Because when a character reveals his thoughts, he's confiding in the audience. *I'm counting on you to understand me—and possibly even help me understand myself.* Suddenly readers are in the thick of it; they feel involved and invested. They have some skin in the game.

What exactly is internal dialogue? Simply, it's the inner voice of a character. Which is, frankly, a very metaphysical subject. In most modern cultures—and, consequently, most modern literature—there's a dichotomy within the self: there's an *I* and a *Me*.

> I like my eyebrows.

> I have to be strict with myself when it comes to pecan pie.

Internal dialogue is the manifestation of this in fiction. And because it presents the most intimate thoughts and realities of your characters, it is beyond elemental: Internal dialogue is the marrow of your story.

Some writing experts argue that internal dialogue should rightly be called *internal monologue*. That's a fine term. However, I note that the Greek prefix is not *di-*, meaning two, but *dia*, meaning across. Add the stem *legein*, meaning words, and you have crossing streams of words. Given that a character might have conflicting inner voices, internal dialogue is a perfectly correct term.

For inexperienced writers, internal dialogue can be confusing, because a character's inner voice can take endless forms. How does one properly represent it? The truth is, there are really very few rules for using internal dialogue. That's freeing. All you need is a basic understanding of the subject, and some reference points.

Let's first take a moment to consider the most famous piece of introspection in literature, Hamlet's fourth soliloquy: "To be or not to be, that is the question ..." The speech serves to tell us why Hamlet is reluctant to avenge his father's murder, and it shows his frustration with a fate he didn't choose: If his father is to be avenged, he's the one who's got to do it. And if he fights, he might die, and even though this life is kind of lousy, death could certainly be worse. So he has to think it over, and, since he's only human, he has to come down in judgment on himself. It is the definitive example of the "on one hand ... but then on the other ..." dilemma. Bits of this profound passage have been quoted, referenced, and adopted as titles in countless other works: *the slings and arrows of outrageous fortune / to sleep, perchance to dream / this mortal coil / the undiscovered country /* and more.

A key element of this passage's success is its economy. In Shakespeare's time, a character's innermost thoughts were commonly revealed by direct speech without corresponding action. It's convenient and quick. The technique is still used in theater today, when a character might deliver a wisecrack or lament as an aside to the audience. In musicals and opera, we sometimes get a whole aria that acts as a soliloquy—a window into the character's heart and mind, just for the audience.

As a writer of fiction, short or long, you can use internal dialogue to even better effect, because you and the reader have a completely private relationship. Instead of calling attention to artifice, internal dialogue smoothes the boundaries between author and reader by letting us inside the characters' heads silently and seamlessly. With internal dialogue, you can:

- Establish your characters and their unique voices.
- Show the difference between what a character thinks versus what she says or does. This can fuel both tragedy and comedy.
- Trace a character's growth and development, or the opposite: a character's degeneration. Change is the name of the game.
- Develop your plot. A shift can become clear in a word or two.
- Reveal things below the surface: pain, secrets, hopes, fears …
- Create and develop suspense. Especially when the reader knows more than the character, the reader can be worried about some impending event or consequence.
- Change the subject. No matter what's going on, a character's thoughts can suddenly drive your story in a new direction.
- Reveal a character's opinions. This one's always fun.
- Describe. A character can look around and comment on his surroundings; he can observe and analyze.
- Develop and reveal character motivation. *Why* are they doing what they're doing?
- Render reflection. Let your character think through a problem or process an event to whatever degree she's capable of. A character

can be a tad less smart than the reader, thus permitting the reader to feel on top of things. Reflection can also be used to:

- Adjust the pace. After a spate of action, let your character(s) pause and reflect. This can even happen while things in your story literally are still in motion—say in a speeding subway train. But even so, it will slow things down and let the reader absorb what just happened.

FORM AND FORMAT

Internal dialogue typically takes three basic forms: first-person narration, third-person narration, and direct thought-speech. The latter is my term for thoughts expressed as if directly spoken to the reader, usually without attributors like "I thought." Can narration be internal dialogue? The boundaries are squishy at best, as you will see, so don't worry about it.

Then there's the issue of tense. Skim through today's best-seller lists, and you'll find the majority of internal dialogue written in present tense, no matter whether the rest of the work is in past. This technique works well, but isn't the only choice.

As for format, the only rule is to avoid quotation marks, single or double, as they're associated with spoken-aloud dialogue and can confuse the reader. It used to be the convention to put inner thoughts in italics. I've done so in my fiction. Now the trend seems to be to keep everything in roman text, the idea being that italics are intrusive and unnecessary.

For both form and format, you can select something that feels right for you and your manuscript's style and voice. Read closely to distinguish the differences in the six versions of this passage:

> Saturday night came, and still Sheila didn't call. Marco sat at the window, drumming his fingers on the gritty sill. He felt like robbing a liquor store. Would a knife be sufficient? He didn't know. [Entire passage, including inner voice, is third person, past tense.]
>
> Saturday night came, and still Sheila didn't call. Marco sat at the window, drumming his fingers on the gritty sill. I should hold up that liquor store

tonight, I really should. Be something to do, anyway. I have my knife. [Narrative is third person, past tense; inner voice is first person, present. And the inner voice is rendered in direct thought-speech.]

Saturday night came, and still Sheila didn't call. Marco sat at the window, drumming his fingers on the gritty sill. *I should hold up that liquor store tonight, I really should. Be something to do, anyway. I have my knife.* [The identical passage as above, with Marco's thoughts in italics.]

Saturday night came, and still Sheila didn't call. I sat at the window, drumming my fingers on the gritty sill. I should hold up that liquor store tonight, I really should. Be something to do, anyway. I have my knife. [Narrative is first person, past tense. The inner voice, in direct thought-speech, is first person, present.]

Saturday night came, and still Sheila didn't call. Marco sat at the window, drumming his fingers on the gritty sill. I should hold up that liquor store tonight, I really should, he thought. Be something to do, anyway. He had his knife. [Narrative is third person, past tense. The inner voice is first person, past (though verging on present), and the narrative resumes in third person, past, in the final sentence.]

Saturday night comes, and still Sheila doesn't call. I sit at the window, drumming my fingers on the gritty sill. I should rob that liquor store tonight, I really should. Be something to do, anyway. I have my knife. [Everything is first person, present.]

Any of these forms are correct, and they all have slightly different flavors—some seem more formal, some less. First person always reads as more informal and immediate. Just be as consistent as you can, once you've made your choice.

ACHIEVING MULTIPLE EFFECTS

Now let's look at how authors use internal dialogue to achieve various effects.

If you want people to like you you have only to spend a little money. I spent a little money and the waiter liked me. He appreciated my valuable qualities. He would be glad to see me back. I would dine there again some time and he would be glad to see me, and would want me at his table. It would be a sincere liking because it would have a sound basis. I was back in France.

—Ernest Hemingway, *The Sun Also Rises*

This passage gives us the protagonist Jake's flat, ironic inner voice. He narrates a fact—he tipped the waiter well—and then meditates cynically on friendship. Jake has just left his friends after an eventful, unsettling few days at a fiesta in Spain. Now we're invited to conclude that his friends weren't true friends. Jake's ruminative time in France also slackens the pace of the story, which had been driving pretty hard up to now.

> The encounter, though, had bruised her. Gavin was the first person, she thought, that I was ever really frank and honest with; at home, there wasn't much premium on frankness, and she'd never had a girlfriend she was really close to, not since she was fifteen.
>
> —Hilary Mantel, *Beyond Black*

Mantel plays with internal dialogue free and easy here, switching from third person to first and back again. The reflective passage gives us a sense of the character Colette's loneliness and inner pain. We also get the hint that Colette is somewhat limited, not resourceful, not very strong, and thus motivated to subsume herself by becoming an assistant to a more prominent—and dominant—person.

> "... Where do you think you'll be for Tet?"
>
> I thought, *Probably in jail.* I said, "I'm not sure about my itinerary."
>
> —Nelson DeMille, *Up Country*

This bit of inner speech establishes the character, Paul's, biting wit and devil-may-care attitude. With extreme economy, DeMille also clues us in that Paul, a Vietnam vet posing as a returning visitor, intends to do something dangerous, foolish, or both.

> ... On my way into the Chinese cleaners I brush past a crying bum, an old man, forty or fifty, fat and grizzled, and just as I'm opening the door I notice, to top it off, that he's also *blind* and I step on his foot, which is actually a stump, causing him to drop his cup, scattering change all over the sidewalk. Did I do this on purpose? What do you think? Or did I do this accidentally?
>
> —Brett Easton Ellis, *American Psycho*

The main character, the psychopathic Patrick, is presented here in all his shockingly casual cruelty. We see that he is contemptuous and self-ish. We get his sarcastic inner voice in the direct question to the reader—*What do you think?* Patrick's personal style is brusque and immediate, and we don't need a crystal ball to perceive that this morsel of brutality is but a taste of what's to come. The reader lives in suspense to the end.

> Also she loved her house. Across the creek was the Russian church. So ethnic! That onion dome had loomed in her window since her Pooh footie days. Also loved Gladsong Drive. Every house on Gladsong was a Corona del Mar. That was amazing! If you had a friend on Gladsong, you already knew where everything was in his or her home.
>   *Jeté, jeté, rond de jambe.*
>
> —George Saunders, "Victory Lap"

This young girl's stream of consciousness as she bops around the house, alone, is rich in information. We see Alison's exuberant spirit as she describes her environment and executes ballet moves; we understand that she lives in a bland subdivision; with the mention of the creek we literally get the lay of the land; we're aware of an unusual neighboring structure. In this short story, Saunders portrays Alison's voice with precision, and as we ingest her unspoiled happiness, we also know that we're reading a story—and in stories, things happen and things change. This inherent suspense suffuses all of Saunders's tales.

> Me: I'm so freaked out and pissed at Coco Nash I could spit.
> Me: Easy now.
> Me: I have to confront her.
> Me: Why? When?
> Me: Now, goddamn it, today! What can I gain by waiting? I've got evi-dence, solid empirical evidence that she means harm to the greatest crea-ture ever to tread ground. That's *why*, for Christ's sake. I almost caught her twice. Three times.
> Me: Wait. I really think Genie should know. Let her decide what to do.
> Me: What, are you crazy?
>
> —Elizabeth Sims, *Damn Straight*

I like to play with fiction forms and norms, and it's funny to portray a character's on-one-hand-then-the-other thoughts with the bluntness of a TV script. This excerpt provides a dash of comic relief, as well as reflection, inner conflict, and exposure of information.

SKILL BUILDER

A good way to develop your feel for internal dialogue is to get in touch with your *own* internal dialogue—the stream of consciousness that flows through your head, sometimes annoyingly, sometimes quietly and productively.

Take fifteen minutes and simply write what you're thinking. If you stall out, remember some recent problem or bit of family drama, and write your internal dialogue on that.

Strive to render your thoughts as realistically as you speak.

Write it. How did it feel? Read it over. What's it like? What do you see?

When you turn to your fictional characters, remember what it felt like to write "out of your head."

BUILDING TRUST

As you can see, internal dialogue is a terrific tool for building immediacy and authenticity into your fiction at the deepest levels. The fact is, readers love to be seduced. And the gorgeous con game of fiction is really a form of seduction, isn't it? Readers fall in love when they completely trust your characters. And you gain that trust when your characters behave as if *they* completely trust the *reader!*

Authentic characters, like excited new lovers, reveal and reveal and reveal themselves, all the while going about their business of living the story you're writing. Good internal dialogue takes your readers deeper than intellect, deeper even than blood and guts: If you do a good job, readers will sense the living marrow of your story. They will become enmeshed in your characters and action, and they will be open to the truth you want to tell, which is the reason we all turn to fiction for enjoyment, beauty, and inspiration.

PITFALLS TO AVOID

- Making a character's inner voice into a sarcastic wisecracker who won't shut up. Such a voice can be entertaining, but only if used sparingly. When your beta readers start to groan because they know exactly what the inner wiseass is going to say, that's when to dial it back.
- Head hopping. Reserve internal dialogue for very few characters. Many writers successfully do internal dialogue for just one character—their protagonist.
- "... I thought to myself." As a writing coach, I'm on the alert for this construction, which screams rank amateur. Who but oneself does one think to?
- Telling huge hunks of backstory via having a character "think about" or "remember" it.
- Putting in anything that doesn't serve the story. If it's important that your protagonist dithers over whether to buy the store brand bleach, fine, but if it's not relevant, just let him buy bleach and get on with it.

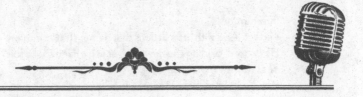

CHAPTER 25
CONFLICT IN DIALOGUE

BY JAMES SCOTT BELL

"So tell me all about dialogue."

"In two pages?"

"Hey, you're the writer. Just do it!"

"Look, let's talk about this later when—"

"We'll talk about it now! Tell me about dialogue."

"Sure. You've just helped. Your dialogue adds to the conflict."

"How?"

"By arguing with me. Put two characters together who have different agendas. That should be revealed in their dialogue. In fact, that is one of the two primary goals of dialogue—to create conflict."

"Oh yeah? What's the other?"

"To reveal character. And you're doing that, too. Our readers will get the idea you're a rather brusque fellow."

"Says you!"

"See? And you don't talk like me. That's another key. Each character should have his or her own way of speaking."

"So I'm doin' somethin' right, is that what yer tellin' me?"

"Almost. I'd avoid overuse of idioms and accents, like *yer* and *tellin'*, unless they're absolutely necessary. They're too difficult to read. A mere suggestion every now and again is all you need. The reader's imagination will do the rest."

"So I'm *not* doing it right, is that it?"

"Calm down."

"I *am* calm!"

"At least you're a man of few words. Dialogue in fiction should be brief."

"What if I've got a lot to say?"

"Heaven help us. But if you must, avoid long speeches. Break the speech up, using other characters' interruptions and—"

"Interruptions?"

"Perfect. And with little actions that demonstrate emotion."

He paused, twirling the tiny revolver in his hand. "Like this?"

"Yes. You're catching on quick."

"Hey, how about those Dodgers, huh? And isn't it a nice day outside?"

"Hold on. Avoid small talk. You're not trying to re-create real life in a story. Remember, you want to use dialogue to move the story, create tension, interest the reader, reveal character."

"What if my character likes small talk?"

"Good point. If your character is supposed to be a bore, it will work, because that dialogue has a story purpose."

"Thank you." He pointed the gun at me. "Now give me your wallet."

"Very good! That is a surprise, a twist. It forces the reader to read on. That's often a good way to end a chapter, don't you think?"

"I mean it, give me your wallet, pal!"

"And there's another great tactic, the off-center response. You didn't answer me right on the nose. Work on that angle a lot. Have your characters give slightly off responses whenever they can. That helps make the scene tense. Listen, fella, why don't you give me the gun, huh?"

"Go ahead, make my day."

"Yech! Avoid clichés like the plague!"

"Is that supposed to be funny?"

"A little humor is always welcome in dialogue, so long as you don't force it. Now hand over the gun."

"Only if you tell me what I should do to make sure my dialogue works."

"Set it aside for a few days. Then read it aloud, in a monotone. Or get a friend to read it to you. Hearing it out loud gives you a different perspective. The gun?"

"Okay. Here. Now what do we do?"

"We figure out a snappy, interesting way to end this dialogue."

"You got an idea?"

"Yeah."

"Let's hear it."

I raised the gun. "Give me your wallet, pal."

Okay, a little bit of play, but with some content to consider. The main point is that dialogue is rich soil for sowing conflict and tension. Never waste it with small talk or throwaway lines. Sometimes even masters of dialogue, after a certain number of books, can seem to be stretching things out because, well, it's just so much fun to write.

Until you have that fortieth novel published (and maybe not even then) write compact dialogue with conflict.

The best tools for creating conflict in dialogue are:

1. Orchestration
2. Subtext
3. Opposing agendas
4. Sidestepping
5. Dialogue as weapon
6. Parent-Adult-Child

1. ORCHESTRATION

When you go to a concert, after shelling out for tickets and dressing up in your evening best, you don't want to sit down and listen to an orchestra of oboes.

Nor do you want to have every instrument play exactly the same note.

What you hope for is the pleasing sound of different instruments coming together in just the right ways, creating the notes and resonance that add up to a great musical experience.

That's what we call orchestration. It is the assembling of parts for a desired effect.

In a novel, the parts you use to orchestrate conflict are called characters.

That's where it all starts. If you create bland, undistinguished characters, your chances of building page-turning conflict will fail.

And great dialogue begins before you write it, with characters you create for contrast.

Pay special attention to how each of your characters sounds. Give them unique voices in your own mind, and that will play out in more conflict on the page. Do this for each main character:

1. Create a voice journal. Use this to give each character a distinctive sound.
2. Write a statement, in the character's voice, of his *reason for being in the story.*

> My name is Sam Gerard and I'm a U.S. Marshal. Why am I in this story? You have to ask? I'm the Big Dog, and I have one job. To bring in fugitives from justice. I don't care about their case. I don't care if they say they're innocent. Hell, they may be! That's not my job. Don't tell me it is. I want to catch guys. That's what I do. I love it. I love my team. And I will not accept failure as an option.

Try it for all major characters. Get to know them as individuals. Find backstory elements that will contrast with the other characters. Look especially at the *Big 5*:

1. Education
2. Religion
3. Politics
4. Type of work
5. Economic status

2. SUBTEXT

A scene should be about more than it is about. On the surface it is what the characters are doing and saying. But underneath the surface, other story deposits are bubbling up toward the top.

You have *previous character relationships*. This character web might be known to you but not the reader. Not yet. But the way the characters speak with this hidden knowledge will create uncertainty in the scene.

There is *backstory*, or events that have happened before the scene. You may have written about these events in previous parts of the novel, or they may have occurred before the novel's time line. But events from the past that affect the present create possibilities for conflict on the surface.

You may also be aware of the *theme* of your novel. Even if you're unclear about it, just giving it some thought will automatically offer subtextual elements. List several possibilities of what your book might be about.

3. OPPOSING AGENDAS

Always know what each character wants in a given scene.

If a character in a scene is just taking up space, give him an agenda or get him out of there. Or cut the scene entirely.

Crafting Dynamic Dialogue

Scenes require conflict or tension, even if it's subtle.

Before you write the scene, note what it is each character wants.

Then spend a few moments playing with those motivations.

List three other possible motives for each of the characters, then mix and match to decide which ones will make for the best conflict.

It is also important to create tension among allies.

One of the danger points in fiction is when two friends, or people who are at least on the same side, have a talk about what's going on.

The trouble is there might not be any trouble between them. So much of the dialogue becomes a friendly chat.

This will violate Alfred Hitchcock's axiom (Hitchcock once said that a good story is "life, with the dull parts taken out."), however, so we have to do something about it.

The fastest way to handle it is to make sure there is tension manifested from the start.

Create tension in at least one of the characters, preferably the viewpoint character.

For example, when you have Allison meeting Melissa, her college friend, for coffee, don't have them sit down and start talking as if nothing's wrong in the world.

Put the trouble of the story into Allison's mind and nervous system and make it an impediment to her conversation with Melissa.

In Melissa, place something that might be in opposition to Allison's needs. Allison needs to ask Melissa's advice about a crumbling marriage. Maybe Melissa is full of news about her sister's impending wedding to a wonderful man and gushes about the prospects.

Spend some time brainstorming about the ways two friends or allies can be at odds. Then weave those things into the dialogue.

4. SIDESTEPPING

You instantly create conflict in dialogue when you avoid "on the nose" responses. On the nose means a direct response, sometimes even echoing the previous line:

"Are you ready to go, dear?" Bob asked.
"I'll be ready in just a moment, darling." Sylvia said.

"Want to play some catch?" Cody asked.
"Yeah, let's play some catch," Jared said.

"I didn't like what Collins did in there," Stan said.
"Me either," Charles said. "It was nasty."

There is nothing inherently wrong with these responses. Indeed, we talk like this in real life and sometimes will do so in our fiction. But notice how you can create instant conflict with a slight sidestep:

"Are you ready to go, dear?" Bob asked.
"I saw you downtown today," Sylvia said.

"Want to play some catch?" Cody asked.
"What's on your chin?" Jared said.

"I didn't like what Collins did in there," Stan said.
"He that troubleth his own house shall inherit the wind," Charles said.

You can avoid direct response:

- with a statement that is unrelated to the prompting dialogue
- by answering a question with a question
- with a line of dialogue that is going to need some explanation

Also consider using silence:

"Are you ready to go, dear?" Bob asked.
Sylvia said nothing.

Or use an action response:

"Are you ready to go, dear?" Bob asked.
Sylvia picked up the mirror.

5. DIALOGUE AS WEAPON

Look for places where you can use dialogue as a weapon, a means for your characters to charge ahead in order to get what they want. Keep in mind that dialogue is action. It's a physical act used by characters to help them get what they want. If they don't want anything in a scene, they shouldn't be there.

Note that not all weapons are explosive. They can be small and sharp, too.

Here's a well-known example from the classic film *Casablanca*. In this scene, a Nazi officer, Strasser, has come to Casablanca to capture Victor Laszlo, the underground fighter. It is rumored he will be showing up in Rick Blaine's saloon. The local French police captain, Louis Renault, allows Rick to operate because Rick takes no sides. He "sticks his neck out for no one."

Strasser wants to find out for himself where Rick stands. That's his agenda. See if you can pick up what the others want in the following exchange:

> RENAULT
> (calling to Rick)
> Rick!
> (Rick stops and comes over to their table.)
>
> RENAULT (CONT'D)
> Rick, this is Major Heinrich Strasser of the Third Reich.
>
> STRASSER
> How do you do, Mr. Rick?
>
> RICK
> How do you do?
>
> RENAULT
> And you already know Herr Heinze of the Third Reich.
> (Rick nods to Strasser and Heinze.)
>
> STRASSER
> Please joins us, Mr. Rick.
> (Rick sits down at the table.)
>
> RENAULT
> We are very honored tonight, Rick. Major Strasser is one of the reasons the Third Reich enjoys the reputation it has today.
>
> STRASSER
> You repeat "Third Reich" as though you expected there to be others.
>
> RENAULT
> Personally, Major, I will take what comes.

Even before Rick enters the conversation, the positioning has begun. Strasser corrects Renault on a minor point to emphasize the dominance of the Nazi regime. Renault lets it be known that his agenda is to "take what comes." That's because (we find out later) he has a nice little setup here at Rick's. It's where he wins at the gaming tables and also selects distressed young women to dally with as payment for getting them and their husbands out of Casablanca. He doesn't want to upset the proverbial apple cart:

> STRASSER
> (to Rick)
> Do you mind if I ask you a few questions? Unofficially of course.
>
> RICK
> Make it official if you like.

The first volley by Strasser is spoken in soft terms. Rick's rejoinder it intended to be a slightly harder parry. He's telling Strasser he has nothing of value for them:

> STRASSER
> What is your nationality?
>
> RICK
> I'm a drunkard.
>
> RENAULT
> That makes Rick a citizen of the world.

Rick's reply is sharp, a touch of the tip of a rapier. Renault knows this immediately and injects a line to deflate the impending tension. Rick's agenda is clear now: Don't be a patsy for strong-arm questions. Renault's agenda is to keep Rick's saloon from being closed down!

> RICK
> I was born in New York City if that'll help you any.
>
> STRASSER
> I understand that you came here from Paris at the time of the occupation.
>
> RICK
> There seems to be no secret about that.

> STRASSER
> Are you one of those people who cannot imagine the Germans in their beloved Paris?

> RICK
> It's not particularly my beloved Paris.

There is subtext in Rick's last reply. There's something about Paris he does not like. We don't find out until later what that is:

> HEINZE
> Can you imagine us in London?

> RICK
> When you get there, ask me.

> RENAULT
> Ho! Diplomatist.

Heinze, the humorless, charmless Gestapo man blunders in with a challenge. Rick knocks it right back at him. And once again, Renault tries to break the tension:

> STRASSER
> How about New York?

> RICK
> Well, there are certain sections of New York, Major, that I wouldn't advise you to try to invade.

Rick's response is priceless. Without giving up his pose of neutrality he jabs with a bit of American attitude:

> STRASSER
> Uh-huh. Who do you think will win the war?

> RICK
> I haven't the slightest idea.

> RENAULT
> Rick is completely neutral about everything, and that takes in the field of women, too.

So far, everyone is in roughly the same position as they were at the start of the scene. The initial jabs have all been met without lasting damage. Renault has succeeded in painting Rick as impartial. Now Strasser, frustrated in his initial queries, shows off a larger weapon—a dossier:

> STRASSER
> You were not always so carefully neutral. We have a complete dossier on you.
> (Strasser takes a little book from his pocket and turns to a page.)
>
> STRASSER
> "Richard Blaine, American. Age thirty-seven. Cannot return to his country." The reason is a little vague. We also know what you did in Paris, Mr. Blaine, and also we know why you left Paris.
> (Rick takes the dossier from Strasser.)
>
> STRASSER
> Don't worry, we are not going to broadcast it.
>
> RICK
> Are my eyes really brown?

Rick meets the challenge with another sarcastic comment. The match is even to this point, even though the Nazi has the stronger power position:

> STRASSER
> You will forgive my curiosity, Mr. Blaine. The point is, an enemy of the Reich has come to Casablanca and we are checking up on anybody who can be of any help to us.
>
> RICK
> (looking at Renault)
> My interest in whether Victor Laszlo stays or goes is purely a sporting one.
>
> STRASSER
> In this case, you have no sympathy for the fox?
>
> RICK
> Not particularly. I understand the point of view of the hound, too.

The scene continues for a few more lines. The Nazi has failed to draw any blood from Rick. The confrontation has occurred but without it breaking into an overt fight (which Rick would have lost). Rick and

Renault have won the exchange. Rick hasn't given the Nazi any reason to close him down. Renault has kept things light enough that Strasser isn't angered or suspicious enough of Rick to put him out of business.

The subtle use of weaponry above can be contrasted with a more overt duel. Mickey Spillane's Mike Hammer was never one for delicacy. Here he's talking to a cop he knows after being picked up for drunkenness in *The Girl Hunters*:

> When I looked up Pat was holding out his cigarettes to me. "Smoke?"
>   I shook my head.
>   His voice had a callous edge to it when he said, "You quit?"
> "Yeah."
>   I felt his shrug. "When?"
> "When I ran out of loot. Now knock it off."
> "You had loot enough to drink with." His voice had a real dirty tone now.
>   There are times when you can't take anything at all, no jokes, no rubs—nothing. Like the man said, you want nothing from nobody never. I propped my hands on the arms of the chair and pushed myself to my feet. The inside of my thighs quivered with the effort.
>   "Pat—I don't know what the hell you're pulling. I don't give a damn either. Whatever it is, I don't appreciate it. Just keep off my back, old buddy."
>   A flat expression drifted across his face before the hardness came back. "We stopped being buddies a long time ago, Mike."
>   "Good. Let's keep it like that. Now where the hell's my clothes?"
>   He spit a stream of smoke at my face and if I didn't have to hold the back of the chair to stand up, I would have belted him one. "In the garbage," he said. "It's where you belong too but this time you're lucky."
>   "You son of a bitch."
>   I got another faceful of smoke and choked on it.
>   "You son of a bitch," I said.

Between the subdued tones of the *Casablanca* scene, and the Ali-Frazier punches of the Mike Hammer exchange, you have an infinite range of possibilities for conflict in dialogue when you see it as a weapon.

Using dialogue as a weapon is also a great way to give the reader *information*. Rather than clunky exposition (simply telling us, in narration or in dialogue, what the author wants readers to know), use a tense exchange. So long as it is organic—that is, true to the characters—it can work seamlessly. Here's what I mean.

In this first example, the exposition comes through narrative:

> Arthur Marks was her accountant. He'd come from Omaha a few years ago and set up a practice in Los Angeles. His troubles in Nebraska—a bit of local fraud leading to sanctions—prompted him to seek a new venue.

That's fine as far as it goes, but too much of this gets us out of the direct conflict of a scene. The enterprising novelist will then consider dialogue. But sometimes the dialogue looks like this:

> Mary opened the door. "Oh hello, Arthur, my CPA from Omaha. What can I do for you?"
>
> "I'm just trying to make it here in Los Angeles after my move from Nebraska. I thought I'd ask you for a reference."

Okay, perhaps not so clunky as that. But you get the idea. Many times, especially in the openings of manuscripts, I'll see this kind of slipping of information to the reader.

The simple and powerful solution is to make such dialogue *confrontational*. That renders the information through conflict, which is the best way to go. Here is the first example rewritten:

> "What are you doing here?" Arthur said.
>
> "It's not because of my tax return," Mary said. "I know about Omaha."
>
> "I don't know what you're talking about."
>
> "Really? Sears? Cooking the books?"
>
> Arthur said nothing. His cheek twitched.
>
> "Why didn't you come clean with me?" Mary asked.
>
> "I just wanted a fresh start," Arthur said. "Is that so hard to understand?"
>
> "It's my money we're talking about here."
>
> "I'm clean! Honest."

A conference student once turned in a chapter to me. It contained the following (used by permission). A woman (Betty) has been planting bombs to avenge the death of her son. She now has a forensic investigator (Kate, who has been closing in on her) tied up and is threatening to kill her:

> Betty looked down at Kate. The triumphant smile on her face faded into a snarl at the mention of her son's death. "Why do you care?"

> "Because if my son had died as a result of finding out about something terrible that had happened to him that I had kept hidden to protect him, I would want to blame the person responsible." Kate thought she would try the empathy tactic. She did feel a great sorrow for Betty and her tragic story. She watched as Betty returned her statement with a hard stare.

In this tense moment, Kate has revealed to Betty facts about the case, but the dialogue sounds unnatural. The long line has information stuffed into it, but it feels more like it's for the reader's benefit rather than the character's.

I told the student to go back and cut all dialogue that is not absolutely true to the character and the emotional beats. What would either of them *really* say? Revised, it looks like this:

> Betty looked down at Kate. The triumphant smile on her face faded into a snarl at the mention of her son's death. "Why do you care?"
> "I do care."
> "Why?"
> "Because if my son had died like that—"
> "Don't talk about your son! He didn't die."
> "I would have protected him just like you."
> "You know nothing."
> "I wouldn't have told him. I would have made the same choice."
> "Shut up now. Don't you dare say another word."

6. PARENT-ADULT-CHILD

A great tool for creating instant conflict in dialogue is the Parent-Adult-Child model. I first read this idea in Jack Bickham's *Writing Novels That Sell* (1989). Bickham, in turn, picked it up from a school of psychology popularized in the book *Games People Play* by Eric Berne (1964). This school is called Transactional Analysis.

The theory holds that we tend to occupy roles in life and relationships. The three primary roles are Parent, Adult, and Child (PAC).

The Parent is the seat of authority, the one who can "lay down the law." He has the raw strength, from position or otherwise, to rule and then enforce his rulings.

As Yul Brynner's Pharaoh puts it in *The Ten Commandments*, "So shall it be written. So shall it be done."

The Adult is the objective one, the one who sees things rationally and is therefore the best one to analyze a situation. "Let's be adult about this," one might say in the midst of an argument.

Finally, there is the Child. Not rational, and not with any real power. So what does she do? Reacts emotionally. Throws tantrums to try to get her way. Even an adult can do this. We've all seen clandestine videos that prove this point.

So it is a helpful thing to consider what role each character is assuming in a scene. How do they see themselves? What is their actual role? (It may indeed be different than what they perceive it to be.)

Most important, how will they act in order to accomplish their goal in the scene?

Answering these questions can give you a way to shape your dialogue so there is constant tension and conflict throughout.

Also consider that the characters might change their roles (try something new) in order to get their way. Thus, this is a never-ending source of conflict possibilities and only takes a few moments to set up.

DO THIS:

1. Look at all of your dialogue exchanges, especially ones that run for a page or more.
2. Analyze what roles the characters think they're inhabiting.
3. Rework the dialogue by getting each character to be more assertive in their claimed role. (Also note that a character can change roles as a matter of strategy. For example, if the Parent isn't working, a character might switch to pouting like a Child in order to get his way.)

Much of the dialogue I see in manuscripts seems loose and without real purpose. That is a waste of potential conflict. When you follow the guidelines in this chapter, your dialogue will take on an added verve that agents and editors appreciate.

CHAPTER 26

FIGHT FOR THOSE ARGUMENTS

BY NANCY KRESS

When was the last time you had an argument with someone? I know you did; we all do, and that includes fictional characters. In fact, arguing is one of the best ways to make your characters seem real to your reader. This is true not only because disagreement is universal, but also because in argument a person reveals so much about the hidden layers of himself.

Furthermore, arguments cannot only characterize, but also aid your plot. Here's how.

FIGHTS AS PLOT DEVICES

While any argument will characterize (more on this in a minute), a carefully chosen argument will also advance your plot. Arguments, by definition, are divisive. Two (or more) people take separate positions on something. Pick characters who you want to be separated for part of your story.

Here, for instance, is part of a critical argument between fourteen-year-old Lily Owens and her father in Sue Monk Kidd's bestseller, *The Secret Life of Bees*. They are fighting about Lily's mother, who died when she was four:

> "I hate you," I screamed.
>   That stopped his smiling instantly. He stiffened. "Why, you little bitch," he said. The color faded from his lips.
>   Suddenly I felt ice cold, as if something dangerous had slipped into the room. I looked toward the window and felt a tremor slide along my spine.

"You listen to me," he said, his voice deadly calm. "The truth is, your sorry mother ran off and left you. The day she died, she'd come back to get her things, that's all. You can hate me all you want, but she's the one who left you."

The room turned absolutely silent.

This argument, which occurs in chapter two, propels the remainder of the book. Lily runs away to search for her mother's family. Without this fight, there would be no novel.

Arguments also can divide characters in less fundamental, but still useful, ways. For instance, your protagonist might alienate the one person who has the information she needs to solve some problem. Or close friends might be angry with each other, letting one feel justified in doing something of which the other might not approve. Or lovers might fight and separate long enough for one to get involved with someone else.

Ask yourself these questions:

- What characters do I want separated, temporarily or permanently?
- What interesting plot consequences might come of their separation?
- What subject might they quarrel about that would separate them for the time I want them apart?

FIGHT TO BUILD CHARACTER

Now that you know who is fighting and about what, you can consider the second important aspect of any argument: fighting style. This is where your character reveals more about his inner self than he knows. He does this by showing the reader how often he fights, with whom, how intensely, and how fairly.

Some people argue about everything. These are the chip-on-the-shoulder folk, looking for a battle; or the know-it-alls, who correct everyone around them and get mad at any disagreement; or the purely mean. At the other end of the spectrum are those who let nearly any insult go by, unwilling to fight. It takes a lot to provoke these people, who may be either calm by nature or powerless. Here is Lily's father, T. Ray, ready and willing to provoke nasty, pointless fights:

Crafting Dynamic Dialogue

> Whenever I opened [a book], T. Ray said, "Who do you think you are, Julius Shakespeare?" The man sincerely thought that was Shakespeare's first name, and if you think I should have corrected him, you are ignorant about the art of survival. He also referred to me as Miss-Brown-Nose-in-a-Book and Miss-Emily-Big-Head-Diction. He meant Dickinson, but there are things you let go by.

This one paragraph tells us so much about both characters. T. Ray is a nasty man who is also jealous of his daughter's education. Lily is canny and self-controlled enough to refuse his provocations—until he starts the fight about her mother, her most sensitive topic. These vivid impressions set us up for the rest of the novel, in which Lily will continue to be canny and self-controlled, and T. Ray will continue to be a nightmare of a father. All beautifully foreshadowed by how often they're willing to battle.

Closely related to when a character is willing to argue is the question of whom he'll argue with. Some people, like T. Ray, will fight with anyone over anything. But the author might have created a different T. Ray by portraying him as abusive to Lily but charming to everybody else. They regard their family as personal property to be treated as they like, but may go to great lengths to impress the rest of the world with their good character.

Other people are usually kind and patient with those they perceive as subordinate (including children), but are touchy and critical of superiors. These are the characters with "authority issues."

Is your rich old lady gracious with her heirs, her cleaning woman, and her gardener, but argumentative and unpleasant with cops and doctors? If so, I want to read about her—she sounds interesting. Show me whom she argues with and whom she doesn't.

MINOR VS. MAJOR SPATS

Another aspect of fighting style is intensity. There are, for instance, married couples who bicker about differences ("You ignored me all evening") and married couples who divorce about differences ("You always ignore me! I'm leaving!"). There are people who shrug off an insult

("That's just the way she is") and people who commit murder over an insult ("I'm avenging my honor!"). Plus, of course, everything in between. Which is your character?

The answer to that, to be believable, should depend on three things. One is personality. How hard does your character take events in general? Does she get really excited over good fortune and really depressed over setbacks? Then we'll find it believable that she gets really angry and reacts accordingly.

The second cause of an intense reaction is the nature of the specific fight that you're creating on the page. Lily Owens lets most of her father's insults go by ("the art of survival"). But when he starts in about her mother, the topic is too important to Lily to gloss over. Lily's reaction is intense. She runs away. Another type of character might merely have seethed silently. Still another might have fought T. Ray more intensively, setting fire to the house with him inside.

Finally, the strength of fights is culturally determined. Where public or even private scenes are disapproved of (upper-class London, old-money Boston, "well-behaved" families), arguments may be muted, even when the subject matters a great deal. In other cultures, volatility is not frowned on, and people may feel free to scream at each other in public. In extreme cases, murder may even be considered a duty, as in avenging a sister's rape.

Where is your story taking place? Are your arguers in tune with local or family culture? Maybe not. You can create interesting effects by portraying the rebels against the local mores: the meek child born into a battling family, the furious feminist in polite 19th-century English society.

FIGHT FAIR, FIGHT FOUL

Some people, like T. Ray, do not argue fairly. They employ name-calling, sarcasm, profanity, threats, ridicule, belittling, lies, evasions, or physical violence. Others keep scrupulously to one issue, argue it logically, listen to each other's viewpoint, and try to stick to the truth. Degree of fairness applies to all kinds of fighting, from marital spats to interstellar war. It tells the reader volumes about character.

In fact, putting these various aspects of fighting style together practically paints a picture of essential character. Here are only three of the possible combinations:

- a man who hates to fight, avoids it when possible, but on a subject of critical importance will fight with deadly intensity and no rules whatsoever
- a woman who bickers constantly with her family but in such a low-key, unthreatening way that they tolerate the irritation
- a political aide who is obsequious and agreeable to those in charge but argumentative and dishonest to those below him in the power structure

Fighting might not be pleasant in real life, but it's enormously useful in fiction. Let the battle begin!

QUICK TIPS TO CREATE A FIGHTING SCENE

- A fight should pit two or more characters against each other.
- A fight can be about something major or minor in the plot line.
- Tailor a specific fighting style to each character. This tells readers more about each character without blocks of abstract exposition.
- Create the right level of intensity needed for each fight.
- If you are setting up a major fight, hit a character's pressure points to show us why she is so upset.
- Keep a character's fighting style consistent with the traits you have already described.

CHAPTER 27

DIALOGUE & SUSPENSE

BY JAMES SCOTT BELL

Let's focus in on ways dialogue can carry suspense and stretch tension. When you read the masters of dialogue—Ernest Hemingway, Elmore Leonard, Robert B. Parker—you will find they do this all the time. Dialogue for them becomes another means of heightening the stakes. Remember, dialogue is an expression and extension of *action*. It is a physical act by a character in order to serve his purposes in a scene. With that in mind, you have several options in your toolbox.

SPARE DIALOGUE

In chapter one of Lee Child's *Worth Dying For*, Eldridge Tyler, a seemingly benign Nebraska grandfather, gets a call. He and his rifle might be needed. Immediately we're hooked. A grandfather and his rifle? What for? Child uses spare dialogue to develop it for us. Tyler asks, "What's going on?"

> "There's a guy sniffing around."
>> "Close?"
>> "Hard to say."
>> "How much does he know?"
>> "Some of it. Not all of it yet."
>> "Who is he?"
>> "Nobody. A stranger. Just a guy. But he got involved. We think he was in the service. We think he was a military cop. Maybe he didn't lose the cop habit."
>> "How long ago was he in the service?"

"Ancient history."

"Connections?"

"None at all, that we can see. He won't be missed. He's a drifter. Like a hobo. He blew in like a tumbleweed. Now he needs to blow out again."

"Description?"

"He's a big guy," the voice said. "Six-five at least, probably two-fifty. Last seen wearing a big old brown parka and a wool cap. He moves funny, like he's stiff. Like he's hurting bad."

"OK," Tyler said. "So where and when?"

"We want you to watch the barn," the voice said. "All day tomorrow. We can't let him see the barn. Not now. If we don't get him tonight, he's going to figure it out eventually. He's going to head over there and take a look."

"He's going to walk right into it, just like that?"

"He thinks there are four of us. He doesn't know there are five."

"That's good."

"Shoot him if you see him."

"I will."

"Don't miss."

"Do I ever?"

Here we get a ton of information, explicit and implicit. We know Tyler is a skilled sniper who has killed before, seemingly without a mistake. We know there's an unwitting victim (Jack Reacher, it turns out) walking around about to get his head blown off. We learn about his background in the military, and a bit of what he looks like. We don't know who is talking to Tyler, and that fact ratchets up the mystery.

DO THIS:

1. Find a high-tension section of your novel that is dialogue heavy.
2. Make a copy of the scene and open it in as a new document.
3. Compress as much of the dialogue as you can. Cut away at words, use fewer complete sentences.
4. Compare the two scenes and rewrite your master scene utilizing as much of the new material as you deem appropriate.

STRETCHED DIALOGUE

You can stretch the tension in dialogue, too. Remember to use the techniques of nonresolution and withholding information.

In *Velocity* by Dean Koontz, Billy Wiles is being played by a clever killer who seems to know Billy's every move. Threatening notes tell Billy what to do, or else.

In this scene, Billy is outside on his porch, as per instructions, to listen to a man named Cottle, sent by the killer with a message.

What is it?

> [Cottle says] "You'll have five minutes to make a decision."
> "What decision?"

Instead of telling us what it is right away, the dialogue continues:

> "Take off your wristwatch and prop it on the porch railing."
> "Why?"
> "To count off the five minutes."
> "I can count them with the watch on my wrist."
> "Putting it on the railing is a signal to him that the countdown has started."
> Woods to the north, shadowy and cool in the hot day, Green lawn, then tall golden grass, then a few well-crowned oaks, then a couple of houses down-slope and to the east. To the west lay the county road, trees and fields beyond it.

Now we get a paragraph of description, setting the scene but, most of all, making us wait for the answer:

> "He's watching now?" Billy asked.
> "He promised he would be, Mr. Wiles."
> "From where?"
> "I don't know, sir. Just please, please take off your watch and prop it on the railing."
> "And if I won't?"
> "Mr. Wiles, don't talk that way."
> "But if I won't?" Billy pressed.
> His baritone rasp thinned to a higher register as Cottle said, "I told you, he'll take my face, and me awake when he does. I TOLD YOU."

Billy got up, removed his Timex, and propped it on the railing so that the watch face could be seen from both of the rocking chairs.

As the sun approached the zenith of its arc, it penetrated the landscape and melted shadows everywhere but in the woods. The green-cloaked conspiratorial trees revealed no secrets.

"Mr. Wiles, you've got to sit down."

Brightness fell from the air, and a chrome-yellow glare hazed the fields and furrows, forcing Billy to squint at numberless places where a man could lie in the open, effectively camouflaged by nothing more than spangled sunlight.

Still no answer! More description. Koontz knows exactly what he's doing. The tension grows from the delay.

In fact, the dialogue goes on for another full page before we get the information. Which I won't give to you here. This section is about suspense, after all.

DO THIS:

1. Find a dialogue exchange in which information is being revealed.
2. Can you stretch this section out so the information comes later, even in another scene?
3. Try adding an interruption to the scene so the information is held up.

THE UNEXPECTED

One of the surest ways to create instant conflict or tension in dialogue is to avoid the "on the nose" response. That refers to a statement, direct response, further direct response sequence:

"Hey Joe, let's go to the store."

"Great! I was just thinking of going to the store."

"You want to go now?"

"I sure do."

"All right! Whose car should we take?"

"Let's take my car."

"Good idea. Mine's in the shop anyway."

"Sorry to hear about that. What's wrong with it?"

"I don't know, that's why I took it in!"

You get the idea. Now, this is not to say you should avoid all direct response in your dialogue, because it wouldn't be real. We do talk this way, and so do your characters. Scenes like the above scene should be cut because there's no conflict at all. You certainly can redo the scene with different agendas and so on. Direct responses can be full of conflict:

> "Hey Joe, let's go to the store."
> "I don't want to go to any store."
> "How come?"
> "That's my business."

So there you have direct responses with conflict.

Now let's turn to the unexpected. Throughout your novel, look for places where you can insert "off the nose" responses.

One way is through simple avoidance:

> "Hey Joe, let's go to the store."
> "How 'bout those Dodgers?"

Seemingly innocuous answers can take on tension if they are avoiding what seems like a simple statement or request. Why would Joe not want to talk about going to the store? What's going on in his mind? Immediate interest is created.

A stronger form of avoidance is to answer a question with a question:

> "Hey Joe, you want to go to the store?"
> "Why don't you give it a rest?"

Instant conflict.

An interruption also creates conflict on the spot:

> "Hey Joe, let's go—"
> "I've had enough, okay?"

The unexpected creates a freshness that elevates the writing. One of my favorite movie examples is *Moonstruck*. Loretta has just agreed to marry Johnny, a likable lug but no great catch. She wakes up her mother, Rose, to tell her:

Crafting Dynamic Dialogue

ROSE
Do you love him, Loretta?

LORETTA
No.

ROSE
Good. When you love them they drive you crazy cause they know they can.

What's funny about the exchange is that you would expect Rose to pro-test that Loretta should marry only if she loves Johnny. But she quickly and plainly lays out the exact opposite case.

Later in the script, Ronny, Loretta's true love, is trying to convince her to come into his abode after a night at the opera. How does he do it? By declaring how great love is? No, he says this:

> But love don't make things nice, it ruins everything, it breaks your heart, it makes things a mess. We're not here to make things perfect. Snowflakes are perfect. The stars are perfect. Not us. We are here to ruin ourselves and break our hearts and love the wrong people and die!

Not exactly *Romeo and Juliet*, is it? But the unexpected makes it fresh and full of tension, if for no other reason than the audience doesn't know what the heck to make of it.

Now some of you may have a question bubbling around in your writer's mind. We usually hear that it's a good idea to cut in order to make our books more readable. That is not quite correct.

The idea is to cut the parts that don't hold the reader to the page. Clunky exposition, bloated dialogue, interchanges with no tension, and so on.

But when you have the reader nailed to the page because something major is happening, keep them there by adding—so long as what you add keeps the moment hot with suspense.

What would a roller coaster be if you got one climb and one dip? A rip-off, that's what. Give your readers the full ride by stretching tension.

CHAPTER 28

TALK IT OUT

BY SARAH DOMET

All novels must have dialogue because it's important to let your character speak in his or her own words. One thing to remember about a dialogue scene is that it doesn't simply contain the words that the characters are speaking. You'll also need to narrate the setting, the body language of your characters, action, and descriptions. Dialogue scenes aren't just conversations but conversations that go somewhere and add to the overall trajectory of your novel.

Many of your scenes will contain small bits of dialogue, but scenes that contain a good amount of dialogue, or are composed entirely of swaths of dialogue, should come into play in your novel as well. Like action scenes, dialogue scenes are useful for quickening the pace of your novel. But keep in mind, dialogue scenes aren't simply scripted blocks of spoken texts. Instead you should be sure to fold in your direct lines of dialogue with descriptions of action, body language, and movement. What else are your characters doing besides talking?

Take a look at this excellent example from Richard Russo's novel *Nobody's Fool*. As you read, pay attention to how the dialogue is punctuated, how lines of speech are intertwined with expository narration, and how the author forwards the scene through this conversation.

> The men on the trailer steps watched several of these aborted attempts, shaking their heads in good-humored disbelief. Sully and Will watched for a moment also, the boy's eyes growing wide and round with wonder and fear.
>
> "What's wrong with him, Grandpa?" the boy asked.

"He had a little accident a couple weeks ago," explained Sully, who had seen the dog a couple of times in the interim. "You want to ride on my shoulders?"

When Will nodded enthusiastically, Sully swung him aboard.

"Look who's here," Carl Roebuck said when he noticed Sully and the boy approaching. "You come to admire your handiwork?"

"It's not my fault you got a spastic Doberman," Sully said, setting Will down on the step. The boy was still warily watching Rasputin circle. Hearing Sully's voice, the dog was now emitting small howls of frustration.

"I think it *is* your fault," Carl said. "I just wish I could prove it." Then, to the two men who were watching the dog, "I know you guys'd love to stay here all afternoon and watch this dog have another stroke ..."

"I would," one of the men said. "I admit it." But he and the other man headed for the gate, and Carl and Sully and the boy went inside the trailer.

Carl Roebuck went around behind the small metal desk and sat down, put his feet up and studied first the boy, then Sully. "Don Sullivan," he said knowingly. "Thief of Snowblowers, Poisoner of Dogs, Flipper of Pancakes. Secret Father and Grandfather. Jack-Off, All Trades. How they hangin'?"

Sully took a seat. "By a thread, as usual," he said. He motioned for Will to go ahead and sit on the sofa. "Don't ruin that," he warned.

Will looked at the sofa fearfully. It was torn to shreds, stuffing exploding from slits in the upholstery. Will climbed on carefully and found both men grinning at him.

"Your grandfather tell you how he poisons dogs?"

Will's eyes got big again.

"He steals people's snowblowers, too."

"Don't pay attention to him," Sully said. "He just can't keep track of his possessions."

Russo does an excellent job seamlessly integrating dialogue into this scene and allowing the conversation to flow, even as the characters move around. Importantly, Russo does not begin this scene with a line of dialogue, but instead offers up enough context in order to orient the reader as to who is doing the talking. Also note how Russo allows body language to do the "talking" when necessary. Will nods his head when he wants to ride on his grandpa's shoulders—this stands in place of a more contrived line like, "Yes, I do, Grandpapa." Later, Will's eyes get big instead of directly answering the question posed by Carl Roebuck. Any time body language can stand in the place of a direct line of dialogue, you should let it. Body language *is* a kind of language after all, and so it can communicate just as well what your characters are thinking as the spoken word can. It also provides a bit of action and momentum.

Also pay attention to Russo's dialogue tags. He never tries to get fancy with them. In your own dialogue scenes, aim for simplicity in your attributive tags. A simple "he said" or "she asked" will do; you never want to draw attention to dialogue tags by getting too creative (example: "he articulated loquaciously"). Remember, your aim is for invisibility when it comes to assigning lines of dialogue to a speaker. You want your reader to simply skim over the "he said/she said," using them only to discern who is speaking.

Another lesson we can learn from Russo's scene: The characters often speak in fragments, not complete sentences. Although you may have learned in elementary school to always write in complete sentences, dialogue is a different beast altogether. People don't always talk in complete sentences, and neither should your fictional characters. At least, not always. It's okay for your characters to interrupt one another, stop midsentence, or speak in short fragments.

Finally, and perhaps most importantly, Russo narrates action in the midst of the conversation between characters. Carl, Sully, and Will walk into a trailer. Carl then walks to a desk, sits down, and puts up his feet. Sully sits down. Will climbs on the couch. All these details are important because nobody has a conversation standing completely still. Unless he is a British beefeater guarding Buckingham Palace. And beefeaters don't speak. At least not while on duty. (I'm sure they yammer on during their off hours when they go to the local pub to knock back a few pints.)

EXERCISE

Take a look at any dialogue scenes you've written in a recent work-in-progress. Give yourself an honest grade from 1 to 10 (1 being the worst, 10 being the best) on how well you did in this exercise. Practice being your own best critic. What tips can you take from Russo's scene above? What could you have done better? It's a good idea to learn from your practice exercises before moving on to the real thing.

Once you've written your scenes, read them aloud. Trust me, the best way to catch stilted, unbelievable dialogue is to read it out loud. If it doesn't sound real, it probably won't read much better either.

Crafting Dynamic Dialogue

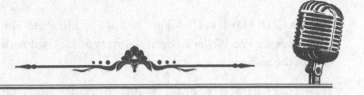

PERMISSIONS

"Believable Dialogue." Excerpted from *Writing New Adult Fiction* © 2014 by Deborah Halverson, with permission from Writer's Digest Books.

"Conflict in Dialogue." Excerpted from *Elements of Fiction Writing: Conflict & Suspense* © 2012 by James Scott Bell, with permission from Writer's Digest Books.

"Constructing Scenes with Dialogue." Excerpted from *Make A Scene* © 2007 by Jordan Rosenfeld, with permission from Writer's Digest Books.

"Creating Active Dialogue." © 2003 by James Scott Bell. Originally appeared in *Writer's Digest*, June 2003. Used with permission of the author.

"Dialogue & Suspense." Excerpted from *Elements of Fiction Writing: Conflict & Suspense* © 2012 by James Scott Bell, with permission from Writer's Digest Books.

"Dialogue as a Means of Pacing." Excerpted from *Write Great Fiction: Dialogue* © 2004 by Gloria Kempton, with permission from Writer's Digest Books.

"Fight for Those Arguments." 2003 by Nancy Kress. Originally appeared in *Writer's Digest*, September 2003. Used with permission of the author.

"Handling Dialect & Jargon." Excerpted from *Novel & Short Story Writer's Market 2012* © 2011 by Jack Smith, with permission from Writer's Digest Books.

"He Said, She Said." Excerpted from *Novel & Short Story Writer's Market 2016* © 2015 by Jack Smith, with permission from Writer's Digest Books.

INDEX

Crafting Dynamic Dialogue